Earlsferry and Elie

A Scottish Golf Heritage

By
Graham Johnston

MAPLE
PUBLISHERS

Earlsferry and Elie – A Scottish Golf Heritage

Author: Graham Johnston

Copyright © 2024 Graham Johnston

The right of Graham Johnston to be identified as author of this work has been asserted by the author in accordance with section 77 and 78 of the Copyright, Designs and Patents Act 1988.

First Published in 2024

ISBN 978-1-83538-299-8 (Paperback)
978-1-83538-300-1 (E-Book)

Book cover design and Book layout by:
    White Magic Studios
    www.whitemagicstudios.co.uk

Published by:
    Maple Publishers
    Fairbourne Drive, Atterbury,
    Milton Keynes,
    MK10 9RG, UK
    www.maplepublishers.com

A CIP catalogue record for this title is available from the British Library.

All rights reserved. No part of this book may be reproduced or translated in any form or by any means, electronic or mechanical, including photocopying, recording or by any information storage and retrieval system without written permission from the author.

This book is a memoir. It reflects the author's recollections of experiences over time. Some names and characteristics have been changed, some events have been compressed, and some dialogues have been recreated, and the Publisher hereby disclaims any responsibility for them.

For the late Ronnie Sinclair whose enthusiasm and perspicacity set me off on this trail.

Contents

Foreword 5

Chapter 1 – Elie and Earlsferry 6

Chapter 2 – The Early Earlsferry and Elie Golf Clubs 12

Chapter 3 – The Litigation 20

Chapter 4 – Earlsferry and Elie Golf Club 35

Chapter 5 – The Golf House Club 45

Chapter 6 – Earlsferry Thistle 56

Chapter 7 – The Recreation Park and Sports Club 64

Chapter 8 – The Development of the Golf Course 83

Chapter 9 – The Golf Club Makers Part 1 George Forrester 92

Chapter 10 – The Golf Club Makers Part 2 Andrew Scott 108

Chapter 11 – The World Wide Influence of Earlsferry Golf
                 Professionals 117

Chapter 12 – The Ladies 288

Chapter 13 – Royalty 300

Chapter 14 – James Braid 306

Chapter 15 – Miscellanea 311

Chapter 16 – The Children 319

Chapter 17 – ... and Finally 321

Chapter 18 – List of Golf Clubs Associated with Elie/Earlsferry
                 Professionals 322

INDEX 330

Foreword

The subject of this book is the History of Golf in Earlsferry and Elie. In current times the two villages are referred to as Elie and Earlsferry and I have deliberately reversed the order. Golf itself started quite clearly in Earlsferry and eventually spread to Elie which was only a minor player in its development in the area. It cannot be stressed too highly the importance of golf to the development and success of Elie and Earlsferry. It occupies a pivotal role in the history of these villages and the East Neuk of Fife. I have tried to make this book both a history for reference and also readable for those who may know something about the origins of the game in the villages. I have concentrated on the early history of the golf course, the various golf clubs that came and went and the association of the golf course with the Sports Club.

The section on the professional golfers who owe their origin to Earlsferry and Elie is gleaned from newspapers of the time and to that extent its accuracy is dependent on the accuracy of the newspaper reports. It is to be hoped that as a result of this research not only will the importance of these pioneers be at last recognised but further information may be forthcoming from the clubs at which they earned their livelihood. It is timed to co-incide with the 150th anniversary of the founding of both Golf House Club Elie and Earlsferry Thistle in 2025.

Chapter 1
Elie and Earlsferry

E lie and Earlsferry are contiguous small villages on the north coast of the Firth of Forth in the County of Fife. Fife is a county on the east of Scotland sandwiched between the firths of Tay on the north and Forth in the south. It is a county with a rich and long history, having at one time been the seat of the Scottish kings. Many small villages along the south shore of the county depended for their existence on the fishing industry and trade via their shores with the continent and especially the Baltic and the Low Countries. The villages lie almost due south of St Andrews on the north coast of the county.

The villages are located on a sandy beach extending to approximately 1 mile. The beach is relatively sheltered by promontories both on the east and the west. It is this beach which attracted tourists to the area.

These two villages were independently administered until 1929 when they were conjoined. Earlsferry is the older, being a Royal Burgh, and can trace its existence back to the 9th and 10th Centuries CE when it was the ferry port for pilgrims coming from the south to visit the relics of the apostle St. Andrew in St. Andrews and there was a very active ferry service from North Berwick on the south side of the Firth of Forth to Earlsferry. There are records indicating that as many as 14,000 people used that ferry in one year. The Earl in the title was once thought to have been the Earl of Fife – Macduff – but Adrian Grant in his excellent treatise "The Genesis of a Kingdom" clearly demonstrates that he did not exist despite Shakespeare's revelations in Macbeth. We are now satisfied that the Earl was Earl Duncan the 1st [1113-1154 CE] and the ferry was initially established to enable him to administer his estates on both sides of the Firth of Forth. The time frame of his existence however suggests to us that there was a settlement in this area in the 9th and 10th centuries CE. We are fairly certain that there is a strong Danish connection with the village since on two occasions in the last century stone "kists" have been found with bones suggesting a Nordic origin. Again Adrian Grant mentions the Danish connection to the area which would conveniently tie in with our understanding of its earlier foundation.

Earlsferry was created a Royal Burgh in the 13th century. At least that is the legend – in fact, whilst it may be true, documentary evidence of such a creation is missing. The explanation given for this is a fire in Edinburgh which destroyed the original charter. Various attempts were made to resurrect that text of the charter and they were sufficient to persuade the Court of Session in Edinburgh that Earlsferry was a Royal Burgh (see "The Litigation" below).

Royal Burghs had certain privileges not least of which was the right to administer the affairs of the Burgh, independent of the influence of either the King or local power stake holders. The granter of the title would define the area of land which was to be governed by the Burgh and the local people would elect a Provost (Mayor) and Baillies (Magistrates) to administer the area of ground. In return the King would expect assistance from the Burghers in the event of an invasion. The position of the Royal Burgh at the seaside enabled the King to have some early warning of attack. The Royal Burgh was the ultimate proprietor of the ground assigned to it by the creator of the Burgh (usually the King). Thus it would have been the town council of the Royal Burgh which would regulate the affairs of the area and be responsible for selling off or leasing land and property to its residents. Most of these burghs kept fairly meticulous records of the grants of property to their citizens. The Royal Burgh also had the ability to raise revenue inter alia by the sale/lease of seaware and the control of shipping wishing to use the Burgh's landing facilities. The control of the foreshore by the Royal Burgh meant that it could sell some of the sand, and especially seaweed which was an effective and cheap fertiliser for the local farming community.

Elie was administratively established in 1864 by the amalgamation of it and two small neighbouring villages – Williamsburgh and Liberty sandwiched between Earlsferry and Elie. It was a Police Burgh. It was administered initially by Police Commissioners and latterly by a Town Council. The land around Elie was owned by the local land owning families. Starting with the Dishingtons of Ardross and then the Anstruther line of Elie House and from 1850s onwards, William Baird, a wealthy industrialist from Lanarkshire. It was the local landowners that controlled the distribution of land to its people not the local council as in Earlsferry.

Prior to 1863 and the arrival of the railway line from Edinburgh and Glasgow to the Fife Coast neither village had much industry. There was a fishing community but the fleet suffered decimation in the 18th Century as a result of sea storms. Elie benefitted from a sheltered harbour (indeed the name "Elie" is thought to be a corruption of the gaelic meaning safe shelter and the area was originally known as "The Ailie of Ardross") which encouraged a degree of trade mostly with the continent but not so Earlsferry.

In the 19th Century there was a small but effective linen weaving community in Earlsferry with many houses having their own looms on which rough linen webs were woven. These were used as backing for the linoleum manufacturing industry in Kirkcaldy, a few miles west along the coast. However by the latter half of the 19th century this had been superseded by cheaper imports of jute from the east to Dundee and Kirkcaldy which led to the demise of the linen weaving industry in Earlsferry.

The arrival of the railway line led to a building boom with the erection of substantial villas especially along the shore line, and employment was available for the young men of the villages as masons - most of the stone for these houses being locally sourced. After the arrival of a direct railway line both villages became a tourist resort for the wealthier residents of Edinburgh and Glasgow and parts farther south who would often spend whole months at the seaside. Most residents of the villages let out their houses in the summer to the incoming tourists – they themselves retiring to sheds in the back gardens.

Earlsferry itself simply consisted of a High Street with houses on the north and south sides. The latter extended down to the high water mark of the beach and the former extended northward towards a piece of waste ground. It was this waste ground which became an area used by the young men of Earlsferry for the practice of golf. At the same time, mid 19th Century, much of the golfing development in the country was being established in Fife at St. Andrews and at North Berwick on the south side of the Forth estuary where there were similar tracts of essentially public ground beside the shoreline.

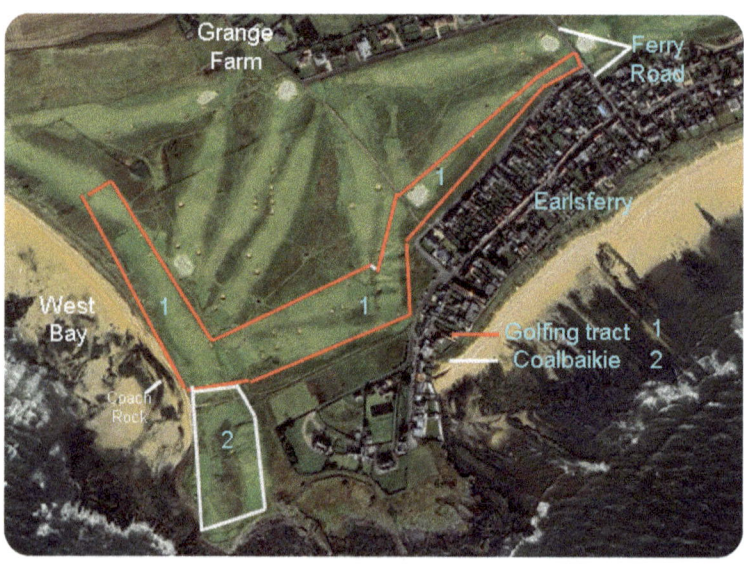

It became a recreation area where the locals would walk, hang out their washing, collect divots to thatch their houses and more importantly, as a recreation, play golf.

For many years, even centuries, it was used by the residents as a playground to hack about a golf ball. The club and feathery balls were hand made by them and a very rudimentary golfing course or tract was established probably between Ferry Road - the eastern boundary of the village and the sea some half a mile to the west. However this ground was not exclusively barren waste land since the tenant farmer of the Grange farm which lay slightly to the north of the village had certain grazing and other rights over parts of it. There were those who thought that he did not have a title to do so. It was this that gave rise to the notorious litigation between the Malcolms of Balbedie and Grange and the villagers of Earlsferry – 1813 -1832.

Chapter 2

The Early Earlsferry and Elie Golf Clubs

In the beginning in Earlsferry ....there was not very much. But what there was, was an area of ground to the north of the houses in Earlsferry High Street that at least in part was of not much use to man nor beast. It was bents, dunes grass of poor quality, sand and perhaps gorse.

It became common ground belonging to the Royal Burgh and its residents and a recreation area principally where the local residents carried out many activities including playing golf. Another purpose was to steep the flax stalks prior to being made into thread for the linen weaving industry.

The young men of the time would use the area of ground to play golf or a form of the game just as waste areas of ground in the West of Scotland became adopted by the local residents as makeshift football pitches.

Thus the tradition of golf was established in that area of ground affectionately known as the "golfing tract". It was said to go back to the 14th Century or "time immemorial...." It was not a formal golfing course as we would know today and the start and conclusion of various holes depended upon the other demands of the area. There was nothing like an organised golf club. The actual outline of the course was fluid, changing direction and the number of holes depending on the demands by others for the ground in question and indeed what crops were grown on some of it. Some of the ground was under tillage by the tenant farmer of the Grange Farm lying to the north of the golfing tract. Again its maintenance was basic and the quality of the ground to make this golf course was rather poor. However what the area may have lacked in quality was made up for by the golf fuelled enthusiasm of the locals.

At that time, elsewhere, golf was a rich man's sport. A suitable area of ground – many, many acres – was required to form any sort of golf course and the golf clubs were hand made by craftsmen whose other job was usually carpentry and wood working. This meant that the aspiring golfer would need a good financial background before indulging. At this time a golf course did not have a specified number of holes – it was only later that 18 became the norm. Earlsferry probably had at best 11 or 12 discernible holes.

The young men of Earlsferry became quite proficient at striking a feathery* (alt. featherie) golf ball on this ground. Competition was intense and their skills were keenly honed on this common piece of ground belonging to all the residents of the area.

*a "feathery" was, as its name implies, a leather skin into which were tightly packed bird's feathers. Its size was somewhat akin to the current size of a golfball.

In the chronological list of golf clubs established in Scotland, Earlsferry comes very high up the list because of the discovery of a newspaper advertisement of 1787. The advertisement is in the following terms:

> **Earlsferry Golf Society.**
> THERE is to be a Meeting of that Society at Earlsferry, on Tuesday the 1st of May, when it is expected all the Members will attend.
> Dinner on the Table at Three o'Clock.
> By order of the Captain,
> P. PLENDERLEATH, Sec.

"Caledonian Mercury" Courtesy of British Library Board

No other evidence has yet been unearthed to increase the profile of this Golf Society. In evidence given to the Court of Session (see chapter 2) one witness talked about his father who was a distinguished landowner in the area and others presumably of similar social standing playing golf on this ground in the 1750s.

Further analysis of the advertisement can, we submit, give some clue to its existence.

So far as we know it was not the habit of the young golfers of Earlsferry who played on the golfing tract to form themselves into an organised club. There was no real need for it. The combatants were well known to each other and head to head matches were, presumably, simply fixed in the local hostelries or the first tee. The need for organisation into a club may well have come later but in the latter half of the eighteenth century and early nineteenth century it is difficult to find any reason for these Earlsferry golfers to form themselves into an organisation or Society. The Town Council owned the golf course on behalf of the residents and the Earlsferry men took it in turn to maintain it in a rudimentary fashion. No subscription was required and the Earlsferry residents were actual proprietors of the ground.

In contrast it was the practice of the gentry to whom golf was also a pastime to form themselves into organised golfing societies especially if they were not resident locally in the golfing area. The existence of the society gave rise to the practice continuing to this day of using the golf course for networking. We can surmise that this Earlsferry Golf Society might have been composed of a number of landed and wealthy persons who may not have lived locally. It is significant, we think, that the advertisement was published in a newspaper with a main circulation in Edinburgh and surrounds. We can take it that if these golfers who lived in Earlsferry wished to have a meeting it would have been advertised by word of mouth rather than in a posh Edinburgh newspaper. In 1787 the probability is that most of the young golfers of Earlsferry would hardly read a newspaper far less than one like the erudite and socially important "Caledonian Mercury". We calculate therefore that the Earlsferry Golf Society may well have been one which was not based locally but which used the golfing tract for its meetings. Later Dumbarnie/Hercules Club of Colinsburgh would have a similar profile.

Despite fairly robust searches there is no further evidence of this golf society. We have some clues. It seems to be the only advertisement that we can find, suggesting that the society, whatever its pedigree, was not long lasting. It is significant that whilst it is clear from the advertisement that the members are expected to attend it does not specify the actual place in Earlsferry that the "dinner will be on the table at 3 o'clock". Subsequent advertisements for such meetings of other clubs and societies tended toward specifying Earlsferry Town Hall as the preferred venue. It may well be that no other establishment in the village could accommodate these members and it was well known that their preferred meeting place would have been the town hall. There certainly was no hotel at that time in the village.

P. Plenderleath is highly probably Patrick Plenderleath who was born in Elie in 1750 and the son of Benjamin Plenderleath who was factor to Sir John Anstruther** (1st Baronet) who at that time would have been resident in Elie House - a large baronial mansion on Elie Estate lying slightly to the North of Elie. Patrick went on to become a writer/lawyer in Pittenweem and died in 1798. Furthermore he became the factor to the Balcaskie side of the Anstruther family**. It is conceivable that this is the correct gentleman with his Elie/Earlsferry connections and learning sufficient to be a secretary for the Society. The advertisement also says "by order of the Captain..". We know nothing about him but if as we surmise he would likely be aristocracy it would not be too far fetched to suggest that the captain might well have been Sir John Anstruther the second baronet who succeeded to the title on the death of the first in 1783. Or indeed more likely Sir Robert Anstruther of the Balcaskie line of baronets to whom Patrick Plenderleath was the estate factor. One of his later successors (5th baronet) is mentioned as being "on the links" for the inaugural competition for a medal presented by Earlsferry Town Council - therefore we subscribe to Sir Robert - the third baronet - as being the most likely captain since the aristocracy took a keen interest in the game. He also became head of Earlsferry and Elie Golf club (q.v.). Patrick himself died in 1798. There is another possibility, and that is, that the Society was based at Dumbarnie/Colinsburgh but that it played on Earlsferry golf course which we know happened later. **there are a number of branches of the Anstruther dynasty. This one was based in Elie House but others were based in Balcaskie and elsewhere.

There is a claim that Elie/Earlsferry golf course started in 1585 and this is based upon the supposed Royal Burgh charter which was conveniently (?) lost in a fire in Edinburgh and which claim was established (?) in 1830 in the litigation referred to above. This however requires rather more speculation than we have so far managed.

Earlsferry Abbey Golfing Society

Following on the Earlsferry Golf Society there appears to have been no further recognised golf organisation until 1831 when there is a reference to "Earlsferry Abbey Golfing Society". Note the "Society" – not a down market "club".

> **COLINSBURGH.**
> The first annual meeting of the Earlsferry Abbey Golfing Society was held on Saturday, the 7th inst., when the silver medal was played for over Earlsferry Links, and won by Mr George Wood, Colinsburgh.

This report of May 1831 is under the sub heading "Colinsburgh". This is a village about 4 miles north west of Earlsferry. That in itself has some significance. Dumbarnie golf course and Hercules Gymnastic club domiciled in Colinsburgh were instituted in 1835 and it is likely that Earlsferry Abbey Golfing Society or even the Earlsferry Golf Society (supra) may have been the precursor of those members of the gentry who used to play that sport at Colinsburgh or even St Andrews.

> *Golf.*—This ancient, healthy, and truly *Scottish* game, once the chief amusement of this and the neighbouring towns, has again been revived in our neighbourhood. Twelve months ago, a few gentlemen, anxious to promote and encourage the practice of this manly pastime, formed themselves into a society under the designation of the " Earlsferry Abbey Golfing Society." The club is now numerous and r spectable; and it is truly gratifying to see our ancient golfing green, lately lonely and deserted, covered with golfers in their scarlet jackets, keenly engaged in this health-promoting sport.

Note the use of the word "Gentlemen". There is reference here to the disporting of scarlet jackets. This certainly suggests that we are looking at a gentrified golf club since these scarlet jackets, almost expected to be compulsory, were expensive accoutrements of the golfer's attire and it is most unlikely that the joiners, stone masons and fishermen of Earlsferry would have aspired to possessing one of these jackets even if they could have afforded it. The suggestion therefore is that the members of the Abbey Society were gentry and that it was unlikely that any of the indigenous Earlsferry men were members of it.

The Abbey part of the title is also confusing. There has never been, so far as we know, an Abbey in Earlsferry. However the Earl of Crawford and Balcarres whose estate was at Colinsburgh was at one time (mid 19th Century) "feuar" of an area of ground known as Dome or Doom Park lying between the chapel at Chapel Green and the 10th Green of the current golf course. The history of this area is obscure but it was thought that the Earl of Crawford (Lindsay) feared that his support of the wrong cause in the '45 might well result in the forfeiture of his estates.

It is said that he divested his estate to his brother but in order to retain some form of holding in Scotland in event of his exile he acquired from Earlsferry Town Council the feu of this area to enable him to have safe landing back in his home country. There is certainly evidence that the estates of the Lindsays were at one time forfeit but we rather doubt whether this was recent enough to cover the feuing of the ground to that family. The valuation roll 1891 makes reference to Earlsferry

Abbey although strangely it is the only reference in the valuation rolls for Earlsferry showing Crawford's interest. Thereafter the area seems to have been divided between the proprietors of the two big houses there, Craigforth and Earlsneuk.

A further newspaper report a couple of years later refers to the Society.

ELIE.
The silver medal belonging to the Earlsferry Abbey Golfing Club was played for over the Links at Earlsferry, on Saturday last, and gained, after a keen contest, by Mr John Swayne. Elie.

It now seems to have become a "Club".

Thereafter references to it peter out and we believe that this was because the club/society was absorbed into Hercules/Dumbarnie club in 1846

COLINSBURGH. A gymnastic club having been formed here sometime ago, a general half yearly meeting took place on Saturday last, the 11th instant, when the members repaired to Dunbarnie Links to compete for one of the silver golf medals belonging to the club, which, after keen competition of two rounds of the Links comprising nine holes each, Sir Ralph A. Anstruther, Bart. of Balkaskie, and Mr John Wood, banker, Colinsburgh, came in equal at 109 strokes. This being the fewest number, they played another round, when the medal was gained by Mr Wood by two strokes. A similar club was lately formed in Elie*, and wish having been generally expressed by members of both that the two should be conjoined, they were accordingly united under the title of "The East of Fife Gymnastic Club", it being the purpose of the club to embrace a great variety of games and athletic exercises. The club, as so united, meets three times a-year—twice on Dunbarnie Links, and once on Earlsferry Links-- competing for a golf medal at each meeting. From the liberality of Charles Halkett Craigie, Esq. of Lahill who has given a grant of a stance for a house *and garden on Dunbarnie Links, besides the privilege of playing over the Links, the members have every facility for practising the different games. Fifeshire Journal 1837 *we are taking it that Elie also covers Earlsferry.*

And according to the Golfers Manual of 1857. Authored by "Keen Hand" (aka H.B.Farnie) and edited by Bernard Darwin.

DUNBARNIE—This Links is irregular in form, but is nearly an oblong square of no great extent. There is a hill in one part, which diversifies the play, and golfers make the most of the green by playing in a zig-zag fashion. There are no whins, but several ditches and other hazards afford some scientific sport.

The Hercules Club, instituted in 1835, with which was amalgamated a Golf Club from Elie in 1846, plays over this course. The United Club meets three times a-year, playing for a Silver Medal each time— Post Town, Colinsburg.

Chapter 3
The Litigation

On or about the middle of February or it may have been March 1812, Robert Carstairs the tenant farmer of the Malcolm family who owned Grange estate in Earlsferry set out from Grange Farm which lies just to the north of the golf course down the road toward Earlsferry, no doubt with his trusted Clydesdale horses and his plough. What he did within the next few hours was to have repercussions for at least 30 years - events which were not eventually resolved until the 1840s at great personal expense and angst to the citizens of Earlsferry and considerable financial benefit to the lawyers. Earlsferry nearly became bankrupt as a result.

"1853 O S"

To understand the significance of what happened we have to go back a few centuries. Earlsferry was not like it is now but consisted simply of two rows of houses one on the north and one on the south side of Earlsferry High Street which stopped at the end of the high street.

There was no building on the shore line and the houses on the north side of the High Street had gardens or more likely yards and middens which extended up a few yards and ended at an area of ground which was really just waste ground. However the citizens of Earlsferry used the area for a number of things. This is the first ordnance survey map of 1850 and it is reasonable to assume that prior to that date and certainly prior to 1812 there was somewhat less building on the north side.

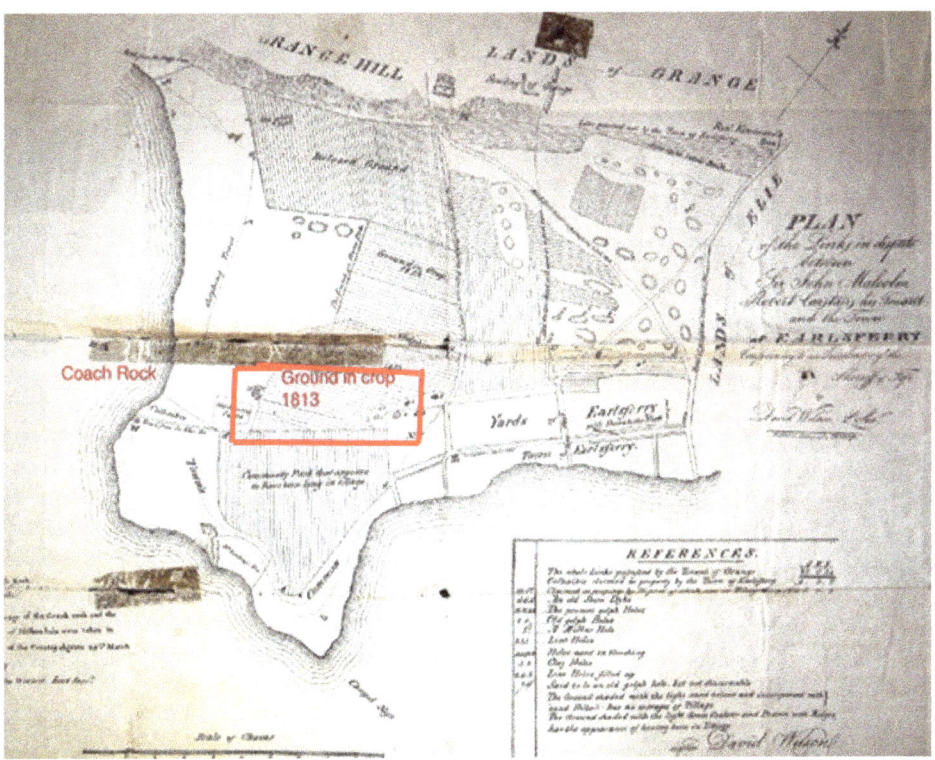

This is what the area looked like in 1813 from a map drawn up for the subsequent litigation.

The tenant of the Grange ploughed roughly the area in the red box. He cut off the links beside the village from the links beside West Bay.

The contours and size of the golf course, the number of holes available to play, varied according to a number of factors. It changed not only with the seasons but also when the playing of golf competed with so many other things happening or expected to happen on this hallowed piece of ground stretching from Ferry Road to West Bay. Sometimes cattle and sheep were grazed on it and sometimes parts of it were ploughed up by the tenant farmer of the Grange. When it was, the golf course simply changed direction until after the harvest or the residents of Earlsferry made a path through the corn or drove the ball over it. Not that the ground actually produced much crop. On this occasion in 1812 the local farmer had cut off the golfers from the east part and the west part of the golfing tract.

The locals claimed that Golf had been played on the links at Earlsferry for many centuries and the links area which borders on the north side of Earlsferry along Links Road was common ground used for a variety of purposes over the years.

It was always considered that this ground was common to the residents of Earlsferry and as such they had a right of access over it for whatever purpose they chose - or so they alleged. However it was golf that predominated on this area.

The proprietor of Grange Estate Sir Michael Malcolm in the 1810s took exception to the playing of golf on what he considered was part of his estate farm and he instructed his tenant, Carstairs, to prevent the good citizens of Earlsferry from playing golf there by ploughing up more land than had been done in the past.

Eventually in 1815, after no doubt considerable disruption to the games of golf, Malcolm raised an action in the Cupar Sheriff Court seeking interdict (injunction) to prevent the citizens of Earlsferry from playing golf on **his** land.

The Magistrates of Earlsferry as representing the people of Earlsferry raised a counter action of declarator claiming that the citizens of Earlsferry had a right to play golf on **their** land and they owned it but lest they did not then they sought a right which they claimed was enshrined in law as a servitude. A servitude is a right to do something over a piece of land you do not own which attaches to the occupation or ownership of an area of land which you do own. That servitude, claimed Earlsferry, was the servitude right to play golf.

One would have thought that the possession of a title deed might have been definitive of this dispute but as no one seemed either to have a title deed or, if they had at one time it had been lost, the litigation was necessary.

There was eventually a hearing of evidence which lasted in all two years during which there were witnesses led by both sides. There was a procession of the good, great, and maybe not so great, of Earlsferry, summoned to appear in Edinburgh to evince the fact that golf had been played on this bit of land for as long as they, no doubt their fathers and grandfathers too, could remember.

Malcolm contended that the evidence of these witnesses for the burgh was tainted because they lived at or near Earlsferry and might be supposed to have been biased in favour of being able to play golf on as large an area as possible so no doubt the first question in cross examination was "Do you play golf ?" to which the answer seemed to have been invariably "Yes" thereby disclosing a vested interest.

The contention of Earlsferry was that the burgh owned the ground but in any event had a servitude right on an adjoining land of commonty called Ferry Links of golfing, bleaching clothes, steeping lint, casting divots and perambulating over it. And that they had a right to a piece of land called Coalbaikie but it or part of it had been ploughed up by Carstairs, Malcolm's tenant, and in addition he had been taking stone from the quarry there.

The citizens claimed that they had ownership of the area on the map called Coalbaikie. This was ascertained by drawing a line from the Coach Rock which sits out to sea and joining it up with the corner of what is now Chapel Green walk. In any event it seems that Carstairs egged on by his landlord, Malcolm, claimed he tenanted, and his landlord owned, the whole area which he had ploughed up to the detriment of the golfers, bleachers, steepers, divoters and perambulators. He further contended that there is no such servitude in law as the right to play golf.

For a technical reason the action was transferred to Edinburgh to the Court of Session, Scotland's highest civil court.

The Elie History Society is privileged to have in their possession some of the original documentation which was before the court between 1815 and 1832. (As an aside, the Clerk to the appeal court is stated in the papers to be Sir Walter Scott.)

In these papers there is reference to some of the evidence given by the witnesses who had been called for the proof and much of it makes interesting reading. This gives us some insight not only to these times but also the origins of the game in Earlsferry. The narrative below is taken from the written submissions of the parties to the Court.

"Admiral Duddingston* who attended the school at Earlsferry 70 years ago [i.e. 1750s] said that he was then often present with his father when playing golf on the said links along with many other gentlemen**in the neighbourhood as he was too young to play himself. When they played golf on the links they did so wherever they thought proper and never were restricted or quarrelled. James Ovenstone said that he was born in Earlsferry where he stayed 20 years then he came to Elie where he has resided ever since. When he stayed in Earlsferry he often amused himself and[sic] playing at golf, that it was the then common practice not only for the inhabitants but for others in the neighbourhood to come here and play. Alexander Jarvis a flax dresser said that about 37 or 38 years ago he left the town of Earlsferry insofar and as he knows that passed the memory of man the inhabitants of Earlsferry have enjoyed the right of golfing on

the links there and the witness, so far back as he can remember, saw them enjoying this amusement and he did himself many times participate in it; that golf was played over the links as above in all seasons. Alexander said that he recollects that on one occasion the east course was interrupted by John Leitch's (an earlier tenant of Malcolm) sowing corn who one season ploughed a part of it but the golfers paid no attention to it, at least he paid none, golfing such that he did not spoil the corn and went round and drove his ball over it. James Forrester says that he recollects corn having been sowed to the West ....but there was always a track left for the golfing which enabled him to go on without interruption and he does not recollect that at any time the golfing was interrupted by corn being sown as a track was occasionally shifted when that became necessary. .....He remembers when John Leitch was the tenant of Grange he made an attempt to interrupt the golfing. He came down drunk and when he did so the gentleman named Lord Balcarres**** and Mr Durham and others paid no regard to this interruption and continue their game during the whole of the week after. James Boyd aged 52 says that they bleached and washed their clothes, linen yarn and spreading and drawing their lint and steeping their lint in different holes in the links that he never knew or heard of any price being paid for exercising these privileges or any levy being applied for and never knew of any interruption either by the possessors of the Grange or anybody else. An attempt has been made on the part of Malcolm to show that so far at least as regards the servitude of bleaching they have required certain sums of money to be paid for the privilege which the town enjoys. The town officer was sent through the town with a bell to warn people to meet and he had been present when the money was drawn but when he was asked to name those who paid for steeping the lint bleached he said that Bailey Sunter, James Anderson now both dead Jean Bishop, David Lyle, now dead Elizabeth Lyle paid for these privileges. By far the greatest number of witnesses paid no attention whatever. Mrs Jean Bishop says that she has known four different tenants at Grange and during the possession of all of these tenants she has been in the habit of bleaching both cloth and clothes on the links and never was *rejected and never paid any consideration for doing so nor does she know of anybody who paid for the privilege.*

*Admiral William Duddingston was a member of a land owning family who principally owned the estate of St. Ford which lay about a mile to the north of the golfing tract. He featured in the Gaspee incident in Rhode Island in 1772 when the British naval revenue vessel he was commanding, "the Gaspee", ran aground and was set on fire by the disgruntled inhabitants of Rhode Island. It was this excursion which many claim was the first skirmish in the American War of Independence. Admiral Duddingston retired from the navy and built Earlsferry House at the west end of Earlsferry High Street - it was demolished in 1960. The estate went bankrupt in 1777. Duddingston himself died in 1817. **the significance of this is that this would have been in the time when Earlsferry Golfing Society was up and running which suggests that any Elie and Earlsferry Golf club may have been even earlier than the advertisement in 1787.****again the landed gentry connection with golf at Earlsferry.

As a footnote the land of Grange at one time belonged to Major George Arnot from whom it was acquired by James Malcolm, son of John Malcolm of Balbedie. James Malcolm's investment was confirmed by charter from the crown and James Malcolm incurred a forfeiture of estates by conviction for high treason****. The estate of Grange and certain other lands were sold by the commissioners of the forfeited estates and they granted a conveyance to David Scott of Scotarvit in 1774. This deed proceeds upon a narrative of the attainder of James Malcolm, the exposure of the lands to public auction and of a minute of sale entered into between the commissioners and the said David Scott. David Scott conveyed the lands of Grange and others to Margaret Malcolm, sister of James and she executed the disposition of the lands of Grange in favour of her nephew, Robert Malcolm. Then the estate of Grange descended to James Malcolm of the Grange who was succeeded by Michael Malcolm as one of the heirs.

**** The Grange House and estate and the Malcolm family were ardent Jacobites and some of the planning of the return of the young pretender in 1745 was carried out there. Subsequently, of course, having backed the wrong side James Malcolm was accused of high treason and his estate forfeited. But it seems that they came back to the family when David Scott bid at the auction and then handed the estate over to Mrs. Malcolm!

Title of the magistrates of Earlsferry is claimed to be based on the extract from the Great Seal which had been lost in the fire in Edinburgh.

The judge gave a note.

The burgh of Earlsferry is of great antiquity and though its possession of lands is very small there are indications of a more extensive possession in former times. Their next neighbour, a most formidable enemy, is Sir Michael Malcolm Bart. This gentleman and his tenant have been encroaching upon the burgh property and privileges for so long a time past that there is much reason to believe that a considerable part of the town's property has in that way been carried off. Sir Michael's titles have been withdrawn, I have not found out what they comprehend. I only suspect that some parts of the town's property had been affected by prescription ....in point of fact the magistrates and inhabitants of the town, if they neglected some part of that, owns property have at least attended with sufficient care to other parts of it and so far as I can perceive they have not lost sight of a great number of servitudes if the rights which they have been exercising maybe so determined. For if the property which has been subject to the administration of the magistrates or the inhabitants of the town belongs to nobody but the town itself the servitudes in question used by the inhabitants may be the property of the town if no other party has an interest to it but it seems to be taken for granted .....that the property in question belongs to Sir Michael Malcolm and that the magistrates and inhabitants had no right in it at all even to the extent of a trifling servitude. I do not think however that such a construction can be put upon the uses to which the lands in question has been applied by the magistrates. I think it is evident that from time immemorial the magistrates and inhabitants have cultivated these lands in a variety of different ways. He goes on to say that in his view it is Malcolm and the tenant of the Grange who have encroached on the common ground owned by Earlsferry people.

The hearing of evidence took two years.

After evaluating the evidence the first judge found:

"that the Burgh of Earlsferry has, past all memory, enjoyed all the rights and privileges of a royal burgh....and that this burgh has enjoyed property past all memory and that in so far as the burgh has been in possession of the ground it is entitled to protection of its rights....[he rejected the evidence of most of the witnesses who were resident in the burgh but founded his opinion on independent witnesses].... there was a lot of contradiction in the witnesses........... There is strong evidence that part of the ground called Coalbaikie had been possessed by the inhabitants of the burgh for a great length of time and ....that although the inhabitants of this burgh and strangers visiting it had played golf on the eastern links and enjoyed other exercises and amusement upon these links, then not ploughed or enclosed yet that during all that period the proprietor and tenant of Grange exercised every right of property by ploughing them at different periods, and killing rabbits on them and that the whole of these links had been ploughed and in regular cultivation except some small hillocks. That there was also a golf course upon the links to the west which although diminished by part of the ground being enclosed and ploughed seems still by the plan to afford a sufficient space for golfing:- that the present course as marked upon the west links seems perfectly sufficient for affording the amusement of golfing such as the population of Earlsferry can require, without having any title to exercise that right except alongst the same or links, where aration (sic an old word meaning ploughing) cannot well take place; but in order to prevent any dispute in time to come appoints Mr Wilson the surveyor who prepared the plan (vide supra) in process at the sight of the parties to put in march stones* ..... such as he conceives will be the least prejudicial to the estate of Grange and may sufficiently secure the exercise of golfing to the inhabitants of Earlsferry;" *These march stones still exist between 6th and 7th fairways and at the side of the 9th green.

The court remitted to the Sheriff of Fife to draw up a plan showing the roads and golfing tract.

There was much significance apparently in the fact that Malcolm having originally submitted his title deeds to the court eventually withdrew them – the inference being that his title deeds actually showed much less land than he claimed.

So the case was submitted back to the Sheriff Court in Cupar. Sensible way of proceeding one would have thought but it did not quite work out that way. The Sheriff of Fife attended with the parties and wandered around the ground and he went on to look at the area of ground necessary for a golf course. At that time there were holes marked out of sorts starting at Ferry Road (here called German's Wynd) going west. He laid out a line of golfing tract which effectively consisted of the present fourth fairway, from the fourth green north west at an angle roughly to the top of the hill at the ninth green and then 12th and 13th and that was about it. The current 10th and 11th would remain because there was no dispute that this was on commonty land owned by the burghers of Earlsferry and Sir Robert did not make a claim to this.

The rest of the land of the current golf course he recommended be part of the estate of Grange although he makes a comment that Malcolm did not produce a title deed to that ground. Mind you, neither did Earlsferry who relied upon the charter granted to it as a Royal Burgh. In any event the strip of ground which the Sheriff reported back to the Court of Session was bounded on the north by what looks like a line down the middle of the rough between 4th and 17th. Then a line from about the current front tee at the 5th to a marker which was down 6th fairway (see stone image above) Thereafter the line went north westerly to the current 15th green and from there directly north to the fence of the field at Kincraig Point. And the land to the seaward side of that line and the ground to 10th green and 11th green would be part of the course.

Earlsferry and its golfers were not happy. Firstly they claimed that the corner of Coalbaickie had always belonged to the Burgh as part of the commonty and Carstairs had ploughed this bit up actually provoking the dispute.

So there was an appeal by both sides. Malcolm, on the basis that the witnesses had been biased and that there was no such thing known to the law as a servitude right of golf. The Burgh took objection on the basis that the track he had marked out was not sufficient to the enjoyment of golf. *{it seems some of the areas marked out the course were too narrow and not enough to hit a golf ball – this is probably where the legend arises that the amount of ground was determined by the normal hit of a golf ball}* The Court then granted a new remit :

"to experienced golfers, or to the Sheriff (*who by implication was not an experienced or even a golfer*) along with experienced golfers and it remitted to Walter Cook W.S. and John Taylor Attorney in Exchequer to examine the ground in question to lay out a proper golfing course thereon sufficient for the exercise of that amusement."

Research shows that these gentlemen were indeed experienced golfers. Walter Cook, Writer to the Signet, was a stalwart member of the R. and A. and on 3rd October 1806 won the autumn meeting at St. Andrews with a gross 100 and John Taylor was a member of HCEG at Muirfield and he won one of their medals on 21st July 1814.

Their plan was a little different from the earlier one and eventually this was the one which the court accepted and gave authority to. From what can be ascertained it was broader than that drawn up by Wilson and the Sheriff and included the corner ground at Coalbaikie.

So there is the outline of the golf course in 1831 and, of course, that was the same date as the establishment of Earlsferry Abbey Golfing Society. It is a guess that this club formed in 1831 was so that they could make representations to Cook and Taylor about the golfing tract.

So it was established that the citizens of Earlsferry could golf on this area of ground set out to the court.

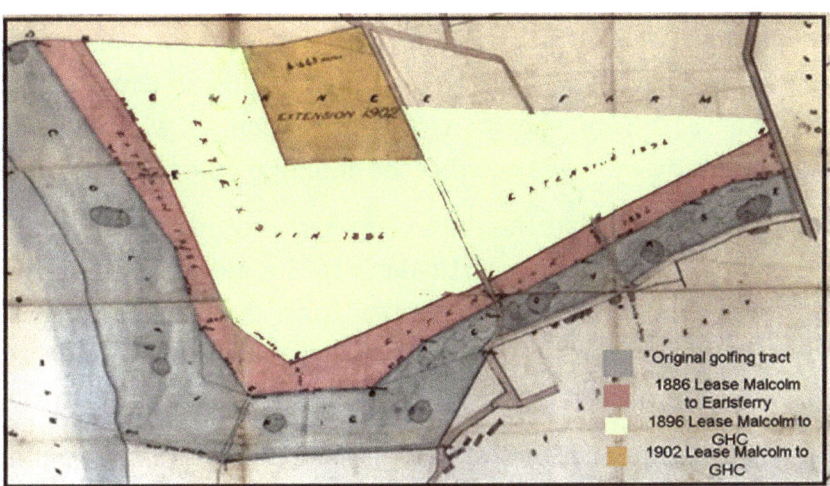

This is the area coloured blue/grey on above plan. It is believed that this was the kick start that golf needed in Earlsferry and even visitors from as far away as Elie could play golf on this area of ground for free. There was some restriction in that the golfers were not expected to interfere with the comings and goings of the farmer and the Grange estate.

The parties co-existed for a few years and there may have been some tension because there was a warning sent out by the Burgh to golfers that if they hit their ball into a field being cultivated they were not allowed to retrieve it lest they do damage to crops.

But the dispute did not end there because in 1878, Sir James Malcolm of Balbedie (the successor to Sir Robert) and Grange, and David Fraser, farmer, Grange Farm, his tenant, sued the Committee of Management the Earlsferry and Elie Golf Club, and George Forrester, clubmaker, Earlsferry, green keeper to the Club, and also the Magistrates of Earlsferry, and James Waddell, Town-Clerk, and community of Earlsferry, for their interest, to have it declared that the golfers have no right to cut or carry away grass from any part of the golfing course of Earlsferry, part of the farm of Grange, and that they should be interdicted (*prevented*) from so doing.

The Malcolms also asked the Court to regulate the hours during which the privilege of playing golf over said golfing course shall be exercised, in such a manner as will enable him and his tenants to pasture their cattle and sheep on said golfing course, without injury or molestation to them – *(one assumes the animals rather than the golfers.)*

Malcolm claimed that the defenders had recently, in the course of the present year, 1878, and particularly in the month of June, cut and carried away large quantities of grass from the said golfing course against the remonstrances of the pursuers, and to their serious loss, and they maintain a right to do so without permission of the pursuers.

In answer to the pursuers' statements the defenders, the Committee of the Golf Club said that the decree founded on by the pursuers proceeded on the basis of a report prepared, under a remit of the Court, by Walter Cook, W.S., and John Taylor who examined the Links and laid out the golfing course which has since been in use. It was admitted that golfing has been practised on this course on the Links since 1832, that it has been practised on the Links from time immemorial, and that the exercise of the right was restricted and regulated by the decree, so far was deemed compatible with the due exercise and enjoyment of the right. It is explained, in particular, that Messrs Cook & Taylor, as their report bears, considerably narrowed the space over which golfing had been in use to be practised. It is admitted, also, that the defenders, the Club, have cut the grass upon certain parts of the course, and explained that the Club was instituted in 1858 *[this is the Earlsferry and Elie golf Club, see later]*, and has had from the first, among other officials, a greenkeeper that was George Forrester the golf club maker, whose duty it is, and always has been, to keep the course in order for play.

With that view he cuts and always has cut, the grass of the putting greens when necessary, and also the nettles and rank weeds and grass which grow in the hollows, of which there are several on the course. He also levels moleheaps, fills up rabbits' holes, and the like. All this, it is said, is absolutely necessary to the due exercise of the game, and no more has at any time been done than is absolutely necessary. From the circumstance that in the present year the Links have not been grazed, the quantity of grass cut may have been larger than formerly, but the area cut is not larger than in former years. The course is about 1500 yards long, and from 50 to 100 yards wide. There are from nine to eleven holes in it.

For eight months in the year (October to May inclusive) there is very little golfing; and, during the remaining four months, the farmer and landlord have the course to themselves on Sundays, and during the night and early morning of each day, and also during unfavourable weather when there is no play. Last summer the bestial were put out from 5 to 10 every morning, when they were removed to an adjoining park. The Links being unenclosed, herds have in any case to be kept {in}. There is, the defenders maintain, no necessity for further regulation, and no room for such regulation, without abridging their rights, as defined by the decree of the Court founded on. In particular, the hours of play cannot be restricted without entirely interfering with their rights, and depriving players of all opportunity of playing."

This case did not come to anything the parties having settled it. How the course developed thereafter see chapter 7 on the Development of the golf Course and it is in our view not insignificant that an extra strip of land was leased in 1886 to Earlsferry Town Council. The new Golf House Club in 1896 leased an area of ground from the Grange estate which broadly included part of the ground which had been in the farm.

So what happened to the right of the Burghers of Earlsferry to play golf on that golfing tract?

The most fascinating is that a burgher of Earlsferry (by that, an owner of property) had the right to play golf on the Earlsferry links. Or at least on the part decided in this court action which does not include the land to north of the 15th Green or the land alongside Grange Road. Of course at that time the Melon Park was not part of the golf course and anyway that was in Elie. It became part later.

Chapter 4
Earlsferry and Elie Golf Club

In Chapter 3 we explained how the traditional golfing tract of Earlsferry became an official golf course subject still to the rights of the owner and tenant of the Grange estate. With the amalgamation of Earlsferry Abbey with Dumbarnie/Hercules in 1838 or so there appeared to have been little organised golf at Earlsferry. The landed gentry and important players of the area played at Dumbarnie twice a year and once as the Hercules Club at Earlsferry in addition, of course, to the strong attachment to St. Andrews. In chapter 3 the litigation with the Malcolms, concluded in 1833, was reported but it had cost the Town Council and Earlsferry residents dearly.

With the finalising of the golfing tract it can be imagined that the permanence of the golf holes meant that more people would have played. But would there have been a necessity for a club?

The Earlsferry men continued to play on their golfing tract without the red jackets. The land was owned and managed by the Town Council and although the coffers were somewhat depleted with legal expenses they still had an income to enable such maintenance that may have been required. A formal club with subscription etc. was unnecessary. It might well have been called the first municipal course. A clubhouse was not a vital part of the scene. The players were all local and presumably just picked up their club/s and wandered to the first tee looking for a game. There was no need for special golf shoes or red jackets. In any event the Golf Tavern was very close to the first tee and operated as a semi clubhouse and it served drink of course. Later, part of Georgeville, the house built by George Forrester next door to Golf Tavern, was to have a sort of clubhouse facility but this was not until much later in the 1880s.

> **ELIE.**
> GOLFING SOCIETY.—On the evening of Thursday the 23d inst., a meeting of golfers took place in our parish school, for the purpose of constituting a Golfing Society, Mr Steward, Earlsferry House, in the chair. A considerable number of gentlemen were present, all of whom seemed hearty in the cause. Various resolutions were adopted for future guidance, among which it was resolved, that 'Earlsferry and Elie' be the name of this Society. A Treasurer, Secretary, and Committee were duly appointed, and after a vote of thanks to the chairman the meeting separated.

As the game started to catch on with the locals, competitions were sought. Various local worthies would put up prizes for competition amongst the Earlsferry golfers but there was then a need for some sort of organisation to manage the competition, police them and award prizes and trophies. We imagine that the formation of the Earlsferry and Elie Golf Club was such a vehicle. By then the residents of Elie had taken an interest in the game and since only Earlsferry residents had a right to play over the course it made sense to form a club with members from both villages and of course make the Elie players pay a subscription! That, it is speculated, was what happened in 1858.

It is perhaps a little surprising that a formal golf club did not emerge until 1858 but there may have been another reason for this. By that time it was expected that a railway line would be built in the East Neuk linking the various fishing villages and also giving better access for those coming from Edinburgh and Glasgow. It would take a few more years yet, but it certainly looked as if the golfing pleasures of Earlsferry might well have been opened up to a number of people who were not actually resident in the Burgh. This obviously gave rise to questions and the Town council may well have thought that a formal golf club would enable it to police the area better. By 1890 the Forth Rail Bridge had made the area far more accessible but that was in the future. Additionally golf was becoming a more popular sport although not to the extent that it became in the next 50 years,

In 1865 a newspaper report is in the following terms *"Earlsferry. The managers of Earlsferry* having sometime ago agreed [to] present a silver medal to the Earlsferry and Elie Golf Club, to be competed for annually, they, along with the captain and a few members of the club, met in the Town Hall on Friday last week, when Sunter**, [in] a suitable speech, presented the medal, hoping that it would always fairly and honestly [be] played for and honourably won. Mr Proudfoot [The Captain] returned thanks in a very complimentary manner to the managers for the excellent gift which they had conferred upon the club. The medal was played for on Saturday, and won by Mr Andrew Rolland. Sir Robert Anstruther and other players were upon the ground, and also a picnic party from Andrews. "* *i.e. the Town Council ** the Provost

This was the Burgh Medal. It would appear therefore that the club was flourishing because in the same year came this report.

"EARLSFERRY. Golf Competition —On Saturday last, the members of the Earlsferry and Elie Golf Club met on the Links here, to compete for a very elegant silver Quaich presented to the Club by L. C. Browning, Esq........ In accordance with the wish of Mr Browning, the Quaich is to be competed for annually in a handicap match for the purpose of putting all the players on an equal footing. This was accordingly done on Saturday, and from the nature of the match, the competition was all the more keen and exciting. Two rounds of the Links —consisting of twenty-two holes*—were played, ...In the evening the members of the Club entertained Mr Browning to supper, in Aitken's Hotel Elie. Mr Proudfoot, Captain of the Club, occupied the chair, and Dr Robertson officiated as Croupier [old term for vice chair who traditionally sat at the bottom of the table] ......In the course of the evening toast and song were given alternately; and altogether a very pleasant and agreeable evening was spent. The supper was served in Mr Aitken's very best style, and gave unqualified satisfaction."

*this was before any holes were built on the east side of Ferry Road.

In 1866 there was a competition organised by the club for 18th August. The prizes were a set of clubs donated by Colonel Babbington and the

Club Medal. We know from a newspaper report of the proceedings that present were Sir Robert Anstruther, Patron of the Club, Babbington himself and the Dean of Faculty of Advocates. The great Tom Morris who had made the clubs which Babbington donated as a prize was also present. This seems to be a fairly prestigious gathering for a small golf club but the article also says "and others from St. Andrews". By October of that year they were also competing for the Balcaskie Medal donated by the patron Sir Robert Anstruther. Things were indeed increasing in pace. One major consideration was that the outline of a golf course at Earlsferry had been laid down many years ago and whilst other clubs and courses were just starting up Earlsferry had a historical pedigree.

It seems that by 1872 things were firmly established and the list of medals was Browning Quaich, Burgh Medal, Robertson Cross, Club Medal, Baird Medal, Balcaskie Medal and the Henry Gold Medal. These had been presented to the club for competition and one of the stipulations of the club was that no player could win more than one medal in each calendar year. At that time the Patron of the club was Sir Robert Anstruther (Balcaskie), Captain was W.R. Ketchen the local banker and lawyer, the secretary was James Davidson the schoolmaster. Significantly the approved professionals were Bob Mackie who was given the task of Greenkeeper and Andrew Rolland (Dougie Rolland's father).

The membership was an interesting selection. There seems little doubt that many of the office bearers and movers and shakers were those members of the gentry who would have been members of Hercules and R. and A.

It is suggested that the playability of Earlsferry golf course was an attraction to these gentry members and they would have shown a preference over Dumbarnie which by then was rather a boring and flat golfing area not exclusively dedicated to the sport, and St. Andrews which was probably, as now, rather over subscribed. It is true that there was a thriving club at Crail but the convenience of Earlsferry seemed to attract the hardened golfer. By 1872 therefore there was a solid thriving club at Earlsferry and it seems from later remarks that it contained not only the "locals" but also some members from Edinburgh and further afield. Of course the arrival of the Railway line in 1863 made Earlsferry golf course that much more accessible to Edinburgh and other urban afficionados. It may well have been that which attracted those from the higher social echelons of Edinburgh.

At this point the course comprised of 11 holes and a standard round was twice round the course. The club aspired to a larger area but that was to come a little later.

In 1873 there was another E.G.M. and this time we know that W.R. Ketchen resigned as Captain giving way to Mr. Henry, a gunmaker who lived in Chapel Green House. The significance of this resignation was to be made clear a few years later.

Again the club had no recognised premises but to all intents and purposes it seemed to be in good fettle. It used Earlsferry Town Hall for its meetings and probably the Golf Tavern for après golf entertainment.

In the background however there must have been some tension because we know that Mr Ketchen, having resigned as captain, wooed the local landowner, William Baird, to grant him and three others a lease over the Melon Park an area lying to the east of Ferry Road and therefore in Elie (the only area of the golf course which was not and is still not in Earlsferry). He established a golf club in 1875 and a number of wealthy and well-to-do patrons were invited to subscribe funds to build a clubhouse (the one that stands today) and thereby incorporate the holes on the east side of Ferry Road into the course.

Now one can imagine how this might have been received in the Earlsferry side of things. Firstly the Town Council were the owners of the golfing tract in Earlsferry and could very much control its use. It had no authority however over the part of the course on the other side of the town boundary. This was the new Elie Golf House Club (GHC) and in due course they had a very commodious and substantial clubhouse from which to play, meet and socialise. It took a couple of years to build but by 1877 it was ready for action. It might have been thought that at that point the GHC held the upper hand but William Baird in granting a lease over the Melon Park stipulated that any golf club playing over the Earlsferry part was to have the right to play over the Elie part. There was therefore a reprieve for Earlsferry and Elie golf Club.

There was one other and much more significant consequence of this move. Because the GHC controlled the Melon Park and a spanking new club house the founder members could choose which worthies they would allow to become members. A number of the former members of Earlsferry and Elie club threw their lot and money into this fledgling but important new social hub. Equally as a number of members of the original club were by reason of their social and economic standing likely to be excluded from membership of the new entity, it left most of the joiners, fishermen and masons still attached to the Earlsferry and Elie club or if they lived in Earlsferry and did not belong to that club. By 1875 the players of Earlsferry had become extremely proficient in the game, some were playing for money – not just a casual sweepstake but serious money - and this was unlikely to be appreciated by the members of the Golf House Club.

There were two other factors which ultimately led to the withering of the Earlsferry and Elie Golf club. The first was the loss to the GHC of these wealthy and influential members. There was a view that by that stage many, if not most, of the members of the Earlsferry Club were from outside the area and the "clubbiness" of the GHC was far more likely to enhance their social standing than remaining with the old club which in any event did not have club premises.

There was another factor which had a considerable bearing on the outcome. Sir Robert Malcolm and his tenant at the Grange complained and raised another court action in 1878 against the Earlsferry and Elie club, the Town council, and George Forrester the Greenkeeper, complaining that the club by cutting the course to make it suitable for golf was depriving the tenant of the Grange from the grass for his cattle. (See Chapter 3.) Earlsferry Town Council having recently been subject to the hazards of the legal process not to mention the costs of the original litigation must have been extremely concerned. However on this occasion they did have the more powerful and, dare it be said, socially and financially more stable GHC to look to for some financial assistance with the defence. The GHC agreed, mindful of the consequences of losing this court action, to help fund the defence. This was a more formidable opponent than the Town Council and one suspects in the background the might of the GHC persuaded Malcolm to come to an amicable settlement and, as we shall see, this involved leasing a larger part of the Grange estate for the golf course. Obviously the members of Earlsferry and Elie Golf club were very concerned about the costs and their individual liability therefor. This probably led to further defections to the other side of Ferry Road to the GHC. The action was speedily settled. One wonders if this was because Sir Robert Malcolm realised the muscle socially and financially of the new GHC. By then (1879) the GHC had demonstrated its power and started its own competitions.

One of the thorns in the side of the good golfers of the former club was that the rules stipulated that one player could not hold more than one of the club's medals in each year. There was some concern about this rule. A further concern appeared to be the proliferation of "professional" golfers in the ranks. This may well have intimidated many of the members of the former club who in any event were unlikely to be local. At the same time as the GHC was starting its affairs it became clear to a number of the Earlsferry and Elie members and those not members, but living locally, that they were not of a sufficient social standing to be admitted to the new club on the Elie side. In 1875 therefore the Earlsferry Thistle golf club came into existence – it gathered in those really good golfers from the Earlsferry lads and it proved to be a very strong club challenging a number of surrounding clubs to matches. (See chapter 5).

In 1881 there is a report that the scheduled competition for the Robertson Cross by Earlsferry and Elie golf club did not take place owing to lack of players. This was a foretaste of what might come. It seems that after this failure the club became moribund prompting this article in August 1883.

> GOLF.—Several old members and other golfers interested in the Earlsferry and Elie Golf Club which has been dormant for some years, have resolved to resuscitate it. For that purpose, a meeting was held in the Town Hall, Earlsferry on Tuesday night. Mr Small, Edinburgh occupied the chair, and the attendance was encouraging. The following office-bearers were elected :—viz., captain, Mr Small; vice-captain Mr M'Lees, Elie ; secretary and treasurer, M Davidson, Williamsburgh ; committee, Messr Dun, Adamson, Given, Balsillie, Gibson, and Bryson, Edinburgh, and Robinson, Colinton.

There were other significant advancements in the golfing scene in Elie and Earlsferry at this time. With the huge increase in interest in the game the manufacture of golf clubs became an important business and George Forrester having returned from USA in 1871 started a business making these clubs. The business flourished and he eventually acquired property in Links Road and built Georgeville part of which he later let out to the Earlsferry and Elie Golf Club as a clubhouse. George Forrester's business rapidly became so successful that he employed many of the young Earlsferry golfers as apprentices in his "shop". These apprentices in the main were excellent golfers in their own right and after an apprenticeship with Forrester many became professional golfers all over the world. However a mere golf club maker was hardly the pedigree to become a member of the GHC so these golfers joined the Thistle - the "artisan" arm. The Simpson family and James Braid were attached to the Thistle rather than the Earlsferry Club or the GHC.

The club seemed to survive however and there is a report in these terms in 1895.

> ELIE.—The members of the Earlsferry and Elie Golf Club yesterday evening finished a most successful two-days' competition for a massive silver cup presented by Colonel Outhwaite, and which becomes the absolute property of the winner. The cup was won by Mr H. Sanderson. The

It is interesting that the Outhwaite family of Craigforth seemed to have taken an interest in the Earlsferry club whilst one would have thought with their pedigree the GHC might have seemed more attractive. The Outhwaites brothers were very good golfers but perhaps the younger was not GHC material because he owned and ran a garage and car business in Cupar.

There is evidence that the Earlsferry and Elie club continued until about 1912 and thereafter was disbanded. The membership that remained either joined the Golf House Club – provided they were accepted and had the right pedigree – and the balance the Thistle Club.

There is no further information about this the first really organised club at Elie but there is little doubt that the GHC and its membership was a considerable threat to the old club and when the GHC negotiated a lease of a larger area of ground in 1896 the writing was on the wall. *(See chapter 8 Development of Golf Course)*

Chapter 5
The Golf House Club

In Chapter 4 we learnt how the Earlsferry and Elie Golf club became established over the Earlsferry course after the hiatus of the litigation with Malcolm and the Grange Estate.

The club was initially comprised locals who lived in Earlsferry but as the arrival of the Railway opened up the villages to visitors, holiday makers and second home owners (even in 1870s) so the membership became rather more cosmopolitan with many members joining, who lived in Edinburgh and Glasgow. It had ceased in many respects to be a local golf club.

At an extraordinary General Meeting in 1872 the then Captain, W.R. Ketchen, a local lawyer and banker who lived in the National Bank Building in Bank Street, resigned. There had been some friction between the Earlsferry Town Council and some of the members and it is probable that Ketchen among others thought the club too parochial and too dependent upon the Town Council of Earlsferry who owned the course. Whether his resignation was well signposted or not we do not know (he had attempted to resign the previous year) but in the background over the next couple of years it emerged that he had created the foundation of a new golf club. At that time Earlsferry and Elie Golf club did not have its own premises – it was not until 1885 or so that George Forrester offered that club accommodation in his house at Georgeville.

It seems that in May 1875 Ketchen along with Major General Briggs, gentlemen called Raimes, Orr Paterson, Browning and Dewar had along with Thomas Currie, the local builder and his son John Currie the local architect met and formed the new club or rather had come out into the open as having leased from William Baird what was then known as Melon Park (at least the southern portion thereof lying to the north of the houses at Williamsburgh). This is the piece of ground lying to the east of the Ferry Road. Baird leased the ground to Rev. William Hillhouse, John Luke, Thomas Currie and W.R. Ketchen.

At that stage they were not trustees for Golf House Club but it became pretty clear that there was an intention to build a clubhouse for the GHC on part of the ground of the Melon Park. This was the final building and it is possible to date this image from between 1877 and 1895 because the fence which is in the foreground was the original fence separating off the southern part of the Melon Park from the northern part. It was only after this fence was removed that the northern part of the Melon Park became part of the golf course. However it was only the piece of the Melon Park lying north of the houses at Williamsburgh and a line drawn from the corner of the quarry to the Recreation Park. In effect this was just what is now the 18th fairway. It was enough however for three holes to have been added in that area.

And so it happened that by 1877 the following appeared in the newspapers of the time -

OPENING OF THE NEW GOLF HOUSE AND GREEN AT ELIE.

The increasing popularity of Elie and Earlsferry as summer resorts, and the yearly augmented number of golf players, has of late years led to a desire for more extensive accommodation than has hitherto existed. Although this want was felt for some years, it remained for Mr Ketchen, for many years the popular and energetic chief-magistrate of Elie, to originate a feasible proposal, and the efforts put forth by that gentleman were so successful that the landed proprietors and the leading gentlemen of the district at once took an interest in the scheme, and at a preliminary meeting held in May 1875 subscriptions to the amount of £200 were intimated. At this stage, William Baird, Esq., of Elie, came forward and offered a lease for nearly a quarter of a century of the Melon Park, which adjoins the Earlsferry Links. This was at once accepted, and the committee with much discretion selected a commanding site at the north-east of the new ground. Designed by Mr John Currie, Elie, the new house, which is in the Italian style of architecture, and has cost upwards of £1000, consists of a handsome club-room 21 feet in length by 19 broad, with a ceiling 14 feet high, and a billiard room 25 feet by 19 feet, both being lighted by large windows ten feet in height and made to open. At the entrance is a wooden portico with glass sides, while at the further end of the spacious lobby are the passages leading to the lavatory and offices and housekeeper's apartments. The house commands clear and uninterrupted views of the course and of the Firth of Forth, and is in every way suitable for the purpose intended.

The consequence of this was that the influence of the Earlsferry Town Council and the Earlsferry and Elie Golf Club waned. No longer did the Town Council control all that happened on the golfing tract and the Town Council would have to give increasing precedence to the wealthier establishment on the east side of Ferry Road over which Earlsferry Town Council certainly had no control. A lot of the kudos perhaps of the GHC was gained by the pedigree and financial clout of most of its members. Initially it was agreed that the management of the golf course (both east and west of Ferry Road) would be in the hands of a joint committee and George Forrester – an Earlsferry man – was appointed first greenkeeper of the new course.

John Laidlay   Sir Ralph Anstruther

The office bearers and committee of the GHC make interesting reading. The Captain was John Earnest Laidlay. He was one of the most important and successful amateur golfers of the era having won two British Amateur Golf championships and numerous (said to be over 130) medals of the various clubs of which he was a member. He lived off private means and was resident then in Grangemuir which is just to the north of Pittenweem. He was also a member of the committee in 1899 when the golf course was initially extended. Sir Ralph Anstruther of Balcaskie was on the committee on both occasions. We know his late father, Sir Robert, was patron of the Earlsferry and Elie Golf Club at one time. James Scott Davidson a charter accountant from Glasgow - again he was also on the committee in 1899. William Jamieson the factor of Elie estate. James Nicholson Loden Kirkwood described as being a colonel in the Indian staff corps who was also on the committee in 1899, Dr. Philip Grierson Borrowman who took over the medical practice of

Dr. Macallum in Elie in 1891 - by 1899, he had moved to Crieff but he still retained his committee membership of GHC. If this committee was representative of the quality breeding and financial standing of the members of GHC the locals did not have a look in.

One of the consequences of the GHC establishing itself in 1875 was the formation of the "artisan" club of Earlsferry Thistle. The local population of Earlsferry who did not qualify as a result of their social status to be invited to join the GHC now formed their own club. It was into the Thistle that the vast majority of the very good local Earlsferry golfers went. (see Chapter 6 Earlsferry Thistle) Also there were a number of professionals who joined the Thistle. At that time 1875 the "professional" golfer was still not defined. Playing for money could not be the main criterion since most of the members of GHC would play stakes on a game. It was Dougie Rolland* who first alerted the golf authorities, such as they were, to the difference between an amateur and a professional in his application for entry to the Amateur championship at Hoylake in 1885.

*See chapter 11 on professional golfers.

> The minutes being read and approved of, the Hon. Secretary (W. R. Ketchen, Esq.) intimated that there were now 102 members, and read an abstract of the funds of the Club, showing liabilities to the amount of £401, and assets, exclusive of the Club-house and furnishings, £101. Mr Ketchen also explained that subscriptions to the amount of £90 were now due.
> The Chairman then proposed Sir R. Anstruther as captain of the club, which was seconded by Colonel Babington, and unanimously agreed to.
> On the suggestion of the Hon. Secretary, Mr Thomas Sime, captain of the Earlsferry and Elie Club, was elected a member of committee in room of Mr Richard Raimes, Edinburgh.

At the annual meeting in 1879 there was this report:

So within a very few years the club membership had risen to 102 But this minute forecast a few rocky roads on the way forward.

This looks like an attempt to bring Earlsferry and Elie golf club into the fold (subject always to the member being acceptable to the GHC) and it looks as if the cost of upkeep of the course had fallen exclusively on Earlsferry Town Council which seems prima facie unfair since at least 75% of the course was now under the control of GHC.

> One of the most successful tournaments yet held under the auspices of this Club took place on Elie and Earlsferry Links on Friday last. Established in 1877 the membership of the Club has continued steadily to increase, and the handsome club-house, which has cost about £1400, is the resort of a large number of visitors during the summer months. The weather on Friday was all that could be desired—the sunshine being tempered with a westerly breeze which was not strong enough to interfere with good scoring. There was a good attendance of visitors during the day, and amongst those who watched the play were Sir Robert and Lady Anstruther and party; Principal Sir Alexander Grant and party; Major Boyd and party; Mr Bethune of Blebo, captain of the Club for the present year; Mr W. H. Cameron, treasurer of the Edinburgh Water Trust, &c. Mr Ketchen, the courteous and energetic hon. secretary, personally superintended the arrangements, which were of the most complete description.

In 1882 came this report.

Again the prestigious nature of the GHC is borne out by the dramatis personae spectating. It must have been a supreme social occasion.

Because of the control over 75% of the course by GHC this gave rise to obvious anomalies. If we accept by virtue of their citizenship of Earlsferry, residents were entitled to play free of charge on the old golfing tract and the Coalbaikie (which in effect is what the result of the litigation with the Malcolm family determined) What should or would they have to pay to play on the extended course? The astute Mr. Baird had made it a provision in the lease to the fledgling GHC that Earlsferry and Elie Club members and any members of a recognised golf club would be entitled to play over the Melon Park - one cannot but wonder whether this may have rankled with the GHC committee. Should the members of GHC pay to play on the golfing tract and Coalbaikie - no such reciprocal right appears to have been granted to the GHC members? The current arrangement would therefore have meant that Earlsferry and Elie golf club members could play on the full course free of charge but GHC members were subject to the control of the town council vis a vis the golfing tract and Coalbaikie. This must have been anathema to GHC members who were paying an annual subscription whilst many of the Earlsferry Golfers paid no subscription to any club, they being entitled to play on the course free by virtue of their residence in the village. It was this that predicated the arrangements that were then negotiated and finalised in the first agreement between Earlsferry Town Council and the GHC in 1909.

These questions obviously exercised the minds of both sides in the enterprise. Earlsferry and Elie Golf Club had many members who were not resident in Earlsferry and therefore not entitled per se to the privilege of playing on the golfing tract free of charge. Their subscription to the club probably allowed them to play on that part of the course but it also entitled them to play on the Melon Park by virtue of Baird's condition. At the same time there was the feeling that the Town Council would rather like to wash their hands of the obligation to maintain the links.

In any event this agreement of 1909 formed the foundation of subsequent agreements up until 1974. The terms and conditions set out in 1909 were as follows:

Firstly the Town Council agreed to hand over the expense of maintaining the links to the GHC – of course, as will be seen later, the bulk of the course was now in the control of the GHC anyway so the Town Council merely handed over the management of the golfing tract and Coalbaikie.

Secondly the GHC were given entitlement to make charges for playing over the links. A scale of charges then followed in the agreement. Remember that this would have applied to all and sundry who were not members of the GHC but there was an interim concession to the members of Earlsferry and Elie Golf Club who should not have to pay more than seven shillings and sixpence for an annual ticket when the non member of either club would have to pay ten shillings for a two monthly ticket or twelve shillings and six pence for an annual ticket. This did not give a right to use the GHC clubhouse.

Thirdly, and here is where the concession was apparent, "that no charge shall be made on any inhabitant of Earlsferry or members of the Thistle Golf club resident in Earlsferry or Elie but other members of the said club *[Thistle]* resident outside Earlsferry or Elie and who are not bona fide workmen in either of these places shall pay the same charges as are levied on the members of Earlsferry and Elie Golf club." There was a further proviso that visitors were not entitled to play over the extended course except on the terms specified in the table of fees.

The agreement was said to last until 1926 and that the rent for the commonty/golfing tract payable to the Town Council by the GHC was to be £3 per annum, that the maintenance of the Seatangle Road (that is the track leading from the west end of Earlsferry to West Bay) shall fall on the GHC and the salmon fishermen* were still entitled to dry their nets on the Coalbaikie. The agreement also provided that the GHC were not entitled to increase the charges in the scale of green fees without the consent of the Town Council.

there was until the mid to late 1950s a very lucrative salmon fishing group based in Earlsferry who had nets stretching out into West Bay.

The next pressing issue, as it were, was the definition of "resident in Earlsferry". With the huge increase in second home ownership did this privilege apply to second home owners who were ratepayers of Earlsferry?

In 1939, after what seemed like a lot of wrangling, there was a further agreement between GHC and the now Elie and Earlsferry Town Council. In 1929 the two local councils had amalgamated (although not willingly it seems). On this occasion, still getting convoluted with the fact that Earlsferry residents had a privilege, it was agreed that (1) No green fee shall be payable by a ratepayer of Earlsferry who was ordinarily resident there, the wife, husband or children of the above, members of Earlsferry Thistle who were ordinarily resident in Earlsferry or *bona fide* workmen in Elie or Earlsferry. This novel concept of bona fide workman was defined to include any shop assistant, clerk, craftsman, artisan, apprentice or person normally employed in manual labour or any other person of similar class – any dispute about this to be decided by the Provost.

Then an attempt to be a bit more precise. This provided that:

1. No green fee shall be payable by ratepayers and residents who live in the area which previously formed the Royal Burgh of Earlsferry [Note women and children abandoned!]

2. A green fee of 30 shillings per annum shall be paid by a ratepayer or resident who lives in the Burgh of Elie and Earlsferry but outside the area in (1) and is not a member of the GHC, Elie and Earlsferry Ladies Golf Club, Earlsferry Thistle Golf Club or Elie and Earlsferry Ladies Thistle Golf Club. In essence you pay 30 shillings per annum if you are not a member of any of the clubs but you must live in Elie and Earlsferry.

There then followed a detailed requirement as to how much members of the Thistle clubs should contribute to the coffers of the GHC. Again there were distinctions this time: ratepayers or residents in Elie and Earlsferry, ratepayers and residents who live within a radius of three miles, those living outside that circle but within five miles. Resident is defined as living for not less than six calendar months in each year. Each of the clubs had to submit a list of their members with the appropriate category and there would be a sliding scale of the amount the clubs were to pay to the GHC.

All these shenanigans were purely and simply to appease the Ferrymen who had this right to golf over the commonty/golfing tract. You bet the GHC could have done without this hassle.

The rest of the history of the GHC can be found in A.M. Drysdale's book of the GHC History.The Golf House Club Elie (1975)

The final chapter in this story happens in 1973/1974. Fife Council possess a common good fund consisting of the assets of the old Royal Burgh of Earlsferry. Common good funds in Fife were assets which had previously been owned by Burghs in their own right on behalf of the ratepayers/burghers and which by successive local government reorganisations became the property of much larger local government behemoths. They are retained for the benefit of the Burgh whence they derived. Elie/Earlsferry had (until recently) two assets in their common good fund – Earlsferry Town Hall, now acquired by a community buy out and "the right to golf on Earlsferry Links". This was and probably still is valued modestly at £1.

With the looming reorganisation of local government in 1974 it seemed very likely that the ownership of the commonty/coalbackie and golfing tract would pass to Fife Council. This was a concern at the GHC* in particular; so a policy was put forward to try to buy out all the leases of the ground occupied by the golf club including, of course, that owned by the Royal Burgh of Earlsferry. After negotiations the GHC agreed to pay the Earlsferry Town Council the sum of £1000 for the area of ground. Similar negotiations took place with Miss Baird who then owned the Melon Park, the Gourlays of Kincraig (this was in relation to the 13th Green and 14th Tee) and the Malcolm family representing the Grange Estate. All parties were happy to agree to this buy out so that in 1974 the whole golf course became owned by the GHC. No longer was a *bona fide* artisan, craftsman, manual labourer, required to be considered in a special position when it came to the golf course. Almost 100 years of uncertainty had been resolved since the acquisition of the tenancy of the Melon Park by Ketchen and his associates (aka GHC).

*It is not specifically stated but there was a perceived anxiety that the Golf House club which was exclusively male might be required by the new local authority owner of the golfing tract to change this rule. Whilst the Elie and Earlsferry Ladies' Golf club had been established many years earlier (1884) it merely had a right to play on the course by virtue of it being a subsidiary of the GHC and even to this day that club pays a subscription to the GHC.

Chapter 6
Earlsferry Thistle

After the conclusion of the litigation between Earlsferry Town Council and the Malcolm family of Grange estate in 1832 or thereabouts the extent of the golfing tract of Earlsferry was at least fairly firmly established. What else was established was that the Ferry men who lived in Earlsferry and had for generations knocked a golf ball about this piece of land were entitled to continue to play on it seemingly by virtue of their residence in Earlsferry and of course it was free of charge – being owned by the Town Council for the residents. They generally looked after it themselves, cutting the grass round the greens and maintaining it as best they could. As the game developed and ceased to be a purely gentrified sport it is suggested that there were Elie people who looked on enviously at the Ferry men with their own free golf course. The gentry would play on it too but we suspect that the Town Council would hardly try to tussle with them and exact a green fee for the privilege of playing on the Earlsferry course. It is known that at least once per year the Dumbarnie/Hercules club would hold a competition on the Earlsferry course and it no doubt gave many of the Ferry men the chance to earn a shilling or two caddying.

> **ELIE AND EARLSFERRY GOLF LINKS.**
>
> The N. B. Daily Mail on Tuesday had the following:—
>
> Although golf has been played for centuries at Earlsferry, the clubs are all comparatively modern. The oldest organisation is the Earlsferry and Elie Golf Club, which was instituted in 1858. Next comes the Elie Golfhouse Club, instituted in 1875, whose commodious pavilion is at the starting tee. If the Club were notable for nothing else it would become so from the the fact that Mr J. E. Laidlay, the brilliant amateur player, is captain. It may be mentioned here that the arrangement of course was largely in the hands of Mr Laidlay, who, together with A. H. Scott, spent many days on the links devising ways and means to make them as perfect as possible. Then there is the famous Earlsferry Thistle Club, which if less "tony" than its neighbours, includes a galaxy of players which few clubs are in a position to beat. There are also two ladies' clubs, one playing over regular course and the other playing over nine holes specially set apart for ladies.
>
> The links at Earlsferry are now firmly established as a home of the game, but at one time the burgh authorities had difficulty in preserving the ancient right of golf "to inhabitants and visitors." Only within recent years, and by amicable arrangement, was ground obtained sufficient to permit of eighteen holes. While not varied by the frightful hazards that make some other links notorious, Earlsferry cannot by any means be described as an easy course. The first two holes are laid out on the high land behind the town, and it is here that the players obtain the finest view of the surroundings. Inland there are the fertile fields and rugged hills of Fifeshire, while to the south is seen the chafing Firth of Forth dotted with islands, the most conspicuous of which are the Isle of May, Inchkeith, and the Bass Rock. Playing to the third hole the golfer descends to the level of the village, and passes on to the seaside, thence returning zig-zag fashion to the clubhouse. The hazards as a rule are judiciously placed. The turf is good, and the grass kept short by constant grazing.

Information on the Earlsferry and Elie Golf Club established in 1858 is lacking but there was a cosy relationship between the club and the council so much so that the council donated the Burgh Medal for competition amongst the members of that club. The membership was likely to be Elie people rather than the real Ferrymen and no doubt the middle class such as they were in Earlsferry would join this club. The arrival of the Railway line in 1863 made a huge difference to the parochial ferrymen and their golf course. Now golfers from Edinburgh and Glasgow could get to Elie relatively easily. They could spend summer holidays here and they could play golf. The Earlsferry and Elie golf club attracted many members from the cities and it seems as though the Ferry men felt marginalised. No longer was this their exclusive golfing patch.

When the Captain of the Earlsferry and Elie golf club W.R.Ketchen (see part 4) resigned in 1871 many of the ferrymen must have realised that their future as players on the golfing tract was likely to be limited by the establishment of the Golf House Club in 1875. When the Melon Park was leased by Ketchen and his associates it must have been clear to the Ferrymen that this new club was likely to dominate the golfing scene in the years to come and that the committee and founders of this new club were most unlikely to welcome into membership the tradesmen, joiners, golf club makers, masons and professional golfers of Earlsferry. The Earlsferry and Elie golf club although enjoying the tacit if not direct endorsement of the Town council was becoming increasingly confined to visitors – whose social profile was close to those who had formed the Golf House Club.

It is a hypothesis that the Ferrymen decided to form themselves into a separate club from the GHC through self preservation. This they called Earlsferry Thistle Golf Club established in 1875. The guess work here relates to an article in the newspapers of 1899 in these terms.

> "the famous Earlsferry Thistle golf club....less 'tony' than its neighbours."

The expression 'tony' is defined as meaning according to Merriam Webster "marked by an aristocratic or high-toned manner or style" or "fashionable among wealthy or stylish people" and whilst not exclusively seems to suggest an American/Canadian etymology. It does however very accurately sum up what happened in the case of the Thistle. The Ferry men realising the strength of a golf club joined this fledgling club and very soon its prowess became legendary. Most of the Ferrymen golfers who had honed their skills on the golfing tract now joined the Thistle. Many of these were enjoying a career in golf at least until they emigrated to spread the word mainly across the Atlantic.

It is speculation but there is ground to believe that the Thistle established in 1875 was so established to form a golf club which was entitled to play over the Melon Park. According to the newspaper report of 1925 celebrating the 50th anniversary of the founding of the Thistle the original members who founded the club were Andrew Anderson, Robert Peebles, Andrew Tulloch and John Ward.

It is an interesting collection of people.

Andrew Anderson was born in Earlsferry in 1850. He was a fisherman originally but the only evidence of his golfing ability was that in the 1901 census he was described as a golf greenkeeper and he was living in the police station at Williamsburgh. This must have been the original police station because the current one was not built until 1937. He was living in this house with his wife Flora and 8 children of whom more later. He is, according to the newspaper article (1925), the only surviving founder member and he was a greenkeeper at the Recreation Park in 1901. He was the father of at least four professional golfers. James Mackay Anderson born in 1882, William Mackay Anderson born 1883, Andrew Mackay Anderson born 1885, and George Mackay Anderson born 1896.

Robert Peebles was also born in 1850 and a fisherman. So it is thought, because there were three Robert Peebles in the area. One in Colinsburgh whom we have discounted – he was a china merchant and seems unlikely to be a golfer. The second was born in 1848 and lived in Earlsferry but we have discounted him because his mother was a widow in 1871. The Robert Peebles we are concerned with lost his life at sea in 1886 thus we conclude that it was this Robert Peebles who founded the Thistle. The 1925 article indicated that only Andrew Anderson was still alive. Like Anderson his son Robert Peebles became a professional golfer. His other son was connected to the golf trade in America although not a golf professional as such.

Andrew Tulloch was much older than his other two Ferrymen. Andrew was 55 in 1871. He was unmarried and was a sailor. He was still on the Thistle committee in 1884.

The fourth founder member was John Ward according to the newspaper article and it states that he was from Elie but there is no evidence of that name in Elie at that time or even later. It is possible that it was meant to be John Warrender who was a contemporary of Peebles and Anderson and also a fisherman although judging by the number of newspaper reports featuring his name he had a tendency to over indulge and get into fights. Not that this would have prevented him from founding a golf club!

So we have this anomalous position that you can play golf on the golfing tract free of charge if you are resident in Earlsferry. But that per se might not have been enough to enable you to play on the Melon Park but if you were a member of a golf club you could play on the Melon Park. It therefore made sense that the tradesmen of Earlsferry would have formed themselves into a club to enable them to play on the extended course which included the Melon Park. It was exactly this complicated anomaly which gave rise to mighty toing and froing between the Town Council and Golf House club in future years when trying to recognise the right of free golf over the golfing tract. (see Chapter 5). The Thistle members therefore would be able by virtue of Baird's stipulation to play over the Melon Park part of the course and also the golfing tract if they were resident in Earlsferry.

> GOLF.—On Saturday last, the members of the Earlsferry Thistle Club played for a very handsome oil painting representing a view in the Links, presented by Mr Aitken, painter. The result of the play showed Mr John Simpson to be the winner with a score of 85. At the meeting in the Clubroom, when the prize was handed over to Mr Simpson, on the motion of Mr Wm. Mackie, Mr Aitken was unanimously admitted a life member of the Club. Such an action as that of Mr Aitken tends much to encourage golfers in acquiring proficiency in the ancient and royal game, and it is to be hoped that that gentleman will have followers during the season now commenced.

All the very good golfers professional or otherwise who played on the golfing tract in the main joined the Thistle which meant that that club could field the strongest team of any club and so they ruled the roost for a number of years. Various prizes were donated to the club and some of the more unusual ones too, e.g. in 1882

And this in 1884 shows the power of the club.

> GOLF.—The members of the Earlsferry Thistle Golf Club competed for medals and prizes on Saturday. 8 couples turned out. At starting the weather was all that could be desired, but while at the "sea" hole, during the first round, a nasty shower rendered play disagreeable and the putting greens thereafter heavy. Douglas Rolland took 84 to the two rounds of 18 holes ; while John Simpson, also a scratch scorer, came in with 84 ; likewise W. C. M. Morris scored 94, and his odds of 10 being deducted, reduced him also to 84, rendering the three a tie. Charles Simpson made the two rounds in 90, and 8 odds being deducted, brought him down to 82. John M'Ruvie was the best non prize-taker with 90, less 5 odds, 85. Charles Simpson was accordingly declared the winner of the "Edinburgh" Medal and accompanying prize. Rolland, John Simpson, and Morris having played one more round to decide their tie of 84, came in with Rolland, 42 ; Simpson, 44 ; and Morris, 50 ; less 5, 45. Rolland, therefore, secured the "Mason" Medal and the second prize ; and J. Simpson and Morris the third and fourth prizes. Since his match with Ball *tertius* last year, considerable interest is manifested in Rolland's play, and Saturday was no exception to the rule. The Links this year are well patronized by lovers of the "Royal and Ancient Game," and the green-

Dougie Rolland was the doyen of the club – Braid, of course, was a member and one of the Simpson Brothers was also Open champion in 1884.

It is worth, at this stage, to put the foundation of the Thistle club into historical context. Research shows that in 1871 George Forrester, an Earlsferry mason by trade, had returned from America and was setting up business as a golf club maker. It is also known that there were a few very good young golfers who had honed their skills on the golfing tract and who were making a name for themselves as players of considerable note. By 1875 therefore there would be a pool of young talent ready to be assimilated into the Thistle. James Crowley had also returned from USA and was making golf clubs, but he moved to Glasgow shortly after the turn of the century, although he kept a property and workshop in Earlsferry. Andrew Scott a former apprentice of Forrester set up a club making business in 1894.

By this time golf was very popular in Earlsferry and many of the great names of that era having been members of the Thistle were pioneering the game abroad especially in USA. Between 1875 and the turn of the century the winners of medals in the Thistle read like a who's who of golf around that time. Braid, of course, was Open Champion but there was a previous Earlsferry open champion in the form of Jack Simpson in 1884 and many Earlsferry men were coming close to winning tournaments in the south of England and abroad as professionals. Douglas Rolland's exploits had been stuff of folklore and the Simpson brothers, the Mackie brothers and the Pearsons, Keddies and others were gaining a world-wide reputation as skilful golfers. It is little wonder that the nursery ground for these titans of the professional golfing scene was the Earlsferry golfing tract.

Of course no professional golfers, club makers or journeymen could become members of the GHC and that was the Thistle's success. So it remained for many years that the Thistle could produce a golf team of scratch players as amateurs but they very soon found that they could earn a good living as professional golfers both in UK and abroad. Their influence in the development of the game in the first decade of the 20th Century cannot be overstated. Similarly the influence of George Forrester, Andrew Scott and James Crowley in the development of design of golf clubs cannot be ignored. More recently Jock Smith and George Murray continued to carry the banner for the Thistle. It is true that a similar cadre of golfers came from North Berwick and St

Andrews and joined the entrepreneurial spirit in USA, but Earlsferry for its size produced more professional golfers pro rata than these other two cradles of golfing talent. It is interesting further that a good number of the Earlsferry men who went abroad especially to USA also inspired their children to become professional golfers. Golf owes much to the lads of Earlsferry and the Earlsferry Thistle which nurtured and tutored the many early pioneers of the game.

Initially The Thistle met in George Forrester's house Georgeville then they constructed a shed but in 1934 they built their own clubhouse which is situated anomalously in Elie alongside the 18th fairway. But they still started their round on the old first tee just outside Forrester shop on the golfing tract. Indeed it took some persuasion more recently to expect Thistle Members to start at the conventional first tee of the current golf course.

Chapter 7

The Recreation Park and Sports Club

One of consequences of the development of railway travel in the latter half of the 19th century was the ability of those living in conurbations to reach seaside resorts and open-air activities which became much sought after. Village resorts especially in Fife and those adjacent to beaches competed with each other to provide facilities to attract more visitors to their area. Visitors meant economic benefits to the businesses. The explosion of rail travel meant that hitherto difficult journeys by road had become substantially easier by rail. A full day out at the seaside and return to home became possible. Certainly from Glasgow and the west the journey time by train to Fife was substantially reduced. The Forth Rail Bridge opening (March 1890) anticipated that the whole of Fife would be much more accessible to the day tripper from east and west and also to second home owners and for lengthy residential holidays. Of course golf courses and beaches were attractive to these visitors but often they expected more. Golf after all was still a preserve of the wealthy and beach batheing in inclement weather was not everyone's cup of tea. It seems that towards the end of the 1880s (the bridge was started in 1882) pressure was being applied to town councils by their constituents to provide some extra form of recreation facilities not only to attract visitors to their area but also to provide the local residents with recreation and welfare facilities.

In the East Neuk between 1886 and 1900 many villages created Recreation Parks for visitors and residents alike – Anstruther, St.

Andrews, Methil, Kilrenny, Auchtermuchty to name but a few involved themselves in creating these parks which might or might not include a golf course. The method would usually have been a petition by ratepayers to their local council asking them to promote such a venture in the interests of the constituents if the council itself had not taken the initiative. And so it was that in Elie in 1888 a few public meetings were held to promote such a venture in the village.

"The public meeting of the inhabitants of Elie and Earlsferry was held in Elie public school on Saturday afternoon (12th July 1889) to consider the advisability of procuring a public park for the district. Between 20 and 30 gentlemen were present. Mr Ketchen (yes – him again!) was called to the chair. ....continuing, the chairman said it was not needful to see much to prove the desirability and even the necessity of a public park for Elie district. He looked at places that fell under the category of "watering places" they would see that those in charge generally recognised the duty and necessity of providing as many attractions as possible to those who visited their shores and neighbourhood. Elie and Earlsferry for some years past fortunately for the inhabitants have become very favourite watering places and they had reached that point in their history when it became a question of the greatest moment whether they would keep the little prestige they had at the moment enjoyed or whether they would allow others to take away their prosperity providing greater attractions.

He did not pretend to say that a public park was an absolute requirement on the score of health but there were other reasons than health to be taken into consideration. The powers that be here have decreed that Elie and Earlsferry are not to become manufacturing places* and they were therefore obliged to make them more and more attractive as summer resorts. They all knew that these places must have considerable natural advantages in the shape of beauty and of situation or they would never have gentlemen from a distance coming there and becoming proprietors and tenants of houses. It required then very little to be said to show that Elie and Earlsferry very must be provided with a recreation park and he hoped to be able to show them how much could be obtained without incurring much expense. They all knew that the Kingdom of Fife had almost been in a state of painful isolation from the outer world on account of its railway system but they were looking forward to reaping considerable benefit from the completion of the Forth Bridge and he wished to impress upon those who had business in Elie and Earlsferry that whilst it was equally true that they should be so much nearer Edinburgh and Glasgow the other large centres of population by the Forth bridge it was equally true that the railways would run to other places having very much the same natural advantages which they possessed. It therefore became imperative that they should try and increase the attractions of Elie and Earlsferry so that they would retain their prosperity as a summer resort. For a considerable number of years now a few of them had been endeavouring to discover how and where they could get a public park.*

Within the last month or two Mr Robertson of Wadeslea had been approached and was quite willing to give a portion of the West Kirk Park between the Melon Park and Park Place. They would have a space of 22 acres. Mr Robertson has secured a lease (from Baird his then Landlord) of the park as part of his farm and he was willing to give the southern portion** of the park for £25 a year for a period of five years or longer if circumstances would permit. These circumstances are that provided he again becomes the tenant at the end of that period then he would be willing to continue the agreement. At the last meeting of Elie Police Commissioners on Monday as they would have seen from the record a large signed petition from the inhabitants was submitted complaining of the annoyance caused by the shows on shooting galleries*** in the High Street and asking that they should be removed on the ground that they were dangerous to the public and interfere with the quiet that was really needed in the early hours of the night for children and invalids. If they had a park these shows and shooting galleries would be removed from the streets. Even supposing they had not these grounds of complaint he thought the inhabitants were quite entitled to insist upon a recreation park.*

He also thought the police commissioners of Elie and Town Council of Earlsferry should take advantage of the powers they had under the act of parliament and to take up this question. He then asked for expressions of opinions from those present. In reply to Mr Glover (he lived in Earlsferry House) the chairman said that the act of parliament gave the police commissioners the power to provide a recreation park by assessment and he believed that the laying on a penny per pound on rental [i.e. rates] would raise all that was needed. If Earlsferry joined with them the share of Elie will be something like £20. ....Mr Currie**** moved and Mr Morrow seconded the first resolution as follows "that this meeting is of the opinion that a public recreation park should be secured and pledges itself through all its power to procure such streets." Mr Glover proposed seconded by Mr. Thompson the following: that this meeting considers the southern portion of the West Kirk Park between the Melon Park and Park Place would afford a suitable site for a public park. The resolution was also unanimously agreed to as was the following " that this meeting recommends that a petition be lodged with the Elie police commissioners and the town council of Earlsferry to provide funds out of the rates or common good." .....Various members were then appointed to a committee.

*"manufacturing places" – this is a reference to a recent proposal to build a paper mill at the Toft to make use of the water from the loch run – by this time the flax mill had fallen into disuse. The application was refused by the town council stating that it did not want industry in the area.

** "southern portion" – this was roughly a line from the current track from park place in a straight line to Elie Golf Course see below

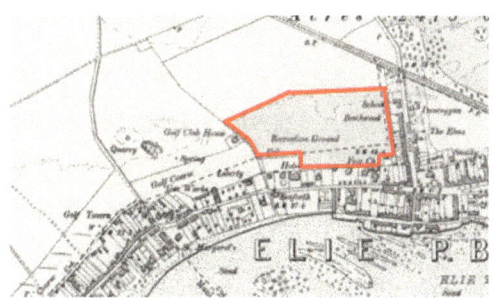

*** "shooting galleries" - these had long been an irritation to the residents of Elie whose sleep was disturbed by rowdy behaviour associated with such travelling fairs. The shooting galleries' successor, the penny arcade and side shows, were later accommodated on ground of the recreation park adjacent to the school during the summer holiday season.

****Mr. Currie was one of the Currie family who were the main builders of the large houses in Elie after the arrival of the railway line. They had premises in South Street.

And so the petition with the 124 signatures was presented to the Police commissioners in Elie (the forerunner of the Town council).

They met and.....

FOR ELIE . THE PROPOSED RECREATION PARK DEPUTATION TO COMMISSIONERS. A special meeting of the Elie Police Commissioners was held on Monday evening, to receive a deputation in support of the requisition by ratepayers in favour of the acquiring of the southern portion of the East Kirk Park as a recreation park. All the Commissioners were present. Mr Ferguson stated that he, as interim convener of the Committee appointed by the ratepayers at the recent public meeting, had to produce a requisition signed by 124 of the ratepayers which he understood represented a large majority both as regards the number of the ratepayers and the value of properties within the burgh. In addition to asking Mr Ketchen (the Clerk to the commissioners) to read the requisition with signatures attached he did not think it would be needful for him to say much in support of the requisition, he had for a good many years been in the habit of coming with his family to Elie as a watering place, and as most of them knew he recently became a proprietor within their burgh. He had been induced to purchase on account of the introduction of the water and the attractions of the place in the shape of a golfing course and the fine beach. As regards the golfing course he believed its recent extension (this would have been the addition of the Melon Park and the increase to 14 holes) would induce others to seek summer residences in their midst as it had done him, ……….As regards the proposed recreation park he was quite certain it was just what was wanted to meet the requirements of the place. As every one knew who frequented the golfing course there was really no provision made for ladies and younger people, and unless such were provided it was quite clear that parties having families would go where such accommodation could be had, and judging from what had been done in the past he could not imagine that the authorities, in the face of the requisition which had been read to them supported, as it was by so many of the ratepayers, could not be attended to and carried out [sic]. Mr Blues said as a ratepayer and proprietor in Elie he confirmed every word that Mr Ferguson had uttered, and most strenuously urged upon the Commissioners to do all in their power to make Elie one of the finest watering places not only in Fife but in Scotland.

Mr Morris (the local Baker)as long connected in trade both in Earlsferry and Elie said he could assure the Commissioners that it was of the greatest moment to the place that all should be done that possibly needed to be, not merely to keep up the credit of Elie and Earlsferry as attractive watering places, but if possible to induce visitors to come to their shores in increased numbers, as not only the prosperity but almost the existence of the place depended on them doing that. Mr Dower confirmed Mr Morris' statements. Mr Leitch (the convenor of the Police Commissioners) *said it gave him the greatest pleasure to receive the deputation, and thanked them for the interest they were taking in the place, and he hoped the Commission would be unanimous in granting the prayer of the requisition. He thought the Commission should now express their views as to how they felt in regard to the matter. Captain Smith was not inclined to have anything to do with the matter. Mr Moon considered that the desire of the ratepayers should be carried out, while Mr Morgan and Captain Bonner, declined to give any expression of opinion in presence of the deputation. Mr Leitch again expressed his approval of the scheme, and thanked the deputation for their attendance, who then retired. Ultimately the meeting unanimously resolved that a special meeting be held on Monday to consider and dispose of the matter.*

Such optimism turned out to be seriously misplaced. Because on the following Monday night ....

The Proposed Recreation Park. —At special meeting of Elie Police Commission on Monday night to consider the desirableness of providing ground for a recreation park, asked by requisition signed by 124 ratepayers, Provost Leitch moved that the requisition be complied with, and urged the necessity of increasing the attractions of the locality for summer visitors. Mr Morgan proposed that the requisition be not complied with, and said the park would only result in an increase in the rates. Mr Ketchen (the clerk) pointed out that the requisitionists asked that the assessment for the public park should not exceed one penny in the £1 so that it was not the case that there would be an increase in the rates above that. The amendment was carried by four to two.

In effect this scuppered the involvement of the local authority in the scheme.

However nothing daunted, the 124 ratepayers took matters into their own hands, leased the ground and set about organising the Recreation Park for the benefit of the villagers and visitors.

RECREATION PARK FOR ELIE.—We are glad to say that the laudable efforts being made to get a recreation park for Elie and Earlsferry are likely to be crowned with success. The public meeting held on Saturday afternoon, (August 1889) although not largely attended was unanimous in demanding that the park should be secured as early as possible. Mr Ketchen, who has done so much for the district in the past, was called to the chair, and in a short but pithy speech, pointed out the necessity of increasing the attractions of Elie and Earlsferry when so many other places were doing their utmost to attract summer visitors. This is the principal trade of Elie and Earlsferry, and in order to keep it up everything possible must be done by the inhabitants to sustain the popularity of the towns. A good deal has been done in the past in this direction, but something more remains, and until a public park is provided, and a larger Hall is erected, the work will not be completed.

Fortunately Mr Ketchen went to the meeting fully prepared with the necessary particulars as to the park to be obtained. Every one will admit that the agreement which Mr Robertson of Wadeslea is willing to enter into, to give 22 acres of the West Kirk Park for £25 annually, is a very moderate one, and inasmuch that the park is in every way suitable and convenient for the purpose asked there should be no hesitation in coming to a definite decision at once. The Elie Police Commission and Earlsferry Town Council will be consulting the interests of their constituents in helping to pay the rent out of the public funds. In no case can the tax exceed a penny per £ of rental for recreation purposes, and in this case it is not likely that that figure will be required. A good part of the yearly rent will be drawn from the Ladies' Golf Course and other sources, and in these circumstances the ratepayers cannot grudge the small sum to be taken from the common good. The Committee, under the convenership of Mr Gorman, who have been appointed to make the necessary arrangements to secure the Park should be heartily supported by everyone interested in the prosperity of the locality. We fully anticipate that a public park will soon be among the number of the many attractions which Elie and Earlsferry possess.

Things moved at a breathtaking speed hence this advertisement merely two days later from the above meeting in 1889.

And the report the following Friday thus: "Elie Recreation Park. This park was opened yesterday by a ladies' golf tournament being played. There was a large attendance of visitors and inhabitants at the park. The ladies' golf course has nine holes and eleven couples started playing two rounds. Sir Henry Morland of Bombay, who agreed to present the prizes, *congratulated the visitors and inhabitants on securing the recreation park which had been opened so auspiciously that day. Although the police commissioners had rejected it, Scottish Enterprise and perseverance had come forward and obtained the park."*

The fact that a tournament could have been organised in such a short time suggests to us that actually there already was a rudimentary golfing area because it seemed most unlikely even with the primitive golf courses that then existed a suitable course could have been created in such a short time. Of course the committee may well have anticipated the decision of the police commissioners and started the ball rolling before the unanticipated rejection. This is compounded by the fact that the initial lease of the property was only the southern section and one wonders whether there was room in that area for 9 holes (even if it was only the ladies who were playing!) However it was up and running and became very popular for various activities.

> GOLF TOURNAMENT.—As will be seen from the posters distributed through the town a golf tournament is to take place on Wednesday, Thursday, and Friday of next week over the Ladies Links for medals and prizes. Since last year the Ladies Golf Club and Recreation Park Committee have amalgamated, and in the future the Ladies Golf Club will be managed by a Committee appointed from the Recreation Park. It is understood that Mrs Asquith has consented to distribute the prizes on Saturday 22nd inst., and a large entry is expected for the various competitions.

One of the early uses was the Elie Annual Sports – this became an institution and was held each year. It seemed to be a most popular event hence this report in 1899.

> **ELIE AND EARLSFERRY ATHLETIC SPORTS.**
>
> Favoured with fine weather the annual athletic sports of Elie and Earlsferry, which were held in Elie Recreation Park, were a great success. Between 2000 and 3000 spectators were admitted.

> THE SPORTS.—The sports come off in the Recreation Park on Friday, the 20th August. The military band and pipers of the Royal Scots (over 50 performers) from Edinburgh Castle have been engaged to supply the music, and that alone should draw a big gate. The success of this meeting will, of course, depend on a good day, and it is to be hoped it will. There will be a general half-holiday all along the coast. The sports commence at one o'clock. The Railway are to grant cheap facilities at single fare and a quarter within a radius of 60 miles on the 20th on all ordinary trains.

And this in 1892

1893

ELIE ANNUAL GAMES. The annual athletic gathering took place in the Recreation Park, Elie, yesterday, in presence of a large attendance of spectators. The weather was highly favourable, and the sports proved a great success. The programme included 23 events, all of which were keenly contested. A special attraction was provided in the band of the 6th (Inniskilling) Dragoons, who played several excellent selections, all of which were much appreciated. Several well-known athletes were present, and the open events were keenly contested. Brodie, Anstruther, was a good first in the 100 yards, while Andersen, Jedburgh, after a good race in the quarter-mile, won the red flag. A ladies' bicycle race was also run, but only two entrants started. Egg and spoon race and obstacle race also provided some amusement.

The competitions for driving the golf ball were strongly contested, nearly a score of pros, and amateurs entering. A wheelbarrow-potato race also afforded great laughter, Pringle, Edinburgh, being the first to arrive with his small load. Much disappointment was expressed at there being no appearance of "lady cyclists", for whom two handsome prizes had been provided. A race for the bandsmen was substituted, and a capital event it proved, the whole of the military going off at a fine sprint for ten prizes. The trotting races for ponies and horses were well contested, four starting in the former and six in the latter competitions. The horsemanship of the Masters Braid in both events was quite a feature, and they deservedly got a place in both events. Nearly £55 were drawn at the "gate," representing an attendance of nearly 3000. The judges of the various events were Colonel Outhwaite and Mr John Foggo, Mr J. Scott Davidson acting as starter.

1896 ELIE AND EARLSFERRY ATHLETIC SPORTS. Charming weather. The Elie and Earlsferry Athletic Sports were held yesterday the Recreation Ground, Elie, in presence of between 2000 and 3000 visitors. The gathering, which proved a most successful one, was under the patronage of Sir Ralph Anstruther, Bart, of Balcaskie; Sir John Gilmour, Bart, of Montrave; Mr Wm. Baird of Elie; Mr J. Scott Davidson of Cairnie; Mr W. R. Ketchen, Largo; and Mr David Adams, Muircambus. The entries were good all over, and some capital sport was witnessed. C. Thomas, Lasswade, was outstanding winner in the flat races. In the mile race he started scratch, and though he lost some distance by falling towards the close he finished in grand style a yard or so in front of T. Graham, Cowdenbeath. The consolation sprint of 100 yards, which was won by J. McEwen, Glasgow, was the keenest contested race of the day. P. Scott, Muircambus, Colinsburgh, was the first for putting the stone and throwing the hammer, his distance in the latter being 86 feet 7 inches, and feet 2 inches farther than the second prizeman. In the golf-driving competition A. H. Scott, Earlsferry, was first with distance of 236 yards, while in the amateurs', Mr H. Zambre, a visitor from London, won with, only three yards less. The pony trot was a bit of a farce. Only three entered, and the "material" two of the competitors had to handle was, as a country gentleman remarked, " a disgrace to the county." Master Oswald Braid, though his pony was somewhat "dour" to start, got first past the post. The donkey race was provocative of much mirth. About dozen "cuddies" were requisitioned from one of the shore people, and riders, being plentiful, start was soon made. Some went forward, others turned back, others went across the field, and so on, but with the kindly assistance of the Mars boys, who are at present on holiday at Elie, and who were accommodated with space inside the enclosure, the stubborn brutes were eventually pushed into the course.

All the donkeys got home in a bunch, but the prize was awarded to Richard Christie, Elie. During the afternoon the pipe and brass bands the Ist Battalion Gordon Highlanders, who were engaged, fee of £25, and the brass of the Mars Training Ship, provided grand musical treat. The revenue from the gate amounted to over £60. In addition to the music the committee might another year introduce variety into the proceedings by engaging a troupe of acrobats, dancers, or some other form of exhibition entertainment.

> **NEW SHELTER AT THE RECREATION PARK.** — A much felt want both on Elie and Earlsferry Links and also on the roadsides round about has been that of resting places other than the damp grass. This has been a matter of comment among visitors, who drew comparisons much to the disadvantage of Elie and Earlsferry. We are glad to notice that a step in the right direction has been taken in erecting a tasteful little shelter or rest in the Recreation Park, which is the gift of a lady. It is of wood, with galvanized iron roof, and will be found a great convenience.

Principally the recreation ground in its early days was used as a ladies' golf course and much is owed to T.M. Anstruther M.P. who opined in 1881 after the opening of the Golf House club that provision was needed for the ladies to play golf. Such that the Recreation park become known as "The Ladies' Course" for many years and even today despite sundry name changes.

This was reported in 1892.

By 1903 bowling had their own patch too.

> Elie Recreation Park Green.—To the golf and tennis of the Recreation Park is added a bowling green. This was opened for play a week ago, but the formal opening was on Thursday, when two rinks from Crail engaged the local players. Provost Don declared the green open in a suitable speech, and Mrs Outhwaite of Craigforth threw the first ball. The visitors won the match by two shots. Elie turf was found very adaptable, but the green requires rolling.

The area was still regulated and operated by the Recreation Park Committee independent of the town councils of Elie and Earlsferry although Earlsferry agreed to make a contribution to the various sports events held there. It certainly had served its purpose by bringing more people into the villages. The committee decided that there should be a more permanent facility to cater for the various users of the park. In 1911 Glasgow staged the Scottish Exhibition of National History, Art and Industry. The venue was Kelvingrove Park. There were a number of pavilions built for this exhibition and sold off at its conclusion. In 1911 Mr. Cook and Mr. Garland (two very well known Elie names) visited the exhibition and arranged to purchase the shell of one of the buildings and transport it to Elie to be erected as a "pavilion" for the users of the park. It was then and subsequently turned out to be an inspirational idea but it was not initially without its pitfalls. In 1913 this article appeared.

ACTION AGAINST ELIE RECREATION COMMITTEE. The record was closed in Cupar Sheriff Court yesterday in an action at the instance of John F. Glass, wood merchant, Glasgow, against the Elie Recreation Park Committee for the sum of £30 3s 4d. It is set forth in the condescendence that the pursuer deals largely second-hand building materials. In 1911 he purchased for removal from the sites then covered by them many of the buildings which formed part of the Glasgow Exhibition of 1911. The defenders entered into negotiations with the pursuer for the purchase of part of these building materials to be used in the erection of pavilion at Ladies' Golf Clubhouse at Elie. Mr Alex. M. Cook, solicitor, Elie, secretary of the Company, went to Glasgow in December, 1911, and agreed to purchase from the pursuer windows and other materials. The pursuer in due course delivered to the committee the windows and other building materials. The defenders contended that the material was not delivered within the stipulated time agreed upon, and the material ultimately delivered did not include the sills, transomes, lintels, and standards of the windows of the Grosvenor Restaurant.

It seems however that good sense prevailed and the action was settled without much pomp and ceremony. So in 1913 the Pavilion was first used and became an Elie institution which is still going. Many alterations and additions over the years but essentially the same structure and material as in its original state.

THE TENNIS COURTS ELIE

However the park was not confined to sports and athletics. There was cricket played we suspect on the area of ground between the Park Place entrance and the current driving range. One less successful venture was an archery range proposed by Mr. Cook and more recently a boules pitch which did not seem to catch on.

By 1909 it was so successful that

> **Elie Recreation Park Committee have enlarged the Ladies' Golf Course by an additional 35 acres, and workmen are now engaged in making the extension of the course.**

The committee sought the advice of James Braid who was in Earlsferry visiting his mother who was seriously ill at the time. His recommendation was *"Mr Braid stated that the ground available for the extension will not permit an increase in the number of holes, but by a rearrangement of the course, with longer distances between the greens, there would be the advantage of more players being able to be on the course at the same time. Meanwhile the Committee await the proposed new plan. The new course is expected to [be] about 3000 yards."* These plans were implemented and it is substantially the same layout as at current.

> **THE RECREATION PARK AND FOOTBALL.**—At a meeting of the Recreation Park Committee last Friday night—Provost Shepherd presiding. Bailie Don asked if the football Club were to have the liberty this season of playing football in the park. He considered that it was only proper that a portion of the park should be given for this purpose. The other members concurred, and it was remitted to the Committee to give off the same portion as last year. It was agreed to put up notice boards in the park to that effect.

It would not have been the same without football.

> **NEW PUTTING GREEN FOR ELIE.**
> Elie Recreation Park Committee has laid out a new 18-hole putting green at the south-west corner of the Recreation Park. This necessitates an alteration in the present starting point of the ladies' golf course.

And in 1922 the putting green was extended.

But not only was golf, tennis and bowling featured in the use of the park but this in 1928.

> **A NEW SPORT AT ELIE**
>
> **MOTOR CYCLE GRASS TRACK RACING.**
>
> The motor cycle grass track racing—a sport new to Scotland—which is to take place in the Recreation Park, Elie, on Saturday, is arousing considerable interest throughout a wide district.
>
> The event is organised by the East Fife Motor Club, with its headquarters at Methil, and with T. Hogg, Methil, as president and J. H. Phillips as secretary. It is largely due to the efforts of R. Braid that Elie has become the venue. Himself a keen sportsman and three times winner of a Scottish championship at St Andrews, he is ex-president of the club, and he obtained the consent of Elie Recreation Park Committee to hold the meeting there.
>
> The track chosen is one-third of a mile in circumference.
>
> The competition, with its 15 events, is catering for machines from 2 horse-power to unlimited capacity. Classes are set aside for experts and non-experts, and there is a good entry. The racing starts at 2 p.m.

In May 1928 there was also a proposal to relieve the congestion of the main 18 hole course so another golf course could be established. It did not come to fruition.

The Recreation park was operated successfully for a number of years and often the Ladies' course were harbingers of changes because in 1958 the Golf House Club had decided to continue the ban on playing golf on a Sunday but the Recreation park (now Sports Club) went in a different direction allowing play on the sabbath. It did not take long for Golf House Club to review that decision. But again it was not without its hiccups e.g.in 1943

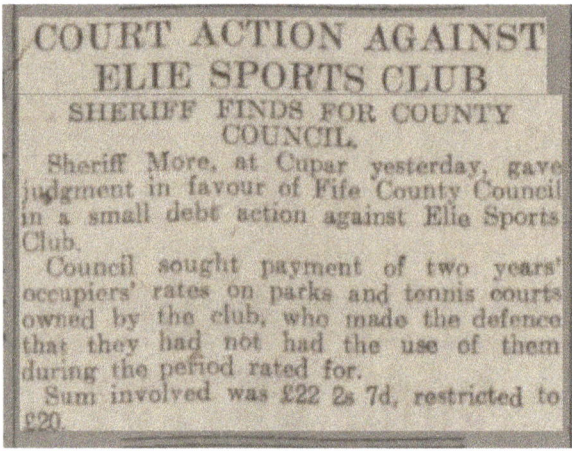

During the second world war the recreation park doubled as a parachute training area for the Polish Parachute Brigade stationed in the East Neuk which included a fuselage of a redundant Whitney bomber for practice purposes although the local children probably had better fun. Part of the course was ploughed up for vegetable planting and even part of it had been "corrugated" by plough to make it unsuitable for landing the airborne gliders of potential invaders.

However in 1962 the financial position of the recreation park/ladies' course/sports club was not healthy and the committee solicited assistance from the Golf House club. In May 1962 the Golf House Club took over and absorbed the Sports club into the GHC. It retained the initial idea of its independence by keeping the committee structure but now the Captain of the GHC was to be a member of the committee and some other representation was necessary on the committee.

Another rough passage prevailed when the committee in 1964 (no doubt under the Golf House Club's initiative) decided to change the nine hole ladies' course into a par 3 18 holes. At this time the attraction of a short course seems to have been in the public perception at least to those like the members of the GHC who saw a par 3 course a nice challenge. Accordingly the whole area was redesigned to produce 18 holes par 3. This however totally destroyed the traditional ethos of the Ladies' Course because it was a prime area for young families and small children to get their first taste of the game without intruding into a conventional golf course and interrupting the play of those more experienced. The whole attraction of the small course then and now is that young families can set off with perhaps one club each and enjoy the freedom of whacking a golf ball around a piece of ground and no doubt learning how to throw a tantrum and a golf club in frustration.

In 1968 the par 3 idea was abandoned and the course reverted to very much what it was in the 1900s.

Whilst this may have brought about some financial stability there were problems. In 1974 when all the leases were bought out by the GHC it was necessary to purchase the Recreation Park. Miss Baird the then owner of the Recreation Park offered very generous terms. The application came from the Golf House club now that the two bodies were amalgamated. A sum was required from the Scottish Sports Council who predicated that the grantees must have a constitution which was approved by that body. There is a suggestion which may be apocryphal that since the GHC was exclusively male in its construction it would not have met the requirement of inclusivity. The whole amalgamation therefore had to be unravelled. Remember, of course, that ladies merely had a privilege of playing on the main course and it was the GHC which ran and controlled things.

Thus it is the suggestion that in order to be able to upgrade the facilities on borrowed money the amalgamation of the two clubs had to be unpicked – at least *prima facie*. In fact the management of the Sports Club became very much an adjunct of the Golf House Club with the Captain of the latter still sitting on the committee.

Since then the nature of the institution of the Sports Club has in many respects blossomed. It became and still is a focal point for youngsters on holiday in Elie to congregate, sip their coca colas, plough money into a juke box (in older times) and shoot the breeze if not a golf ball. Parents of young children anxious to be their chaperones could sip their lattes and watch as their offspring made their first tentative steps towards Wimbledon or the GHC. A driving range was added and reassembled in a different location, golf teaching facilities were upgraded, and paddle tennis courts were installed to add to the racquet sport. Meantime the bowling club goes from strength to strength with probably one of the finest greens in Fife meticulously cared for by the GHC green keepers.

The originators of the Recreation Park would reflect now that it was worth the gamble of going it alone and one suspects that the relative town councils looked on enviously at the institution wishing they could administer it. Actually it is just as well the councils did not have control since now administration would have been in the hands of Fife Council and the autonomy of the Recreation Park would have been seriously compromised.

Chapter 8
The Development of the Golf Course

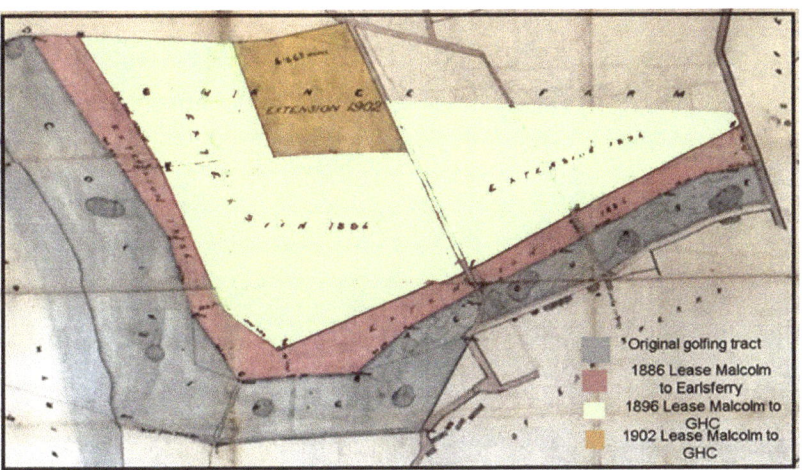

The relationship between the Grange estate and the Town Council was, after 1832, cordial but not without its problems. One of which seemed to be that the farmer objected to golfers whose ball had strayed from the course from trampling down his crop to retrieve the ball. The Town Council pronounced an edict cautioning against such a practice. If your golf ball went into the field it was deemed lost. From the original golfing tract as defined by Messrs Cook and Taylor, and as decerned by the Court of Session in 1832, Earlsferry Town council in 1886 after the settlement of the subsequent litigation from Malcolm arranged a lease of part of the Grange farm to increase the width of the golfing tract. There was now a free run from the eastern boundary of the village (Ferry Road/German's Wynd) following the north side of the village, along the side of Seatangle Road and then up to a point which looks like half way down the current 13th fairway and then back to Ferry Road again. It is a little strange that after a vigorous battle between the estate and the Town Council, Malcolm seemed happy to concede more land from the farm and estate albeit on lease. We suspect that was because Malcolm and his tenant realised that the ground was rather unproductive and it might be better to generate income from a lease to the Town Council (£25 p.a.) than to try to soldier on with poor quality land. In any event it saved bleating about the cut grass. In addition the Malcolm family did not live locally especially after the destruction of Grange House by fire in the mid 19th Century. They had alternative accommodation in Invertiel and Lochore. This merely increased the size of the golf course without changing its contours.

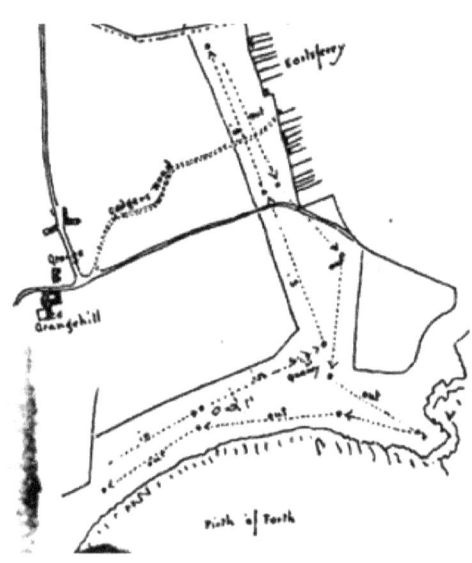

By then the existence the golf course was well established. However at best there could only have been 11 playable holes in that layout on the west side of Ferry Road. With the development of golf equipment, moving on to rubber wound golf balls and greater ability of the golfers, the lengths of holes were often too short. Extra ground was needed. We know from a previous chapter that Ketchen and his committee who established the GHC had acquired a lease from the land owner (William Baird) of the southern part of the Melon Park.

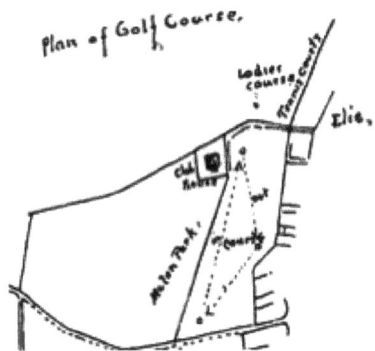

This included later a smaller portion to enable the club house to be built but the incorporation of the southern part of the Melon Park resulted in three more holes being available to the GHC.

This contemporary photograph (probably 1894) shows the additional ground of the southern part of the Melon Park and as can be seen there is a fence from the corner of the quarry to the Clubhouse

old glass negative coloured by Greg Davis.

Whilst Baird only leased the southern part of the Melon Park to Ketchen in 1873 he granted a further lease in 1899 over the area lying to the north of the Melon Park and it was this area that

enabled the golf club to expand to 18 holes which by then had become the norm. The original southern portion of the Melon Park did not include the area on which the clubhouse was subsequently built in 1877 but Ketchen and his committee negotiated with Baird for an additional piece of ground on which to build the club house.

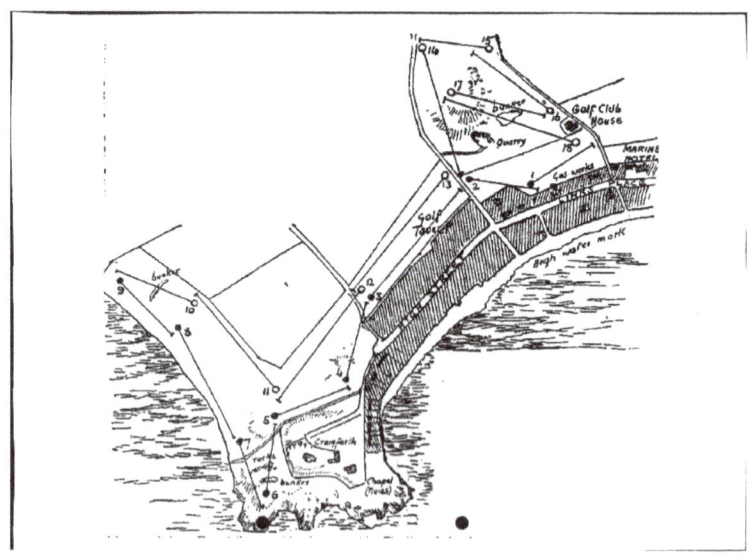

from Elie History Archives

This is the earliest plan we have of what the full 18 holes looked like. We do not know the origin of the plan so it is at least possible that it was just that – a plan – and the new layout was not initiated but it is worthwhile examining it.

This early plan shows the full 18 holes but is very different from the layout which was eventually decided upon. It can be seen from this plan that the first tee lies to the south of the current 18th green and play is directed firstly to a green close to the gas works (the gas works and its prominent Gasometer has been removed but it lay at the far end of the car park to the south of the Club House). The second is a short hole to what is now the 3rd green. Thereafter the 3rd, 4th and 5th holes follow the line of the current 4th, 5th and 6th. Next the golfer turns left over the hill to Lundar Law, and the seventh hole is to a green just over the Seatangle road. Play then proceeds along the shore line of West bay and then the golfer returns to the 10th, 11th, 12th and 13th making back toward the Melon Park. The 14th looks a challenging hole over the edge of the quarry to a green which looks as if it is where the 2nd tee is currently, the 15th is a short hole but it is difficult to envisage the 16th green right beside the club house and the 17th as does the 18th crosses the large bunker (later removed) underneath the hill at the current 1st If this plan is accurate it seems that since the second shot to the 18th green is blind over the hill anyone standing outside the golf club would be in imminent danger.

It is difficult to date this plan but it must have been before the ground acquired by the GHC from Malcolm in 1896. It is reasonable to suppose that this was the first 18 hole layout which was played on in September 1897 by A.H.Scott in a match against Andrew Kirkcaldy. It is possible therefore that the 1896 leased ground had yet to be incorporated into the new layout.

Although it seems that at least in 1897 a full 18 holes was available according to the report.

SCOTT V. KIRKCALDY FOR £50.

Earlsferry green was the venue of one of the most important challenge matches of the season last Friday, the first stage of the home-and-home match between A. H. Scott and Andrew Kirkcaldy being played off in presence of a large and fashionable crowd. This is the first first-class game which has been played over the recently extended course, though there was a talk some time ago of a professional competition being organised. The match was brought about through Kirkcaldy losing his temper at Balcomie, when Scott beat him in an exhibition game, the St Andrews man challenging him for a big stake. Both players paid particular attention to their practice during the days before the match, and on this score they started equally matched.

Then in 1900 the following map of the course was published related to a competition at Elie.

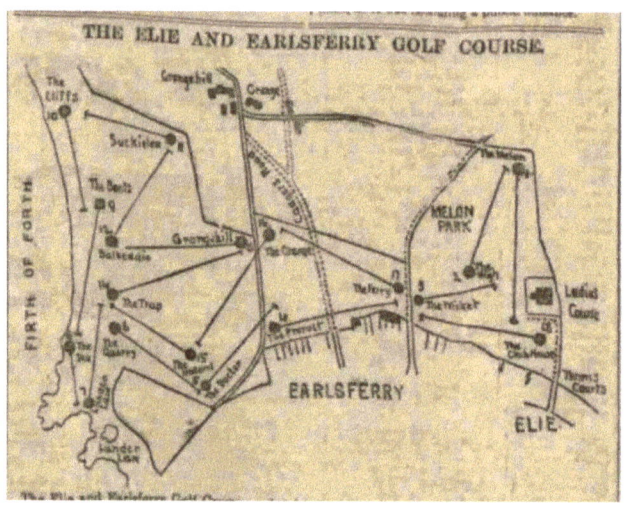

Although a full lease of the northern part of the Melon Park did not seem to have been signed until 1902 the ground was incorporated into the course before that date. The layout shows a change from the first layout. It also meant that the lengths of the holes were substantially increased and the need for double greens was superseded. Advances in golf equipment and players' abilities meant also that the ball could be hit farther and holes which had perhaps been no more than 120 yards came well within the reach of most golfers with the then equipment – not least when the "gutty" replaced the "featherie" as a matter of choice and the Haskell wound ball by then was beginning to be used. Although there is a record from the Elie Games in 1900 that the winner of the longest driving competition, Andrew Scott managed 237 yards (maybe wind assisted). The report does not say whether it was a gutty or Haskell. The additional land enabled longer holes and an 18 hole layout comfortably fitted into the available space. Again this layout comes closer to the current and long established layout albeit that from the 6th green the golfer turns left to drive over Lundar Law to the current 10th green. Furthermore the additional ground acquired in 1902 is not included.

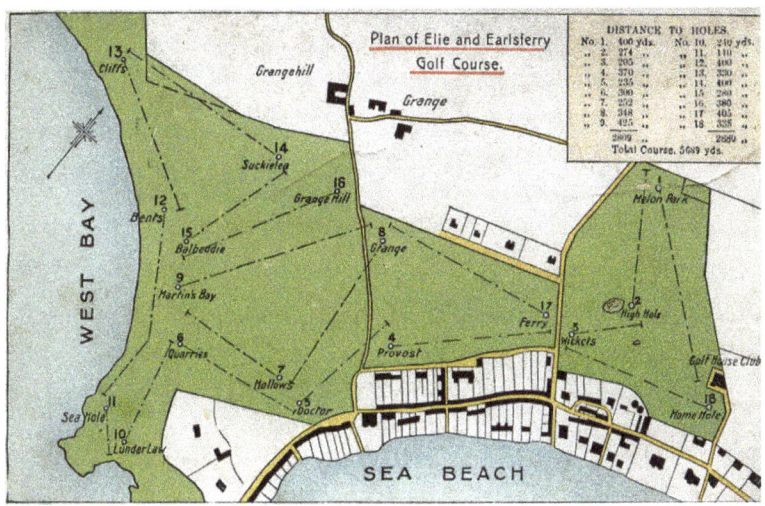

The actual layout of the golf course now shows the incorporation of the 1902 acquisition and the consequent extension of some of the holes. But there have been some cosmetic changes.

At the first hole from the Clubhouse there is a hill immediately confronting the drive off the first tee. At one time there was an extensive bunker underneath this hill. If you fail to get over the hill your fate was sealed by the sand. However failing to carry the hill from the first tee carried its own penalty and the bunker was dispensed with although it can still be seen on some contemporary postcards.

Over the years various other minor changes have been made but not so dramatic as to change the layout of the course. Problems for example have been encountered at the area of the 10th tee, 7th tee and 6th green of players from the 12th tee hitting dangerously close to those putting on the 6th green. Various solutions have been mooted over the piece but none has yet been satisfactory enough without serious changes to the layout. Frequent cries of "fore" emanate during busy periods.

In 1950 the 16th fairway was altered to enable players to have a better view of the green.

> The greenkeeping staff of Elie and Earlsferry golf course are carving a chunk out of a bank on the sixteenth fairway so that players will be able to see the green for their second shot.

More recently the 4th fairway has been recontoured to persuade the player to hit right rather than flirt with Links Road which borders the fairway. This has reduced the danger to walkers along Links Road and parked cars no longer have to flirt with the errant golfer/golfball. There have been a number of changes to lengthen the course but the limits of the area of ground made any serious change impossible. There has been a new back tee at the 5th, at the 15th and 18th adding a few yards but not affecting the par. The 14th hole has also been recontoured –

The Fourteenth hole saga -

Criticism had for long been levelled at the fourteenth hole because of the lack of definition of the green. The approach shot to the green is a little uphill and it was difficult to sight the back of the green. When F.G. Griffiths was captain in 1952 he considered realigning the 14th green. The proposal was put to the AGM that year and given a resounding thumbs down. Things take time in Elie and it was not until 1970 that this problem again came up for discussion at the AGM. There were two alternatives suggested. The first was to move the green back towards Grangehill farm where the back tee of the 15th is currently. This would almost make it a dog leg par 5 (something which Elie golf course lacked). The other alternative was to build a bank at the back of the green so there was a better sight line. The committee and the greens convener had obviously spent quite some time examining these alternatives. After much debate at that AGM it was put to the vote. The Secretary asked for all those in favour of moving the green up towards Grangehill thereby making it a par 5. There were 80 hands raised. He then asked for those in favour of building a bank at the back of the green. After some pause and two recounts 80 hands were raised. The secretary paused, mindful of the constitution of the club, and announced that since the vote was tied the captain had a casting vote. The Captain thought for little while and said, "Well I don't think we should change it - just leave it as it is." Again a pause before the lawyers all jumped in to point out that none had voted for this alternative and it did not break the deadlock. A flustered Captain and Secretary consulted sotto voce. – "Well," announced the Captain, "I vote for the bank at the back." Problem solved.

Chapter 9
The Golf Club Makers
Part 1 George Forrester

By the middle of the 19th century golf was beginning to become a more widespread pastime and not confined to the moneyed classes but all the same golf clubs were not mass produced. Local joiners and carpenters in the area of golf courses began to make golf clubs for their villagers. By this time Forgan in St. Andrews, Forrester in Earlsferry and various producers in North Berwick and slightly later Gibson in Kinghorn set up business to make clubs on a commercial basis. They supplied the aristocracy and the local young men with their clubs.

These makers also employed many of the local people in their "shops" and they became apprenticed to the makers. At that time, mid to late 19th century, certainly in Earlsferry, there was a falling off of openings for employment locally. The weaving trade, so long the Earlsferry staple, was declining with imports from abroad supplanting the need for expensive linen. The building trade, which had employed and trained many masons, had become less important as the large houses along the sea front had been built for the arrival of the railway line and many young men, previously masons, were glad of an apprenticeship making golf clubs. Fishing had become hazardous and not so rewarding. At the same time the makers of these clubs had started to innovate in the design and manufacture of them and the process started to become more automated although most clubs were still carefully finished by hand. The development of iron clubs – firstly the niblick and then the mashie – increased the number of different clubs available and whilst they were of metal cast by a blacksmith, the shafts (usually hickory) and finish of the clubs were the province of the golf club makers. The best way to test your golf club making work was to have a shot with your own creation.

At the same time there was a large increase in the interest in golf by many of the upper echelons of society encouraged by the playing of the game by Royalty. Elie was a favourite golfing venue of the Duchess of Connaught (one of Queen Victoria's daughters-in-law) and her daughter, Princess Patricia. This also increased demand.

George Forrester

The first major golf club maker in Earlsferry was George Forrester.

George Forrester 1848 -1930 was one of the earliest and the most innovative and influential of the golf club manufacturers certainly in Fife and probably in the world. There were earlier and contemporary manufacturers but Forrester was a clever and skilled businessman who not only had the technical expertise to produce golf clubs, he also had an acute business knowledge which stood him in good stead.

However unusually he did not start out as a joiner or carpenter, as many of the others did, but he was initially apprenticed as a mason to David Given (whose son and nephew also excelled (q.v.) as golfers). At that time, late 19th Century, the mason's trade was prosperous with the building of many houses along the beach front of Elie and Earlsferry from stone sourced on the golf course or beach and financed by visitors from the cities via the railway network. To chart his progress we need to go back in time.

He was born 6th April 1848. His father James and mother Agnes lived in Earlsferry in the Main Street. He is described as being a manufacturer's agent but in a later census it is amplified by the word "linen". We can assume therefore that he would be responsible for selling the various items of linen weaving undertaken by the residents of Earlsferry.

There were 12 "weavers' shops" in Earlsferry at this time where there were a number of looms and people would also have looms in their homes and as a cottage industry produce linen which was then sent "over the hill" to Kirkcaldy where it was used in the linoleum manufacturing industry. In addition to this job he is also described as a grocer and latterly an innkeeper and having a grocer's shop which presumably was manned by his wife. In Earlsferry High Street at this time (1865) there were nine grocer's shops and the Forrester's shop appears to have been number 47 High Street. This would place it somewhere between the Town Hall (no 30) and Cadgers Wynd. Subsequent valuation rolls after James Snr's death (1876) shows his wife Agnes as proprietor of house and garden which was tenanted by Mrs. Methven a grocer. Methven's grocer shop was in Earlsferry High Street and it looks very much as though this may have been the Forrester's grocer's shop. Father Forrester and mother were reasonably prosperous. No doubt as a young man in Earlsferry he would be found mostly on the golfing tract where many of his contemporaries honed and perfected their golfing skills. He was no mean golfer again strengthened by his work as a mason. Apparently he first began to make clubs for his own use entirely while still serving his apprenticeship as a mason. Shortly after finishing he went to the United States in pursuance of his trade as a mason/stone-cutter where, we were advised by his family, he became involved in the rebuilding of Chicago after the fire of 1871.

The fire destroyed 17,500 buildings and 73 miles of street so there was a lot of rebuilding to be done and consequently work for masons. That is what we were advised by his great grandson, who lives in Oxfordshire, from family lore. On looking at the records from USA, George was based in Baltimore. At least in the census of 1870 he is shown as living in Baltimore with an occupation of Stone Cutter – now it is possible that this census is wrong and we have picked up the wrong Forrester but his birth year co-incides with the information on that census sheet. We think he travelled from Liverpool arriving in New York on 21st October 1869 and the census in which he is shown as being in Baltimore - coincidentally the ship on which he made the Atlantic crossing was called the City of Baltimore - was taken in the summer of 1870. Guesswork suggests that he did not move on to Chicago until later if at all. However he was back resident in Earlsferry in 1881 census along with his wife. He is described there as a golf club maker so that suggests that between 1870 and 1881 he must have come back to Scotland and set up business. (see advertisement below). It is safe therefore if that information is accurate to assume that he spent very little time in USA and according to an article in "The Golfer" magazine he started his business as golf club maker in 1871. He was clearly no mean golfer. He is noted as having won various golf competitions at Earlsferry in 1872 . We think it safe to say therefore, that he did not spend much time in America not least of which because the great fire of Chicago was in October 1871.

The full report is thus:

FORRESTER, OF EARLSFERRY. (From " The Golfer " Portrait Gallery.) The name of this famous club-maker has extended far and wide—wherever, in short, sterling club and ball are held in due repute......His knowledge of the art has, in fact, been gained through pure experience and many an unsuccessful experiment. Then, in his ignorance of the proper material for his heads--a subject in which he is now an admittedly past master—he not unfrequently found them go in the first round. But he persevered, with the success to which we are all pleased to bear testimony. ......On returning home, the old love of club-making once again seized him, when he began trade as a maker for the public in 1871. He at first found it up-hill work to push trade as the golfers of that day seemed to be of opinion that unless clubs were the handiwork of one two makers of old standing they would be worthless. Some indeed predicted that Mr. Forrester's first year in the trade would be his last--rather erroneously as we know. Even in the trade processes he was occasionally at fault. The mere matter of staining the heads was still a jealously guarded trade secret: and the same may be said of what else. Not many years ago the golfing world was struck with indignant amazement at the thought of turning clubs with a lathe. But Mr. Forrester was alive to the value of this and among the first in the country to have one at work. When the boom in golf began so suddenly it was difficult to secure efficient workmen; hence the use of machinery was almost compulsory. In Mr. Forrester's opinion, clubs made after a proper pattern and finished on the new principle —not known to many makers—are in every respect as good and well finished as the most expert workmen can turn out, and perhaps even more as the rapidity with which they are smoothened up gives them a far superior and ship-shape look. Beech is the most popular for heads, but Mr. Forrester's own favourite is lunderwood*, which stands up admirably, even in wet weathers. It is a rare wood and cannot be sold in large quantities, but stands in the front rank for durability. It is a little more expensive at first, but, as so often is the case, in the end cheaper. Other woods, of course, are used—even oak and cherry—but many require to be faced with leather. Lunderwood* requires nothing of that kind, as the spring is splendid, and drives as far as any beech head. Mr. Forrester knows persimmon wood very well. It is of a dark colour, but rather inclined to " fease " or break away in the face in wet weather. …… For shafts Mr. Forrester's favourite wood is hickory but the prime stuff is difficult to procure…… Of Mr. Forrester's various patents it is impossible to speak in other terms than those highest eulogy [sic]. His centre balance is most ingenious in theory and has stood the test of an immensity of play in all parts of the kingdom. His patent putter too is having an increasingly rapid sale. The principle is very ingenious on the ball being directly in the line of the shaft. It would be absurd to say that it is graceful as the old shape, but it is a highly finished , thoroughly workman like tool and has been found effective in practice. And the golfer who is not familiar with his balls must, it is feared have given up the game before the invention of guttie."

From East of Fife Record 1897.

*"lunderwood" does not seem to be a recognised wood but the fact that it is repeated in the text suggests that it is not a misprint. We wonder if it might be linden wood?

After Forrester started in business as a golf club maker he began to take on apprentices so we can assume that his business took off. Valuation roll searches suggest that he originally tenanted premises on Links Road and it seems fairly safe to assume that he acquired the property because by 1886 he is shown as owning a house and premises on Links Road and the golf club house (Georgeville – see later). We know that he had a smallish workshop behind what is now Georgeville and latterly it was called Cosy Cottage which was immediately behind the Golf Tavern. By this time not only was his business flourishing, but he was also officially the green keeper of the Earlsferry Golf Course. By 1875 the current Golf House Club and Thistle golf clubs were established and co-existed with the Earlsferry and Elie Golf club (vide supra). The Golf house club had its own clubhouse but until 1885 the Thistle did not. Forrester offered the club space in his house, Georgeville. For whilst the current Melon Park (holes 1,2,3 and 18 on the current course) were acquired on lease by the Golf House club the main focus of golf at that time 1875 – 1912 was still the Earlsferry golf course and the clubhouse at Links Road. The property itself was constructed in such a way that there was a small caretaker's flat for the steward of the club which still exists.

George's business flourished not least with the assistance of such luminaries as James Braid, Dougie Rolland and the like. Although Braid was a joiner to trade he did not have much expertise in making golf clubs initially and it looks likely that he relied on George Forrester. Bernard Darwin, Braid's biographer, tells the tale of how Jamie Braid as he was known became the champion golfer. Braid was a tall man for his era and one of his difficulties was finding a golf club which was long enough for him to be able to swing naturally. He found himself often outdriven by his contemporaries. Apparently one day a similarly tall golfer, Mr. Berwick, visited Forrester's shop complaining that he could not seem to hit the ball well enough with his longer club. Forrester ever ready for business offered to buy the club from him for 6d. Very shortly thereafter Jamie visited George's shop and tried out the driver with remarkable results in that he then started outdriving even the most prestigious opponent. Forrester sold it to him for one shilling and sixpence.

During this time he also acted as the green keeper for the golf course and although not officially recognized as such probably the first professional of Elie Golf House club. James Sunter (q.v.) became the first and only officially recognized professional in 1921.

The late Ronnie Sinclair of the Elie Golf House club has done extensive research into Forrester's golf club making and inter alia he notes:

"One of the oldest and most treasured items in the Elie Golf House Club collection is a Forrester play club circa 1875. His early patents include the smooth face cleek (registered design 153408) in 1890, the ball back cleek in 1892, and the first real socket head wood advertised as the "unbreakable drilled neck driver" in 1896 (registered design no. 269117). This development revolutionised golf club design at that time. Forrester had also constructed specialised labour-saving machines for making golf clubs and golf balls. He had created brass moulds that he used to make gutty (gutta percha) golf balls and invented and constructed a machine to wind rubber elastic ribbon into balls around which he moulded a cover. The other machines Forrester built had a significant impact on club making. Traditionally, golf club shafts had been attached to the wooden head by means of a long tapered and glued scarf joint. This long joint was then reinforced by wrapping it with pitched string. Forrester recognised that there was room to improve this method and he developed a way of attaching the shaft to the wooden head by means of a tapered hole in the head. He constructed machines similar to pencil sharpeners to form the

taper on the end of shafts, as well as bespoke machines to taper-drill the heads."

By the time he died in 1930, Forrester was reckoned to have had more registered design applications than any other club maker. He actually misled the public slightly by claiming that they were patented.

His business acumen extended to granting authority to others to stock his golf clubs and there are many advertisements recommending his clubs. Here are just a few:

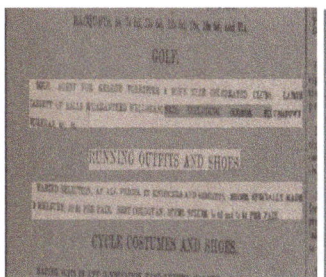 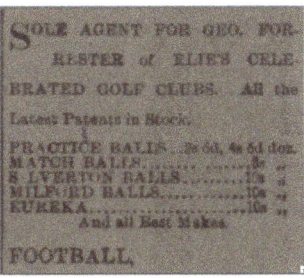

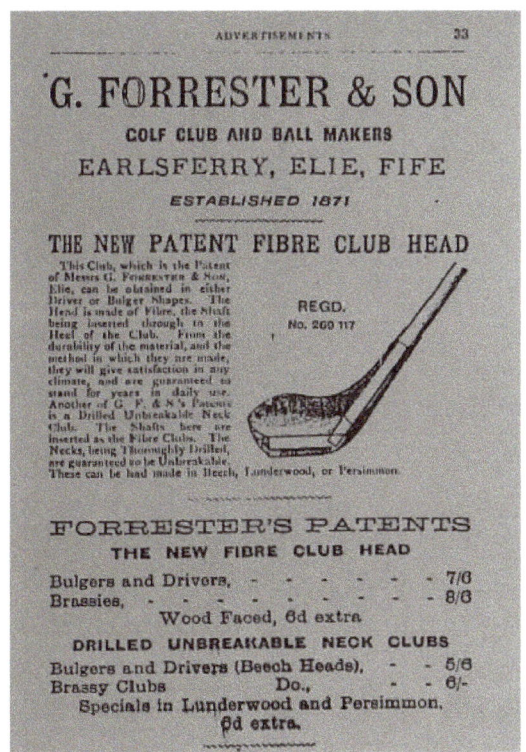

His enterprise was not restricted to golf clubs. In these days golf balls were also manufactured by the golf professionals - from the featherie through the gutty and eventually to the rubber wound ball which survives today. Forrester invented a machine for a rubber wound golf ball to compete with the "Haskell", the first such golf ball. Here is a report from the newspaper in 1907:

THE EARLSFERRY AND ELIE RUBBER CORE GOLF BALLS. In the days of the gutta golf ball, Messrs George Forrester & Son, the well-known clubmakers, of Earlsferry, manufactured balls which had many patrons among votaries of the game. With the advent of the rubber core ball the trade in the Earlsferry gutta, like other guttas, practically collapsed. The rubber core ball, with its hundreds of yards of tape rubber, is a much more difficult ball to make than the gutta, or even the old feather-stuffed ball, and special machinery is required. As golfer after golfer stalked into Messrs Forrester's shop, and tabled a florin for a rubber quick flier, Messrs Forrester & Son came to the conclusion that they could not allow their ball trade to fall into the hands of outside makers, and they forthwith commenced to make experiments. Their first task was to construct a machine for winding the tape rubber. The difficulty was got over by the invention of an ingenious machine, which is driven by a gas engine, and this problem solved, Messrs Forrester applied their minds to the work of getting the gutta cover to consolidate properly with the rubber. This difficulty has been mastered, and the firm now claim that their rubber core "Traveller" and "Dreadnought" balls will retain their shape and merits of flight although they may be very much cut with the irons....... Messrs Forrester's cheaper balls are the "Pioneer" and the "Star of Burns". The senior partner of the Forrester firm an enthusiastic golfer, and is one of our oldest club and ball makers. Among those who were trained at his bench may be mentioned:— Robert Simpson Carnoustie; Charles Ralph Smith, West Middlesex Golf Club, Southall; A. H. Scott, Earlsferry ; William Mackie, David Given, Bogside, Glasgow; William Sime and Isaac Mackie, who are now in America. Mr Forrester likes to hear of the success of his old apprentices, and when they come from distant places to spend a holiday at Earlsferry, they always make it a point to while away an occasional hour with their old master. Messrs Forrester's "centre-balance" club is as well known as their "Kasi" putter. The senior partner is as proud of his machine for the manufacture of rubber core balls as he is of the "Traveller" and the "Dreadnought", and does not hesitate to tell his patrons that his consolidating system of covering the rubber with gutta produces a ball which will fly for 25 rounds with a golfer.

He also featured in a criminal case in Cupar sheriff Court where a number of Earlsferry youths 1909.......

James Fair, John Mather, Wm. Mather, and Thomas Small admitted having stolen five dozen golf balls from the shop of George Forrester, Earlsferry. The Sheriff remarked that they seemed pretty bad boys. The Fiscal said it seemed there had been a clique of boys at Elie, who had been carrying on for some time a system stealing from Mr. Forrester's shop golf balls, and selling them as found balls. The Sheriff —How do they get the balls from the shop? The Fiscal —They are golf caddies, and they were recognised as privileged boys by Forrester. He had no suspicion that these boys were stealing his property. Proceeding, the Fiscal said he blamed the golfers who bought the balls from the boys at 4d, 6d, and 9d. They must have known they were encouraging the boys to steal. He had said over and over again that if he gets a clear case of a person buying these balls he would bring a charge reset against him. The Sheriff—The boys cannot give you the names of the persons to whom they sold balls? The Fiscal —No. They do know, they conveniently forget. As showing the extent to which that matter had gone, might mention that Mr Forrester during the season had had removed from his premises golf balls of the value of £36. It had been gigantic affair. The Sheriff—Mr Forrester, must have been very lax in looking after his golf balls. The Fiscal said box was carried a time, and the balls divided amongst the boys in the clique. The parents of boys said they had punished them. 1907 East of Fife Record.

His inventions and sophistication continued. See these two articles in 1896

AN IMPROVED Putter -- THE AMBIDEXTER CLEEK. —The busy and ingenious clubmaker at Elie, Mr George Forrester, patentee of many useful clubs already in the hands of golfers, has just brought out an improved putter. In appearance it is very much like that which Taylor uses, only the blade is deeper, and its bend in the neck is slightly different. The twist at the hose of the club is made in such a way as to throw it well forward, leaving the entire surface of the blade clear to view......Mr Forrester has also brought out a new doublefaced cleek to suit either a left handed or a right-handed player. The sole is broad, and the space between the two blades is hollow. The balance of the club is in no way destroyed. We have often recommended the carrying by right-hand players of a left hand in important matches, in case of a difficult shot close against a paling or a wall; but in this powerful driving cleek of Mr Forrester in the bag, the carrying of an extra club is thereby obviated.—Golf. 1896

NEW Putter.-- The ingenuity of Mr George Forrester has evolved a new idea in the formation of an iron for putting. It is so constructed that unless with a sketch before you it is difficult to explain. However, it has a neck bent or crooked backwards, and a flange on the upper edge which, projecting over the line of the bottom edge by about three-eighths of an inch, makes it, when in the hands of a player, present apparently a solid front to the ball. Missers of short putts who have often good reason to suspect that the angles of their old favourite have played them false will find this a trusty weapon; the ball gets a straight blow, and is thus more under the mastery of the player.....They are made at Anderson's cleek factory, Anstruther, a guarantee of their finish and quality. The previous patents brought out by Mr Forrester have been welcomed on every green, and there are few golfers who do not carry some examples of his ingenuity in their kit—the Concentrated, Counterbalanced, Bulger, and Bulldog; and now that the Acme has been added to the list, many will be anxious to add it, to make the outfit complete. 1896

Further evidence suggests Forrester's inventiveness and he created a controversy in 1927 about the origin of the mashie golf club. Forrester claimed in a letter* to *Golf Illustrated* that he invented the "mashie" in 1884.

*this letter has not been found

> **ORIGIN OF THE "MASHIE."**
>
> To the EDITOR of THE WESTMINSTER GAZETTE.
>
> SIR,—In your interesting article last night on the "Niblick," you ask the origin of the mashie. When I was in Elie twelve years ago I was told by one of the club-makers there that one wet season, when the grass was very long, they brought out a new club to "mash" the long grass, and called it by its well-known name.—Yours, &c.,
>
> February 25.   D. M.

In a letter to the Westminster Gazette in February 1911, the author – who had visited Elie some 12 years previous – reported:

"The dispute or mystery seems to have been started in 1911 with an article in Westminster Gazette of February 1911 by Horace Hutchinson about the "niblick" in the course of which he posed a question as to the origins of the "mashie".

The next evidence of this question appears later in 1927 with a series of articles in "The Scotsman" newspaper. This seems to have been provoked by a letter in Golf Magazine from Forrester in which he claimed that it was his invention.

WHO INVENTED the MASHIE? Considerable interest attaches to the claim definitely put forward by Mr George Forrester, Elie, now retired from business but for many years one of the best-known clubmakers in the country, that he is the inventor of the 'mashie' because the origin of this club has always been a matter of doubt and discussion. Did Jack Morris, the famous Hoylake professional, not in the early eighties so amend an iron as to produce a club which has been regarded in some quarters as the authentic progenitor of the whole race of mashies and mashie-niblicks of to-day ? Associated with Morris in the matter, if one is not mistaken, was Mr A. F. Macfie, who after an interval of many years had his name added a few seasons ago to our roll of Amateur Champions as the first of them all, in virtue of his having won the pioneer tournament that gave the great event its birth. That was when the mashie was new. As one remembers the mashie story; a consignment of iron heads from Scotland had just been delivered at the professional's shop at Hoylake, and Jack Morris and Mr Macfie exchanged ideas as to altering them from the curved face of the period to a flat face with more loft. Each of them acting independently had the thing done according to his fancy, and each of them produced a club similar in purpose and in finish, and that was thought to be how the first mashie came about. A question of dates may arise here. That Hoylake invention, one thinks, belongs to about 1882, certainly early in that decade and if the year mentioned is correct, it is a little bit advance of the claim of Mr Forrester, who states in a letter to Golf Illustrated, "The mashie was invented by me in 1884. The reason I thought of such a style of iron was owing to the long grass which was not allowed to be cut*; therefore we required an iron with more loft and shorter "blade than was available at that time so as to mash it out". It is probably natural at about that period the same idea may have occurred to different minds in different places. Possibly there are other claimants. Mr Forrester's use of the verb " to mash " may leave less dubiety about the origin of the club's name. There is something onomatopoeic in it just as there is in cleek and baffy.1927

*see chapter 2 The Litigation .

The Bygone Weapons - It is possibly one of the last-named clubs to which an Edinburgh club member specially refers in a communication on the mashie question which we have received. "It may interest you to know," he writes, "that I have in my possession a rough hand-forged iron club of that nature of a very much earlier date. It may be an early form of niblick. It belonged to my father , who, so far as I know, did not play golf after the early sixties. I do not know by whom the club was made but as such clubs were in use many years before the eighties. It seems to me that the only claim that can be made by or on behalf of Mr Forrester, Mr Macfie, or Jack Morris is that one or other of them produced a club more nearly like the mashie or niblick of to-day. " The iron club was, of course, by no means new at the beginning of the 'eighties'. It was no doubt upon the niblicks of the day that [two gentlemen] made their experiments, but even in the later years of that decade one does not find in writings where there might be expected any references to the mashie. The Chambers instance has been referred to. Mr Horace Hutchinson, writing of the 'seventies, has definitely said that there was no such club as a mashie. It looks, therefore, as if the period which evolved the club was the early days of the 'eighties, and that the products of Mr Macfie and Jack Morris were certainly among the pioneers, and, so far as one can discover data on the point, they appear to have been the first of the kind to which the word mashie was applied. "We have been told, however, that at St Andrews in the later 'eighties men had grown so fond of "cleeks and irons in all shapes and sizes" that the baffy had become despised. The play-club and the different spoons of which the baffy was the one used a short distance from the hole, when it was necessary to get the ball quickly in the air to carry a hazard were indispensables in their day, and it is recorded of Sir Robert Hay, who was a baffy specialist, that he continued to use that club after it had been superseded in common use by approaching with irons. 1927

By then Forrester had retired and his business and machinery sold. You might wonder why his son James Forrester, himself an excellent professional player, did not succeed to his father's business. There is from the family a rumour that father and son did not get on together but none has been able to pinpoint the area of controversy.

IMPORTANT SALE of GOLF CLUB MAKER'S PLANT belonging to Mr GEORGE FORRESTER, Earlsferry, Elie, who has retired from Business, comprising Crossley Gas Engine (3 H.P.). Buffeting Emery Sandpapering Cutting Ior Lead and Horns, and Polishing Machines Turning Lathe for reducing Club Shafts Double-Acting Copying Lathe complete: Iron Spiral Stair. Band Saw, Water Engine (Double Cylinder), Shafting. Vices Anvil, a Large Quantity Golf Clubs. Shafts, and Club Heads. Irons. Brass Plates, etc, etc. Roup Commence 11 a.m. CLARK & DUNCAN, Auctioneers. Elie. 22nd February 1926.

He died in 1930.

DEATH OF EARLSFERRY EX-PROVOST MR GEORGE FORRESTER'S INTEREST IN GOLF. *At the age of 85, Mr George Forrester died yesterday morning at his residence, Georgeville, Earlsferry. He was a former Provost of the burgh and a well-known clubmaker. A native of Earlsferry, was apprentice mason there, and as a young man went to America, returning later. He began business as a clubmaker, and in these days it was clubmaking by hand. His business became large and flourishing, and many of the younger generation of clubmakers were apprentices at his bench. Mr Forrester was one of the few surviving members of the old Elie and Earlsferry Golf Club (sic), which was formed in 1858, and became defunct a number of years ago, and was the first greenkeeper to Elie Golf House Club. For three years was Provost and during his term of office many improvements were carried out in the royal and ancient, burgh 1930.*

His estate was reported to be £4844 which is equivalent to £347,000 today so relatively speaking he was very successful.

Georgeville

A famous picture of golfers in front of George Forrester's showroom and workshop which also served as the clubhouse for the Earlsferry and Elie Golf Club until the demise of that club round about 1912.

Elie History Society Archives

The photograph is dated 1905.

The longest lasting legacy of George Forrester must be the considerable number of young men who trained as apprentices to him and went all over the world to spread the message of the importance of golf. (see Chapter 11 on the Earlsferry golf Professionals.)

Chapter 10
The Golf Club Makers Part 2
Andrew H. Scott

Andrew Scott 1875 – 1934 had been an apprentice of Forrester in the early days and he set up notionally in competition to Forrester in Earlsferry in 1895.

Although George Forrester was in many respects a pioneer of golf club making especially in Scotland not far behind him was Andrew Scott who probably benefitted from coming rather later to the scene than Forrester. The fact that Scott was trained by Forrester and eventually set up in competition to him might have been of some angst to Forrester although the latter was so far ahead of his time that the threat must have been minimal. However Scott gathered many of the accolades that started to come the way of the golf club makers once the popularity of the game became more widespread. It is probable that Scott was a better golfer than Forrester and that in itself may have led to his increasing fame culminating in his appointment as Royal Warrant holder to the then Prince of Wales who was later King George V. For fuller details of Scott's career see Chapter 11 on Earlsferry Professional Golfers.

Golf Club Making

It was his golf club making that was probably his most successful area. Having received an apprenticeship with Forrester and gained some experience with Charlie Hunter in Prestwick he setup his own business in 1895 at the young age of 19. Initially he probably had a small shop/workshop at what is now Cleek Cottage and indeed it was outside this shop that the photograph was taken for the coronation of Edward VII.

1899

THE SCOTT STRAIGHT LINE PUTTER. Mr Andrew H. Scott, the golf professional at Earlsferry has brought out a new putter which he calls the "straight line." It differs from the usual form in that the line of the putter comes back past the heel, the head on the tool is longer than usual and the same depth at the heel as at the point. There is very slight curve on the shaft of the putter to enable the player to see the line clearly, and the back is cut out in upper portion that the weight of the head may be opposite the line of impact. The putter, while having nothing of the eccentric form like many of its patented predecessors looks a serviceable tool.

Andrew H. Scott, Elie and Earlsferry, has brought out a new patent for a driver and brassey. Claimed the patentee that the neck of the clubs will be unbreakable. It to be hoped that Scott's theory will be success. Scott one of the most promising and brilliant players the East of Fife. 1894

ELIE. MR SCOTT'S IMPROVED GOLF CLUB. The "Railway Supplies Journal" *of Tuesday says:— It is fortunate that the interests of golfers are looked after by one with, experience and skill as a practical exponent of the game, and a manufacturer of golf-clubs and balls are of no mean order. Those among our readers for whom the present notice is specially intended do not need to be informed that Andrew H. Scott, of Earlsferry, Elie, although a young man who has scarcely reached his majority, has attained a first class position as a golfer, and a not less distinguished renown as a golf-club and ball maker. It is upwards of two years since his unbreakable neck club was patented, and it is now known throughout the golfing world, and has been and is being sold in great numbers. Its chief feature is the manner in which the shaft is fastened to the head. The shaft runs down through the neck to the sole, thus making it practically unbreakable, and at the same time bringing the shaft into a direct line with the centre of the head, whereby it is better balanced than ordinary clubs, a most important and essential quality in a good club. The neck is also shorter than in the old style, and very much neater, scarcely any whipping being required. Moreover, as the shaft goes right down to the sole, a longer handle is obtained than that of the ordinary club, with consequently more driving power. The celebrated amateur, Mr H. H. Hilton, has a high opinion of Scott's Patent Club, and says that he can drive further with them than any other. Mr John H. Outhwaite writes:—"I consider them the best I ever played with." Another gentleman, after using one of these Patent Drivers for some little time, says: "I find that my driving has greatly improved both in length and steadiness." Many other testimonials from well-known golfers and golf authorities might be quoted. It is the only golf-club for which letters patent have been granted. It is stated that over 7,541 are in use in all parts of the world. It should he added that Mr. Scott makes brassies on the same principle. His "Invincible" Cleek also deserves notice.

This a new idea in iron clubs, and is a registered design of Mr. Scott's. Its chief feature is that the bottom edge is rounded instead of being left sharp; hence, it does not hack the ball or cut up the turf, as is the case with ordinary cleeks. Although still young, Scott has come rapidly to the front as a player, and will, no doubt, maintain his reputation in the future. He has a capital style, acquired on the green which has produced such famous golfers as Rolland, the Simpsons, and last but not least, Braid, who gave such a splendid exposition of the game at Hoylake recently. *no doubt a venerable and authoritative journal

1908

Of all the clubs in the "kit" of the golfer, no one is more difficult of mastery than the mashie. A favourite saying of a player was that anybody could drive; "it needed a man wi' a heid to thoroughly understand the use of a mashie." Andrew H. Scott, of Elie and Earlsferry, has put on the market a mashie that differs in many respects from the "tool" that is the bane of the duffer and even men of low handicap. Belonging to the thinking class of professionals, Mr Scott has put his theories into practical effect in the case of his latest invention—to the manorial advantage of a very large community of golfers. The "Special Midget" looks perhaps shorter in blade, but it is quite as deep and as long in the face as the mashie with which the player of to-day is acquainted on the striking surface, the iron is marked in ball facsimile in neat pattern—a clever idea that should influence the eye after the "globe" has been struck. Further, the socket interferes very little with the face of the "Midget" as the heel of the mashie is so hollowed out that there is no curtailment of blade. "Socketing" with the "Midget" is hardly possible. As is usual with articles manufactured in the workshop of Mr Scott, this is a thing of beauty, and should be in the hands of many golfers—amateur and professional.

Later he applied for and was granted permission to build a small factory on the ground at the north of his property in Earlsferry High Street bordering on Links Road. This factory stood until the 1960s when it was demolished to make way for a housing development.

Generally recognised as the weakest point in wooden club manufacture was the attachment of the head to the hickory shaft. It was obviously at that point that the club was under greatest stress during a hit. The head was wont to fly off and only go slightly less far than the ball. Forrester, Crowley and Scott and many others sought to address this problem by invention of various methods of attaching the two. Scott took the view that his patent 21444 was the answer if this advertisement is anything to go by.

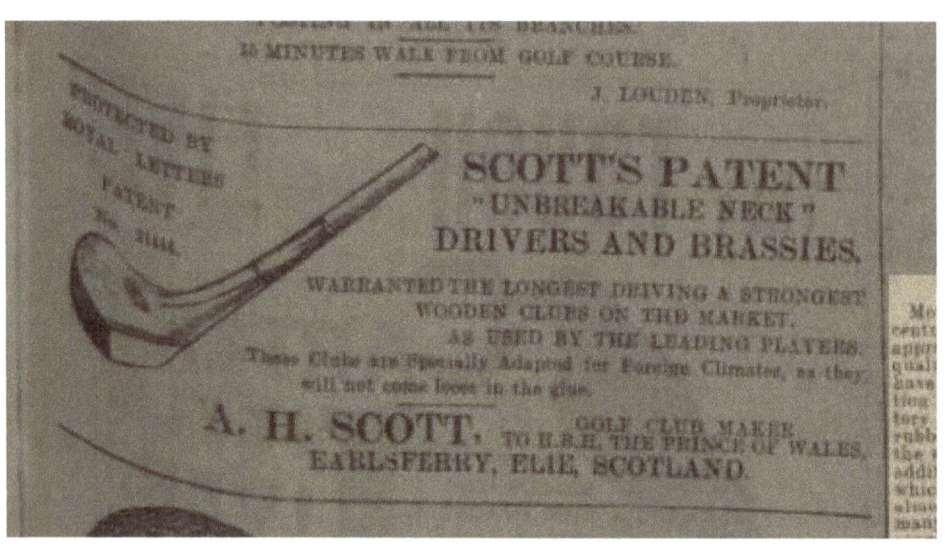

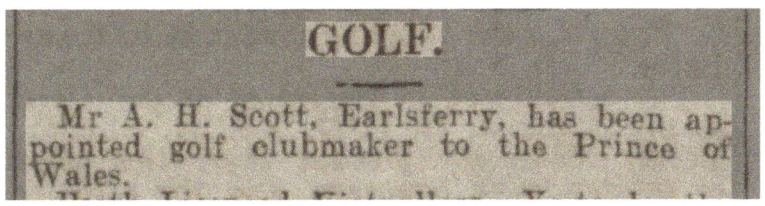

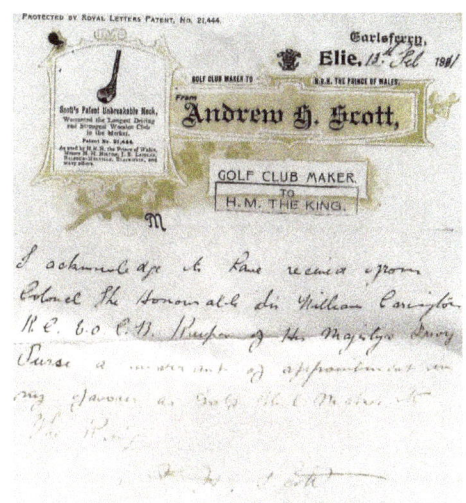

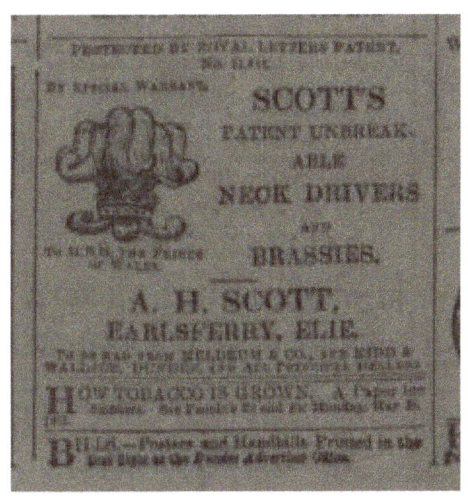

EAST OF FIFE RECORD APRIL 8, 1904. " HOW GOLF CLUBS ARE MADE." The above is the title of an article in the "British Trade Review" for March. The writer made a call at Mr Scott's golf club factory in Earlsferry, and witnessed the works in the various departments. The machines are driven

by a 10-horse power gas engine. Some nine or ten years ago golf club heads were made entirely from beech or apple tree, mostly the former. A decade since hardwoods were looked upon as useless for driving purposes. Times are changed and beech is a thing, of the past. The material favoured in these days being stonewood, persimmon, and dogwood. Of a hard and tough substance, these are able to stand a great deal more usage than the Scotch beech. Imported from the United States persimmon and dogwood are sawn into planks three inches thick, are stored in sheds and allowed to season for a period of 13 or 18 weeks.....After a period of three months these blocks are again taken to the band sawing machine to be shaped and cut into equal lengths to suit the head turning machine. The head turning machine or copying lathe is of very ingenious contrivance, capable of turning out 40 heads net an hour. The head is shaped from an iron model which works against a centre, while the wood block operates against the knives or cutters. By changing the model any pattern of club can be manufactured.... Skilled workmen are called upon to fit in horn and lead and prepare the head for the sand papering machine..... Expert workmen adjust the head and make a thorough inspection of it before it is glued on to the handle. The shaft is also dealt with. Hickory logs are cut into shafts seven eights of an inch square, and three feet eight inches long. Mr Scott is the inventor of several patents, including one relating to the unbreakable neck, and used by members of the Royal Household and many prominent players. Concluding, the writer says:—"It is just nine years since Mr Scott commenced business on his own account and his business is now one of the largest and best known club making business in Scotland, turning out thousands of Clubs every year. Two years ago he had the distinguished honour of being appointed golf club maker to H.R.H. the Prince of Wales. Mr Scott is a golfer and teacher of considerable power—among his students being Miss Glover, the present lady Scottish golf champion.

> In the exhibition of golf clubs and requisites which was held at St Andrews last, week] while the championship competition was going on, Mr A. H. Scott was awarded a diploma of merit for the clubs he exhibited.

June 1910

The Golf House club in Elie have a fine collection of Scott's clubs collected by the late Ronnie Sinclair.

James Crowley (Sen)

1861 – 1937

The other important golf club maker who at least started in Earlsferry was James Crowley.

James Sen. was born in January 1861 and he features in the 1861 census. He was born in St Margaret's Cottage in Earlsferry. He married Margaret Manson in 1886 and then arrived in New York on 31st March 1887 which looks like his honeymoon.

Whilst there they had a son James Robertson Crowley born in New York, 28th November 1887.

He died on 4th December 1937 and is buried in Kilconquhar church yard.

He began his career as a joiner (carpenter) in Elie and Earlsferry and is still so listed in the 1901 census though recorded as a clubmaker in Links Road, Earlsferry, in a trade directory of 1893. He lived a couple of houses down from George Forrester.

He moved to Glasgow in 1911. Based on his youngest son, Alfred's school record he may have moved earlier. However, he is living in Stevenson Drive, Glasgow, in the census of that year described as a clubmaker but he is still listed as having a business in Earlsferry, James Crowley and Son, as late as 1921. Presumably he ran two establishments as he was a major reseller of clubs in Glasgow in the 1920s with a shop at 54 Union Street and latterly at Gordon Street. Like Forrester and Scott, during his time as a golf clubmaker in Earlsferry he dominated the club making scene and applied for a number of patents and registered designs. The golf house club have a good collection of Crowley golf clubs which now are rare. James was an innovator in manufacture of golf clubs his most famous being the Eureka. The Elie Golf Club have one in their collection. 1895

Bibliographic data: GB191126072 (A) — 1912-09-26

★ In my patents list   ▦ Report data error   🖨 Print

An Improvement connected with the Socketed Wooden Heads of Golf Clubs.

Page bookmark	GB191126072 (A) - An Improvement connected with the Socketed Wooden Heads of Golf Clubs
Inventor(s):	CROWLEY JAMES ±
Applicant(s):	CROWLEY JAMES ±
Classification:	- international: A63B53/02
	- cooperative: A63B53/02 (EP, US)
Application number:	GBD191126072 19111122
Priority number(s):	GBT191126072 19111122

Abstract not available for GB191126072 (A)

A NEW GOLF CLUB —Mr James Crowley, Earlsferry, has brought out a new Golf Club. The shaft comes right through the heel of the club, and gives all the better spring. The heads can easily be renewed, and no twining is required, the shaft being firmly fixed. To prevent the head from splitting up there is a pin holding it a little in front of the sole. The club, which is called the "Eureka," has been tried with most satisfactory results.

Chapter 11
The World Wide Influence of Earlsferry Golf Professionals.

There was, of course, a limit to the number of former apprentices of the golf club makers who could set up in competition to their masters. Many of the Earlsferry young men had become very proficient at the game as well as the manufacture of clubs. These young men, often for want of an alternative career, would become golf club makers in different parts of the country. In due course, as the popularity of the game continued exponentially, these young men found that a living could be earned by playing in competitive and exhibition matches.

The clear distinction nowadays between professional and amateur had yet to be formulated but it was recognised that if your main source of income was golf you could be designated a professional. More than one controversy emanated from this distinction (see Rolland). Then the Open golf championship on this side of the Atlantic started to attract these professionals and very often when they were "in town", as it were, golf clubs would promote matches and provide a purse for these professionals to play. Challenges would be offered by the top class players and money matches arranged on that basis. Sometimes the watching members were charged for the privilege, other times they watched for free, but it became a very good way of advertising your course and club.

They still had to make clubs, so they often became attached to fledgling golf clubs initially as teachers or club makers but in addition to advise and plan layout of courses. Their skill at greenkeeping was also a factor to be considered. They became jacks of all trades, teaching, making clubs, selling equipment, looking after the course and designing others. It was not unusual for professionals/teachers to winter in warmer climes at another club and there seemed to be much exchanging of golf courses for those plying their trade as teacher or golf clubmaker. Some were peripatetic moving to where the business was and others anchored themselves to one club and some became the club manager eventually. There was indeed substantial reward for the well-known professional and thus winning tournaments added to the appearance fees they could demand.

Another important development was the growth of the game in America. Again still to some extent a game played by the moneyed classes but nevertheless there seemed to be enough money and enough land for people to get together and build a golf course and establish a golf club. It seems that the trend started in New Jersey and rapidly spread to most of the eastern seaboard.

By the turn of the century James Braid in particular had become the icon of the game – although he never travelled to America – many of his contemporaries in Earlsferry having learnt their club-making skill and being proficient golfers themselves were attractive to those across the Atlantic seeking to establish a golf club. The employment of a Scottish golf professional became *de rigeur*. Thus many young men from Earlsferry made the trip, some on spec and some already engaged by clubs in America. There was no shortage of work and the word filtered back to Earlsferry that a good living was to be made in the land of opportunity. It is intriguing to see that often an experienced Earlsferry golfer in America would chaperone a younger man from Earlsferry on one of his trips back home and then employ the youngster initially at his club and then wherever there was a job. It was often the case that when one Earlsferry-born professional moved clubs he would encourage his former club to employ another of these Earlsferry men. Most of these young men born and brought up in Earlsferry had been apprentice to George Forrester or Andrew Scott before seeking wider horizons. Research which is ongoing suggests as many as 55 or so young men went across the world having learnt their trade and their golf in Earlsferry. The golf tract in Earlsferry produced many exponents of the game who carried the word to the new world. From a rough perusal of the census of Earlsferry in 1891 there were 147 males and 174 females. Of the former only about 68 could possibly be considered to be capable of gainful employment and yet between then and 1920 at least 55 young men became golf professionals.

It tended to run in families. One of the brood (see the Mackies) might make a speculative journey across the Atlantic. There was a degree of encouragement. Witness this advertisement in 1896:

> PROFESSIONAL GOLF PLAYERS who intend paying America a visit will find it to their advantage to call on Messrs A. G. Spalding & Brothers, 126 Nassau Street, New York, immediately on their arrival.

Notable by its absence is what "advantage" might be gained but Spalding was very much at the forefront of the fledgling golf industry in the States.

Ships' passenger lists between 1890 and 1910 show a number of professional golfers and golf club makers travelling to America and in Earlsferry once the word got back from some of the early starters like Crowley and Mackie it became known that a good living could be made.

From the maps showing where these golfers went it is clear that the majority stayed in the eastern seaboard and some moved north to Canada. The golf courses in the Northern states were out of play during the winter and professionals attached to these clubs were often employed in more southern climes and J.D.Dunn (a native of North Berwick) organised a travelling circus of professional golfers during the winter in Florida to play and teach at the golf courses which he managed. These courses were known as the "Plant System" and were attached to Hotels.

There was no doubt that a very good living could be made in America by teaching and playing the game. Most of the young men from Earlsferry whose wills we have managed to access have shown that they were comfortably well off. Far better we suspect than the life of the normal Earlsferry son. However what is important is the huge influence that the Scots, not only from Earlsferry but North Berwick and St. Andrews had on the development of the game in America between 1890 and 1930. It is also notable that the tradition of the Scottish professional golfer was often carried on by the sons and daughters of these pioneers.

The Anderson Family

There were four Anderson brothers. Their father Andrew Senior was the green keeper for the Recreation Park in Elie and the family (a large one) mostly lived in a small cottage in Elie. In 1900 or so Andrew and his brother James built two attached houses, Glencoe and Jamesville. Andrew was one of the founders of the Earlsferry Thistle Golf club and although like his sons, a good golfer, he did not aspire to being a professional. His sons were of a different breed.

ANDREW MACKAY ANDERSON

1885 - 1968

Andrew was the third eldest of the Anderson brothers. He was born in 1885 on 9th January although later it would seem he became a couple of years younger.

We do not know much of his early years although there is a record of him being in Dunfermline in 1901 and he is described as an architectural assistant and living with his uncle, Henry Stewart, an Inspector of police, who was married to his aunt Johanna who was his father's sister. Why he went off to live with his uncle is not clear but we also know he was enrolled in Dunfermline High School aged 9 in 1893. For some reason therefore his father and mother sent him to his uncle to be looked after. One can speculate but Andrew and Flora his mother had a large family and they were registered as living in Wiliamsburgh which also seemed to double as the police station. We are not sure of the connection but it is axiomatic that his uncle was an Inspector in the police.

Thereafter he surfaces in Canada and we note that he marries in 1906 a lady called Margerit Malcolm or Bersea who seems to have been an adopted daughter of the Bersea family.

> F. Tennant, of Arrow River, Man.
> BERSEA—ANDERSON—At the manse, Hanley, on May 11, by the Rev. R. H. Wareburg, Margerit Malcolm, foster-daughter of Mr. and Mrs. G. Bersea, to Andrew McKay Anderson, of Dunferline and Williamsburg. Elie Fife, Scotland. 276-1

This means that he was at the tender age of 21 and must have crossed the Atlantic between 1901 and 1906. However with the popularity of the surname and Christian name there may well be a person of similar name and age. On the other hand the detail in that newspaper announcement of Andrew having been associated with Dunfermline and Wiliamsburgh seems too much of a co-incidence so we reckon this is the correct Andrew Anderson. They were married in Winnipeg from whence a few years later he crosses into USA. We reckon this string is accurate. There is a clue that he may have been living in Humbolt but the census entry is not specific enough to make the connection although the ages are right. We know from one of the family trees on Ancestry that he and Margaret had one child but the plot very much thickens because it seems that that daughter Margaret Malcolm Stewart Anderson born 1907 and whose father was our Andrew was adopted by the same "parents" who adopted/fostered her mother. This would make sense if her mother had died and it may be that is what happened.

The next sign of him is that he crosses the border into America from Winnipeg and is shown in the crossing of 1910 that he is a widower and he notes as his next of kin, Bersea, his former father-in-law. He is described as a professional golfer and indicates his final destination to be Boston Mass.

We are fairly certain from our researches that he then remarried Catherine (sometimes with a K) Margaret Keith who was from Dalkeith in New Jersey in 1911.

We pick him up when he is registered for service in world war 1 where he declares he is living at AMC Apartments, Bell Avenue, Bayside Long Island where he was a golf professional so it possibly the correct Andrew Mackay Anderson although there is an anomaly in his stated date of birth said in the application form to have been 1887 instead of 1885 as we know of his birth. It is complicated further by the existence of Andrew Mitchell Anderson who was a golf clubmaker from St Andrews who was circulating around this time. He pops up again in 1921 census in in Ontario, Wentworth where he is described as a teacher but then in parentheses "golf". The personnel in the household matches what we know of him. This looks like the correct Andrew Anderson. Two years before he volunteers for the first world war and in his attestation form are details consistent with what we know except again the date of birth is two years out of date. We cannot find another such man born on 9th January 1887 so again from this form it looks the correct person. In his alien registration card again the details tie in and again his date of birth is wrongly stated. He even states where he is employed as a professional at Upper Montclair golf club in New Jersey which was up and running quite a bit before 1918 although much additional work was undertaken shortly thereafter.

He decided to go to Canada to join the Canadian armed forces and this may have been at the instigation of his older brother, James, who had already joined up and was killed at the Somme. In any event he crossed border, was called up and served in France before being demobbed and was registered as living in Canada where he ultimately settled. The 1921 census shows him as living in Ontario, Wentworth and his occupation golf teacher.

He and Catherine (aka Margaret) had a number of children before she died in 1943.

She seems to have died in Burlington Ontario and it is highly likely that Andrew was employed as a golf professional there. Indeed there is refence to his brothers also working there. It seems therefore that he was involved in Burlington for some time and there is evidence that he died in Milwaukee in 1968.

Henry (Harry) John Stewart Anderson

1888 – 1948

Henry or Harry was the second youngest son of Andrew Anderson and Flora Mackay who was born in Liberty in 1888. His elder brothers all had the middle name of Mackay, being his mother's maiden name, but Harry did not.

We do not know of his early prowess on the golf course but we manage to pick him up when he goes off to Australia in 1912 where he meets and marries Mary Watson in Tasmania in 1913 and they have a daughter, Nancy. It seems that they then cross to Vancouver landing in 1915 and thence across the border to USA via Niagara. The purpose of this visit is said to be visiting his brother in New York and he is described as a Merchant.

By 1920 we think he was in New Jersey since he seems to have been naturalized in September 1923 and employed as a butcher. But in 1930 census he, along with his wife, is shown as living at 116 East State Street, Kennet Square Pa. and described as a golf professional. Indeed, in his obituary it is stated that he had been pro at Kennet Square Country Club for some 18 years when he died in 1948. Thus he must have joined Kennett Square Country Club in about 1928. The club had only been established in 1922.

According to his obituary he then joined Poquessing Country Club which no longer exists. And also at Burnham golf and Country club

Lewistown – now Lewistown Country Club. He died in 1948 at Maple Dale Country club whilst giving a lesson. He lived latterly at 133 West State Street, Kennet Square PA.

He had devoted his life to golf in Pennsylvania other than a short time during world war 2 when he was employed in the war effort at Pusey & Jones shipyard in Wilmington Delaware. He was survived by his wife who died in 1967 and his daughter, Nancy who died in 1962.

James McKay Anderson

1882 – 1918

James Mackay Anderson was born in Williamsburgh on 11th February 1882. He was the eldest of 7 children. He is described as being a mason apprentice. On 1st November 1901 he married Helen Gerard Dunn at Glencoe Villa in Williamsburgh. They had two children - Helen Junior who survived but a few weeks and William Dunn Anderson who was born in 1907 and died in 2000*. We do not know whether he was apprenticed to Scott or Forrester but he was obviously a proficient golfer and he applied for and was successful in getting the job of professional at Lanark Golf Club. We are grateful to Lanark GC for the following information.

According to Lanark Golf Club records, James McKay Anderson was interviewed on Saturday 16th April 1910 for the position of Greenkeeper and was paid his train fare to attend.

EXTRACT FROM GOLF CLUB MINUTES

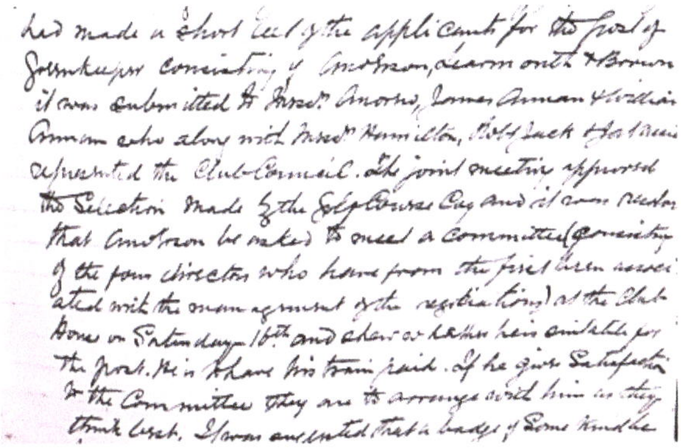

[Handwritten minutes extract]

In 1911, the PGA records show James as being elected to the Scottish Section showing Golf Club House, Lanark as his address. [There is also] an entry in Jacksons Register of British Professional Golfers 1887-1930 which shows that J Anderson was at Lanark until 1914.

This is another extract from the Club Minutes in July 1913 mentioning James Anderson, Professional, and giving him the right to sell golf balls at the Club.

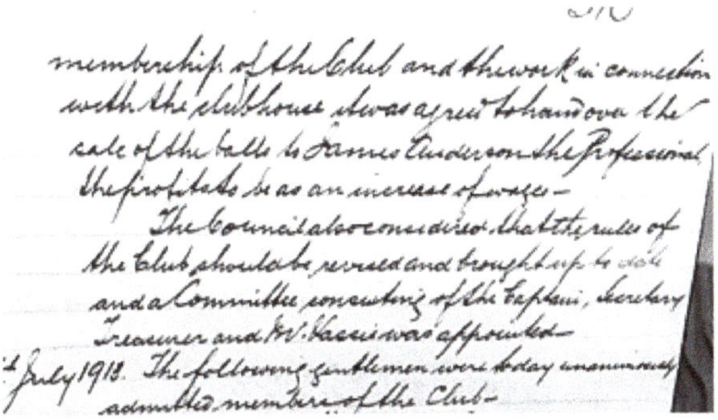

[Handwritten minutes extract]

In the National Records of Scotland, ...James' wife Helen sadly died at the age of 33 during childbirth in the Golf Club House, Lanark on 31st October 1913.

Shortly after that, in 1914, James left Lanark,...to live in Elie - Fife, perhaps to take care of his children and returned to his former profession of Mason. James then joined the 1st/6th Battalion Black Watch in January 1915 and on 12th August 1916 he went on to marry Elizabeth Paisley** in Elie which is where his parents stayed. From July 1917 he was on active service at the front, and in April 1918 it was reported in The East Fife Observer that he had been taken prisoner.

East Fife Observer 25th April 1918.

Missing.

Recently Private James Anderson and his brother Private George M Anderson, sons of Mr & Mrs Anderson, Glencoe, Elie were officially reported missing. Later news received by the wife of Private Jas. Anderson states that he is now a prisoner of war in Germany. In pre-war days he was a professional golfer in Lanark, while his brother was employed by Mr Garland, joiner Elie.

Almost 8 months later, James' wife and parent's hopes were dashed and the East Fife Observer reported the following news on 5th December 1918.

Another Prisoner of War Victim.

"Though no official confirmation of the intelligence has yet been received there is too much reason to fear that another local victim has to be added to the prisoners of war who have made a supreme sacrifice. The mother of Private James Anderson 6th Black Watch – Mrs Anderson – and his wife residing in Glencoe Villa were made aware that he had been taken as a prisoner of war near Cambrai some months since and have been regularly sending him parcels which however it appears he never received. A comrade Private William Stenhouse Northumberland Fusiliers at present in Kirkcaldy has vouchsafed information to the effect that Private Anderson was killed outright by a bomb which dropped from an aircraft fully two months ago and that about ten other soldiers were also killed or wounded at the same time.

His family have been looking forward with eager anticipation to see him coming home soon and this sad information has naturally disconcerted them. Private Anderson joined up in the Black Watch in January 1915 and had been on active service at the front since July last year. Previous *to enlistment he was a golf professional at the golf course in Lanark, was 37 years of age and leaves a widow and three young children. What makes it all more distressing is that his brother Lance Corporal George M Anderson also of 6*[th] *Black Watch has likewise been taken a prisoner after he had been wounded in action and the family are in dubiety as to his present whereabouts.*

On Tuesday Mrs Anderson proceeded to Kirkcaldy to see if she could obtain any further information regarding her husband. Much sympathy is felt for the family in the state in which they now find themselves placed."

On the 19th December, they went onto report that James's brother, George, returned home.

James is remembered on the war memorial in Elie, http://www.iwm.org.uk/memorials/item/memorial/5729

At the moment, there are over 90 names, including James McKay Anderson, added to the list of brave PGA Professionals who made the ultimate sacrifice.

** Elizabeth Anderson probably emigrated to Canada since the address on the war pension form is c/o Smith, Sawdy Athabaska Laundry Alberta so far we have not managed to trace her later movements.

William McKay Anderson

1883 - ?

William McKay Anderson born on 4th August 1883. He was two years younger than his brother James M Anderson (q.v.).

In that census he is shown as a golf clubmaker apprentice although we cannot be certain to whom he was apprentice. However it is more likely to have been Forrester at that time. We find that he married Marion in New Jersey in 1914 although she was Scottish having come there from Scotland with her parents in 1898. We first find them living in 1920 in New York, Queens where he is described as a golf professional although at that time we do not know where he was. He was naturalized as an American citizen in 1918 where it is said that he was professional golfer at Bellport Long Island. It looks therefore in his declaration when he arrived that he already had employment at Bellport. We next pick him up in the 1930 census living in Grand Avenue Newburg Orange county when he is described as a green keeper. This is about a drive and six iron from Powelton Golf club where he was employed.

He appears in some competitions but his problem and ours is that there was another Scot Willie Anderson who won the US open three times in a row. He was from North Berwick.

Along with other professionals, during the winter he would travel south to Florida.

Jack Ballantyne

1912 – 1952

Coming a little later than most of our subjects and technically not an Earlsferry man John (Jack) Ballantyne was born in Auchtermuchty in 1912.

He served an apprenticeship with Andrew Scott and again became a proficient golfer. He lived with his mother in Main Street Kilconquhar until he was married so one supposes he made the daily trip to Earlsferry in his job with Scott.

As a leading amateur of Earlsferry Thistle Golf Club, he played for Fife in inter-county matches. He was a former holder of Elie Burgh Medal and many other local trophies, but he failed to realise his ambition to win the Elie and Earlsferry Links championship, although in 1949 he was leading at the end of the first round. On that occasion he took ill and lost his lead in the second round, which he finished in state of collapse. In 1950 he turned professional and set up business in Elie as a golf clubmaker. He was one of the tenants of the sheds situated alongside the wall of the Golf Club car park which stance he shared with Tom Reekie (q.v.) In 1951 he won the Auchterlonie Putter in the series of competitions organised by Fife, Angus and Perth Golf Alliance.

He collapsed in the street in Glasgow where he had journeyed for an interview for the post of professional at Buchanan Castle Golf club. He was survived by his wife Mrs Miriam Ballantyne who continued the shop after his death, eventually retiring in the 1990s. She died in 1995.

Andrew Bell

1872 – 1922

Andrew Bell was the youngest child of Alexander Bell and Margaret Downie. They had 10 children. Andrew was born in Elie on 27th July 1872 and lived at 3 Fountain Road, Elie. This makes him a contemporary with many of the young men who took up the game. We do not know where he did an apprenticeship but he obviously was trained and also became a good golfer. He is described as a joiner in the census but we pick him up again in 1901 census in England where is he is shown as a golf club maker and living in West Bromwich. By this time he is married to Winifred S. We cannot find the marriage details to find out her maiden name but she was born in 1861 give or take a year or two in Sydenham Devon. It is not clear where he is working but it says "on his own account".

We next find him along with his wife Winifred in Leamington Spa at 11 Archery Road and we know that he was employed as a golf professional at Leamington Spa golf club.

> The professionals of the two clubs also played a match at Leamington, which resulted in a victory for J. W. Whiting (Walmley) over Andrew Bell (Leamington) by 3 and 1. Whiting was round in 74, which constitutes a record for the present extended course from the medal tees.

> The Committee have appointed Andrew Bell, lately of the Leamington G.C., as professional player and coach to the Club, in addition to F. Newton. Bell will enter upon his new duties on Monday next.

Indeed there is a report that he was teaching the members of Atherstane golf club in 1896 and also a report that he played a match against Evason at Water Orton Club.

> **Water Orton Golf Club, Warwickshire. (1902 - WW1)**
>
> The club was founded in 1902.
>
> To celebrate the opening of the club an exhibition match was played between William Evason, the 18 year old professional from Penn Common, Wolverhampton, and Andrew Bell. The Scot won by one hole.

In 1913 he moved to Warwickshire golf club but we do not think he was there very long before the outbreak of war. He joined up in 1914 initially for three years but he stayed on until demobbed in 1919. He then went to live in London in Putney with presumably his wife but he died in February 1922, we suspect as a result of illness contracted during world war 1. He and his wife seemed not to have had children.

Post script from a perusal of the records held relating to Andrew's war pension it is noted that he was married (again!) in 1918 to Minnie Mary Holmes. We can find no evidence of the death of his first wife and in the marriage certificate he is described as being a bachelor. However it is clear from the pension records that Minnie was the recipient of his pension when he died in 1922. Indeed on Minnie's death in June 1955 one of the executors was what seems like their daughter Barbara Lilian Bell and we know that she was born in 1920. We cannot find the death of his first wife but of course it would have been during the first world war where records were difficult to keep. The other executor is his eldest child born shortly after he and Minnie married in 1918. She married in 1943.

William Brown

1877 - 1958

William Brown was born in Earlsferry in 1877. He lived with his wife Marrion (sic) at Craig Cottage at Chapel Green. In the 1901 census he is described as a golf club maker and Marrion Innes is described as golf club maker's wife! They have at that time one child William Rolland Brown born in 1900. They were married in Musselburgh in 1899. I think we can assume that he was apprentice to Forrester. By 1911 he had moved to Walton on the Hill in Surrey where he was still a golf clubmaker and it is reasonable to suppose he had been recruited by James Braid. By that time they had two children John Innes Brown, born 1902 and Douglas Rolland Brown, born 1906. It becomes a little complicated because although he was born illegitimate there was a court action in Cupar in 1893 which established that his father was William Brown and his mother Isabella Rolland or then Smith. They subsequently married but William seems at times to have acquired the middle name Rolland as it suited him because although his marriage certificate shows that he is William Rolland Brown his birth certificate shows him simply as William Brown.

However what complicates things is that he and Marrion had a son whom they called William Rolland Brown. He was born in 1900. He died in 1908. William died in 1958 and Marrion died before him as a result of an accident.

The elder son, John Innes Brown, was described as a golf professional when he married in 1922.

By 1939 he is described as a bus conductor which suggests he did not succeed as a golf professional. It might have been that by that time the golf clubs in anticipation of war were down sizing but in 1939 it was a little early for that.

And by the time of his father's death in 1958 he was a turf accountant. He had a son Donald Innes Brown born in 1923 who was described in the 1939 census as an apprentice golf professional but we cannot find where he was earning his living. He, as had his brother, had been assigned to Walton Heath and trained under Braid.

The Crowley Family

James Crowley was one of the earliest of the golf club makers to make the journey to America. He was making golf clubs in Earlsferry on his own account but we are not exactly clear as to when he established the business. Whilst Forrester had been to America earlier than Crowley he had not gone there as a golfer or golf club maker. He first went to America in 1887 and in some respects pioneered the trail in that he was the first genuine joiner/clubmaker to make the journey.

James Crowley (Sen)

1861 – 1937

James Sen. was born in January 1861 and he features in the 1861 census. He was born in St Margaret's Cottage in Earlsferry. He married Margaret Manson in1886 and then arrived in New York on 31st March 1887 which looks like his honeymoon.

Whilst there they had a son James Robertson Crowley (q.v.) born in New York 28th November 1887.

He worked for Philadelphia Cricket and golf club among other places and we have seen a letter from that Club indicating that he had been with them for almost four years and the letter is dated 1904 and we assume therefore that he started in 1900 – where he was before that date is difficult to ascertain. He is shown in the census of 1900 as living in Earlsferry, but it looks as if it was a rather peripatetic existence and that whilst his wife was with him to begin with she went back to Fife with James Jnr and had more children. This suggests that James Sen perhaps must have come back and forth across the Atlantic and it makes it even more unusual in that he is shown in the 1891 census as living in Earlsferry along with his wife. But he had a son James Robin(ert) son born in New York on 29 November 1887. When in Earlsferry they lived in Links Road but it is not exactly clear where but certainly close to Forrester's workshop. He also had property at St Margaret's Cottage on the High Street actually next door to Linmara the residence of James

Braid. It is likely that the property was on the extended back garden of the property in the High Street. He died on 4th December 1937 and is buried in Kilconquhar church yard. Other than James Jnr who was born in New York all the other children were born in Earlsferry between 1890 and 1900. Yet during this time James Snr was working a golf professional in USA. He arrived in 1887 with designation as joiner so he must have managed to get some sort of work.

He also had a number of properties in Earlsferry and it is highly likely that he may have been one of the early second home owners who took up part time residence in Earlsferry during the summer months. He at one time in addition to St Margaret's owned Ravenscraig (next door to 19th Hole) and a plot of land to west end of the village which he acquired from the Earlsferry House owners. He is also shown as having bid for various derelict properties which often went on the market. He was one of the early air b and b people perhaps. Details of his golf club making appears in chapter 10.

John (aka Jack) Christopher Crowley

1895 – 1966

Jack was James (q.v.) and Margaret Crowley's second son.

Although he was born in Earlsferry his father and mother and rest of the family moved to Glasgow in 1909/11. His father had set up a golf club making business both in Earlsferry and Glasgow but he was principally known for the Crowley Sports Emporium in Gordon Street in Glasgow – it was probably one of the first genuine sports shops although golf was its main concern and it continued well into 1970s. It is probably a pub now.

Jack became involved in the business along with his father. They continued the Elie/Earlsferry connection by having one of the "huts" beside the golf course along with Forrester (earlier) Reekie, Scott and eventually Ballantyne.

> THE Firm of JAMES CROWLEY & SON, Golf Club Makers, fifty-four Union Street, Glasgow, has been DISSOLVED as at thirty-first March nineteen hundred and thirty-three, by mutual consent, by the retiral therefrom of the Subscriber James Crowley, one of the Partners.
> The Business will continue to be carried on by the Subscriber John Crowley on his own account, and under the firm name of JAMES CROWLEY & SON.
> Mr. John Crowley is authorised to uplift all the debts due to, and he will discharge the whole debts and liabilities of, the Firm.
> Dated at Glasgow, this 31st day of March 1933.
>
> JAMES CROWLEY.
> JOHN CROWLEY.
>
> Witnesses to the Signature of the said James Crowley and John Crowley—
> MARY S. J. LAWRIE, Typist, 34 West George Street, Glasgow, C.2.
> ANNIE C. MACLEAN, Typist, 34 West George Street, Glasgow, C.2.

Jack had a most unfortunate first marriage to Ann Stewart from St. Andrews whose father was a golf club maker. He married her in 1927 but she died tragically that year during childbirth and the child was stillborn. He remarried in London, Marion Brown Whitelaw in 1929.

He took over the business from his father in 1933 and the business continued after his death in 1966 which was shortly after his second wife's death in September 1966. He and his family still retained a foothold in Earlsferry having acquired Ravenscraig from George Forrester Executors.

> **CHARGE UNDER ACT OF JAMES VI.**
>
> **CASE AT CUPAR.**
>
> A charge under an old Scottish statute was brought at Cupar Sheriff Court on Tuesday, when it was alleged that John Christopher Crowley, golf club manufacturer, 9 Stratton Drive, Giffnock, Glasgow, did, on August 17, at Carnbee Reservoir, Fife, " it being a stank or lock within the meaning of the Act of 19 James VI., attempt to steal trout or other fish." It was stated that he was liable to a fine of forty pounds Scots.
>
> An agent, on accused's behalf, pleaded guilty. Accused, he said, had been looking for a place to fish and after making inquiries had gone to Carnbee Reservoir. No one was able to tell him whether fishing was forbidden there or not, and he thought that the custom in the West of Scotland of paying on the spot would be carried out. He had no intention of fishing without making payment. The owner appeared on the scene, and accused apologised for the liberty he had taken.
>
> Hon. Sheriff Grosset imposed a fine of £1.

As a last anecdote let us look at the newspapers of 1937 when he fell foul of the law although it is understandable if he pled that he did not remember the statute of James VI.

James Robertson Crowley

1887 - 1962?

James Robertson (otherwise Rolen or Robinson*) Crowley was born in New York on 29th November 1887. His father James Crowley (q.v.) and mother had arrived in New York in early 1887 and his father was a joiner/golfclubmaker. Since he was born in New York he was an American citizen. His father was working as a golf professional latterly at Philadelphia Cricket Club where he stayed until about 1909 when he came back to Earlsferry. His wife and family came back to Earlsferry rather earlier and James Sen was back and forth across the Atlantic until about 1908. His son James Jnr probably was apprentice of sorts to his father who had set up business as a golf club maker initially in Earlsferry and latterly when he moved to Glasgow in 1911. (*this is as a result of the illegible handwriting of the minister who baptized him !)

> James Crowley, the professional golf player who has charge of the Waubanakee links in this city, has arrived in town. Up to the present time no golf has been played at the links, owing to the cold weather.

We also know that James Crowley Jnr i.e. J R Crowley arrived back in USA in 1905 and was shown that his last residence was in Barrhead and he was going to Burlington, Vermont – there are actually a number of Burlington Golf Clubs in the northern USA. We think from that that he may have been attached to Fereneze at one point but he certainly also had affiliations to Whitecraigs and Cowglen where his father also taught. He is designed as a golf club maker. This is certainly James Jnr because of his age in the manifest. But it is interesting that the Burlington Newspaper Vermont shows an entry in May 1907.

> The committee anounces to players that James Crowley, last year with Woodbury, N. J., club, has been engaged as professional and will be found on the grounds after May 15.

We reckon by this time James Sen was back in Scotland and had moved through to the west. He is shown in the 1911 census living in Shawlands. However this is where the plot thickens because James R Crowley Golf Professional is shown as on an assisted passage to Australia in 1909.

There was a J. Crowley entered in a golf competition in 1910 playing out of Whitecraigs. Now we suggest that was James Sen because James Jnr is shown as going to Australia on an assisted passage in 1909 and he was unlikely to return the following year after that. We aso have evidence that he went to New Zealand and then back to Australia but came back to UK in 1915. But this is where we lose track of him.

He must have returned to Australia since we have evidence of him being there in 1927 but thereafter the trail vanishes. We can find no further reference to him meantime. There is a vague reference in the newspapers of 1918 which relates to Alfred Crowley and John Crowley. It says that Alfred had been killed in the war and John had been wounded in France and then it continues "his eldest son is also serving in France". This would suggest that this is a reference to James R, their eldest son. We know his service number 40931. We now know he joined the Royal Dublin Fusiliers and was in action in France. He was wounded and discharged in 1919. His death is rather more difficult. We have a reference to a death which could be our James but other than that we are not certain. During his time in Australia there is evidence that he was in quite a bit of trouble with the legal authorities. The extracts from the newspapers at the time make interesting reading and it is more than likely he was quite welcome to have returned to UK.

JAMES CROWLEY is charged, on warrant, with larceny as a bailee of 20 golf clubs: 4 drivers; 3 brasseys; 10 iron clubs: and 3 dreadnoughts, value £6 14s., the property of John Patterson, professional golfer, Melbourne Golf Club. Sandringham, at Sandringham, on the 15th inst. Description :—Scotchman, professional golfer, about 25 years of age, 5 feet 4 or 5 inches high, medium build, fair complexion, brown hair, clean shaven; wore a black serge sac suit and black tweed cap.—O.5737. 5th August, 1912.

Walker, Sydney Police. Committed for trial at Quarter Sessions.

JAMES CROWLEY, alias JOHN WILSON, alias JAMES ROBINSON, alias JAMES ANDERSON (40), charged with stealing an overcoat value £5, the property of William Allen, has been arrested by Constable 1st Class Arantz and Constable O'Donnell, Sydney Police. Sentenced to twelve months' hard labour. Identical with offender John Anderson, alias James Robinson, alias John Roberts, alias James Crowley, alias John Crowley (vide Police Gazette, 1927, page 319).

EDWARD JOHN DWYER (25), charged with stealing the sum of £20 2s. 6d., the property of the

> ream | ... on it; and a leather suit-case,
> ions; | "T. E. Dence" in ink on inside; total value, £150.
> d six | Identifiable.
> com- | Wentworth Falls.—Stolen, between 11 p.m. the
> e on | 28th and 7 a.m. the 29th ultimo, from a locker at the
> buck | Wentworth Falls Golf Club's rooms, Wentworth Falls,
> ers"; | the property of John Harley McLaughlin, Union
> pair | Bank Chambers, Pitt and Hunter streets, Sydney,—A
> and | leather linen-lined dress suit case; two shirts; three
> oots, | collars; a tie-pin; twelve pairs socks; twelve handker-
> boy's | chiefs; a razor, numbered 1340, "Taylor" written on
> eshoe | the case; a military hairbrush; pair tan boots; pair
> lver- | brown stockings; pair Relax broad garters; and
> ford, | thirteen golf balls; total value, £16 12s. Mostly
> ancy | identifiable. Suspicion attached to James Crowley,
> ons; | 35 years of age, 5 feet 6 or 7 inches high, medium
> hem; | build, fair complexion, light-brown hair, clean shaved,
> ated | thin features; wore a grey suit and a light felt hat;
> six | a golf instructor; a native of Scotland, and speaks
> ated | with a Scotch accent.
> | West Maitland.—Stolen, between 11.30 p.m. the

John Allen Hawkes Donaldson

1903 - 1966

John Donaldson was born in Newburn on 9th February 1903. His parents lived in Lahill Lodge and his father was a coachman. He served his apprenticeship with Andrew Scott in Earlsferry. His family moved to Colinsburgh and in 1911 his father is shown as being a gas stoker. He had a brother James William Given Donaldson who was born in 1906 and at that time Donaldson senior was described as an insurance agent living in Colinsburgh. We expect that whilst doing his apprenticeship he may well have lodged with someone in Elie but we do not know with whom. He became a professional golfer presumably after he had finished his apprenticeship with Scott and initially we think he was attached to the RAC club in Epsom and he was living in Banstead but there is a newspaper report of his exploits.

"..........the 25-years-old John Donaldson, until recently assistant to another East Lothian man, William Watt, at the scene of yesterday's struggle (RAC Club Epsom). Only a few months ago Donaldson became a fully-fledged professional with the neighbouring Cuddington Club."

"A 25-year-old player named John Donaldson, a native of Elie, in Fifeshire, who has been located in the London district for several seasons, finished second this week in the qualifying rounds of the Southern section, which embraces most of the stars of professional golf. It was a very enlivening performance on the part of a man hitherto almost unknown and until recently assistant, but as it was due mostly to remarkable putting, which produced record score of 67 for the Royal Automobile Club's course at Epsom...... On the 18 greens Donaldson took only putts." 1929

He seems, according to that report, to have been in the London area for a few seasons and it is reasonable to suggest he had been assistant to William Watt at Epsom before appointment to Cuddington in Surrey as that club's first professional. He held that post until 1966.

<u>Cuddington Golf Club.</u> This course was opened on 1st January 1929. It was designed by H S Colt in conjunction with John Morrison and Frank Harris Brothers who produced a downland course of good length and variety. The greens were large and offset to emphasise the correct line of play......The Club's first Professional was **John Donaldson** who remained at Cuddington until 1966. John Donaldson was succeeded by his Assistant, Harold Guy, who himself gave great service to the Club until 1982. [Cuddington G.C. website] There is a reference on his appointment to his brother having also been engaged as his assistant.

He married Ellen Biddlecombe in April 1930 presumably shortly after his appointment and they lived in Banstead in Surrey. She was 18 years older than him being born in 1885 and so far as we can find out they did not have any children.

In 1943 there was this excerpt from a local newspaper:

John Donaldson, the local professional, unfit for war service, but able to do his stuff in a munition factory, unfortunately nearly sliced off the middle finger of his right hand during the week, and so could not play in the match.

He played a lot locally and some of his exploits were reported.

1938

£1,040 TOURNEY. Remarkable Round by Young Pro. Archie Compston, twice winner of the first prize, headed the qualifying list of the Southern section of the £1.040 "News of the World" tournament the R.A.C. course, Woodcote Park, Epsom, yesterday. Perhaps by reason of his achievements of the past, Compston›s feat of totalling 141 for the 36 holes attracted lesser notice than that the 25-year-old John Donaldson, until recently assistant to another East Lothian man, William Watt, at the scene of yesterday's struggle. The local professional had held the lead over the field, but his erstwhile pupil took all the attention when with 67, he placed himself ahead of all until the burly Compston shouldered his way to the front to the extent of one stroke. Only a few months ago Donaldson became a fully-fledged professional with the neighbouring Cuddington Club. Donaldson improved two strokes upon the joint record of Charles Whitcombe and Henry Cotton on Wednesday.

However, in July 1944 he is shown to have married Elizabeth Hope Dorothy Brown and there does not seem to be a record of his first wife's death until 1973 when she died in Hampshire. We presume therefore that they were divorced and he remarried. She was born in 1910 so slightly younger than him at the time of their marriage. Again, so far as we know he had no children but he and his second wife took up residence in 1945 in Dorking in Surrey where he lived for the rest of his life and where his second wife died in February 1968. John died in 1966 which must have been very shortly after he retired from Cuddington.

James W.G. his brother died in 1975 in Elie.

The Duncan Family

There were a number of Duncans in Earlsferry and Elie about this time. John and his brother David were the sons of David and Jane(otherwise) Jean Duncan. Their father died as a result of an embankment collapsing whilst working on the railway line to Elie. He can only just have started as a labourer in the railway since his occupation at John's birth was miner. We are not sure where in Earlsferry they lived when David was born but it looks very much as if after his father died the family that is mother Jane (Jean) and his siblings George and John lived at 12 Liberty at least until David and earlier John had moved away from Elie.

David Duncan

1862-1918

He had one brother called John who became professional at Stirling GC (q.v)

He initially trained as a tailor but was a successful amateur golfer with the Thistle club playing in a number of matches. We are not sure he did an apprenticeship with Forrester but his prowess as a golfer may have made him decide to seek his future in the profession. At that time word was about that a good living could be made from the burgeoning activity of golf. He probably was semi professional at that point getting prize money etc. He went south to Northampton in about 1895 at the quite elderly age of 33 which suggests that his lack of employment in Earlsferry made him change tack and he became professional at Northampton golf club which seems to have been established in 1893 or so. On 21st December 1894 this was reported

THE Northampton Golf Club, which was started about two years ago, has been compelled, owing to the quantity of grass which grew this last season, to remove its links, and on Tuesday last week, Tom Morris came down and laid out a fresh course on what appears to be a most eligible site, in the immediate neighbourhood of the town, on land commonly known as the Hills and Hollows. The grass never grows to any length, and the soil is very light and sandy. The course will be a most sporting one, and, as the veteran says, altogether it will be as good as any in the Midlands. It was hoped that Old Tom would have been present at the annual dinner, which was held the previous week. but as he was unable to get down that week, a few of the more ardent members of the club entertained him at a small dinner given on Wednesday last when an enjoyable evening was spent. His tenure was not without incident.

He seemed to have made an impression.

NORTHAMPTON GOLF CLUB. LADIES' AUTUMN MEETING. The competition connection with the autumn meeting the lady members the Northampton Golf Club commenced on Thursday at the links on the Kettering Road. The first event was a competition for challenge belt*, presented by Mr J. W. Janson, open to ladies affiliated to any Golf Club Northamptonshire, the second prize being memento given by the Northampton Golf Club, value one guinea. The green was in excellent condition, which was owing much to the exertions of Duncan, the club professional. Oct 1897 Northampton Mercury

*one can hardly envisage the ladies of the golf club wearing a challenge belt....!

Fire at Northampton Golf Links. Rather serious fire was discovered on Tuesday at the pavilion on the Golf Links on the Kettering-road, Northampton, which are occupied by the Northampton Golf Club, and before it could be extinguished the pretty and commodious pavilion was completely demolished. The pavilion was a wooden building 17 feet by 12 feet, roofed partly with wood and partly with corrugated iron, and it was replete with every convenience for golfers. The fire was caused by a defective stove-pipe.... Mr. Cox, of Moulton, was the first to notice anything wrong, and the manager (Mr. Duncan) was informed. Northampton Mercury July 1899

We are not sure how long he stayed at Northampton but although he married Lucy Pegler who was a nurse in Staines in 1896 he must have stayed on in Northampton at least until the fire. There seem to have been no children.

He moved to Staines and lived with her parents whilst she worked as a domestic nurse. It is not clear what he did there but he was described as a professional golfer and lived quite close to a number of golf courses at which some of Earlsferry friends and contemporaries had been stationed. e.g. West Middlesex C.R. Smith et al. Indeed in 1911 James Braid re-designed West Middlesex golf course and it may be that Duncan was part of that but the census reports that he was in business on his own account which suggests that he may have been a teacher giving lessons wherever required on a fee earning basis or competing on the "circuit" although we cannot find any reference to his exploits.

However he died in Stirling Royal infirmary on 20 July 1918 at the age of 56 and we assume from that he was living at that time with his brother. His wife never remarried and died in Surrey in 1969.

John Duncan

1861 - 1939

The Duncan family – David, Margaret, Thomas, John and Isabel

We are not sure where in Earlsferry they lived but it looks very much as if after his father died the family that is mother Jane (Jean) and his siblings George and David lived at 12 Liberty. Clearly he must have moved to Glasgow. This about Kelvinside G.C.

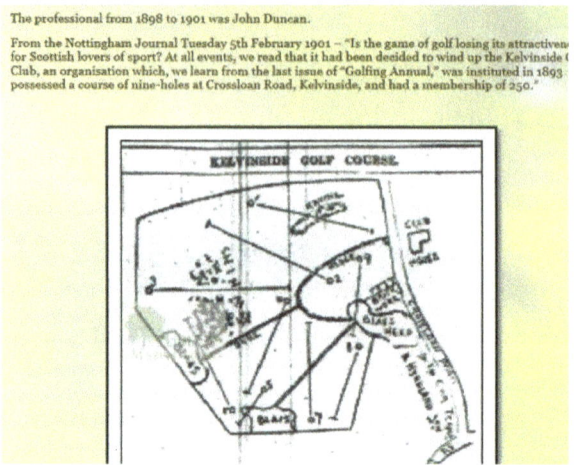

He appears again in the 1901 census as living in Church Street in Maryhill in Glasgow and his profession is stated to be golf club maker which ties in with the demise of Kelvinside Golf club. By that time he had married Margaret Hutson from Rothesay Isle of Bute in 1898.

They had a child later, Thomas Hutson Duncan in 1904. (see later)

He became professional at Stirling Golf Club in 1901.

"John Duncan …… worked at the Club for 34 years, asking for permission to retire at the age of 74. To this day the John Duncan Trophy, commissioned by the Club in his memory, is played for." from Stirling Golf club's website.

JOHN DUNCAN TROPHY, This competition, instituted to mark the retiral of Mr John Duncan, late professional to the club, took place on Saturday.. June 1939

Not long after he retired he died after a long illness.

OBITUARY MR. JOHN DUNCAN. A native of Earlsferry, on the line of Fife, which has given golf to the world, Mr Duncan was in his 78th year. He came to Stirling about thirty-nine years ago and had been professional for over thirty-nine years on the King's Park course. He had been for many years an elder St. George's Church. St. Ninians.... Golfers in Stirling and Scotland will learn with regret of the death of genial John

Duncan, ex-professional of Stirling Golf Club, took place at his home. Kincraig**Bannockburn Road, St. Ninians on Tuesday, after a long illness. Mr Duncan probably initiated more men and women into the mystery the wee gutty ba' than any British professional. John retired in March 1935, ...and he was [viewed as] a regular "institution" ...and his workshop was a little parliament of its own.

** no surprise that he names his house after his homeland

The Elder Family

This family has been very difficult to trace but judging by the photograph in the Canadian papers they were prolific golfers and we are fairly certain owed their roots to Earlsferry. It is not helped by the tradition of naming their children after their fathers and grandfathers.

Robert Elder

1876 – 196?

Robert Elder, born in Dunfermline in 1875 but shortly moved to Earlsferry we know was a golf club maker based in Eastwood perhaps at East Renfrewshire golf club near Glasgow and we assume had trained with Forrester or Scott. He started as a grocer's apprentice in 1891. He obviously turned professional fairly young hence this in 1896 the time when the Elie course became 18 holes.

> **ELIE.**
> PROFESSIONAL MATCH AT CAMBUSLANG.—On Monday night a professional golf match between Willie Smith, Carnoustie, and Robert Elder, of Elie, was played at Westburn Links, Cambuslang. Smith won the match by five holes up and four to play.

His father (George) was a joiner and lived in Earlsferry at St. John's which co-incidentally was immediately next door to a grocer's shop.

His early career as a professional seemed to have taken him to Glasgow and he was professional at Pollok Golf club for 14 years and according to the website of that club – "

> 12/02/02 Mr Elder, recently dismissed by Mr Annan of Sportsman Emporium, applied for position as Professional. Such action placed the Club in a difficult position. Having given excellent service as a clubmaker, Elder was appointed as Professional. The club purchased the workshop and fittings at the price Mr Annan had paid.
>
> 29/06/04 **GREENKEEPER** Having received reports from various clubs on course management cttee decided 'change in greenkeeping was desirable'. Taggart was given two weeks notice, Elder appointed Greenkeeper. House purchased £12.00, insure less than 15s.
>
> 05/08/18 Elder & Johnstone, having started work of 'National Importance', had left the service of club.
> Elder available on Saturday mornings. "

1929

Thereafter and indeed contemporaneously he seemed to have been at Cathcart Golf Club. In these days it was not unusual for a professional to be at more than one club. We know he went to Canada having travelled there in 1929. Hence the photograph.

Father Robert, sons George (b1901), Jock and Robert were all professionals in Canada. His sons joined him not long afterwards and they all had good employment as professionals in Canada.

His brother was George Peebles Elder (q.v.)

In 1949 he was reinstated to the amateur ranks presumably after retiring.

We can therefore adopt Robert Snr. as a true son of Earlsferry even although his children were born elsewhere.

George Peebles Elder

1878 – 1956

There is much confusion with this man because there seem to have been two George Elders about the same time. The one we are interested in is George Peebles Elder since that was his mother's maiden name. His father is shown as being a joiner initially and living in St John's in Earlsferry High Street.

George was born in 1879. He was born in 1878 although being the 27th December his birth was not registered until January 1879. His wife's maiden name was Cochrane and she came from Dennistoun. They were married in Dennistoun Glasgow in 1907 but his address there is shown as Fox Rock Dublin. He is described as a golf club maker. Before 1900 he was assistant to Jamie Braid at Walton Heath and may have come with him from Romford. According to one report in 1903 he seems to have resigned from Hamburg and so took up somewhere else in 1903..... *while it was only the other day George Elder resigned his post near Hamburg......*We are assuming that this is the right George Elder.

We have received information from Foxrock History society which accords with his presence at Dublin until 1908.

> and obliging.... ...We consider him fully competent to undertake Green keeping in all its branches, and his work done here reflects greatly to his credit".

£1 0s 0d PER WEEK

Clay having left "of his own request" in August 1906 the Club advertised for a successor, and on 23 August a letter was sent to Mr G P Elder, Earlsferry, Fife :-

> "... ...your application for Professional and Club maker has been laid before the Committee, and out of a number of applications they have decided to appoint you,"

then, to avoid raising his hopes too high,

> "if on interview you are approved."

Elder arrived on 1 September for a week's mutual examination during which he could see "the links, accommodation, etc.", the Club magnanimously paying his expenses. It would seem from a letter of 29 August that no less than the great Harry Vardon had spoken on his behalf, and on 7 September Elder, presumably approved at interview, was appointed as :-

Professional and Greenkeeper at £1 0s 0d per week... ... subject to a week's notice.

> "You will be expected to work on the Greens and Course ... ...and to keep the entire links in good order. You will also be expected to exercise supervision over the caddies."

then come the opportunities,

> "You will be permitted to charge a shilling per round of nine holes for coaching, and to make, repair, and sell Clubs and balls".

however, lest dreams of potential wealth distract him, the letter ends with the stern reminder,

> "it must be strictly understood that the proper care of the Greens and Course is your first duty and that it must not be interfered with by any other work.".

He must have expressed some views about his accommodation as on 9 October the Committee accepted a tender of £119. 0s.0d. to build "a new Professional's workshop" and the contractor was requested "to put the matter in hand at once".

COURSE DESIGN

He was evidently well thought of as within a few months of his appointment he was taking the 10 o'clock train from Foxrock to Gorey, changing at Bray, in response to a request "to lay out the Golf Links" for the Gorey and District Golf Club. They were to pay him "his expenses and ten shillings for the day." (The Gorey club was instituted in October 1906, but survived on the original land only until around 1920.)

Mr Elder was still with the Foxrock Club in 1908, when with opening rounds of 84 and 88 in the IPGA Championship he failed to qualify for the quarter finals by 5 strokes - perhaps not surprising in view of his many demanding duties to the Club.

LATE OF BUNDORAN

It seems that Elder left the Club in 1908 and his place was taken by H J Magee who in a contemporary article is described only as "late of Bundoran". A more elaborate description appears in the 1911 edition of Porter's Office Guide :-

Thereafter it is a bit piecemeal. The 1900 census shows a George Elder as living in Walton Heath which might accord with his employment as a golf club maker and we think that he is the George Elder who won the Craigforth Challenge cup in Earlsferry Thistle in 1899. He beat Isaac Mackie who was a contemporary.

He is shown as having travelled across to Canada in 1904 but there is no record of what he did in Canada. He was still employed at Foxrock until 1908 so he must have come back from Canada.

In 1925 he went to Australia with his wife and we are pretty certain he is identifiable in the ship's manifest as it shows his address as c/o Cochrane in Dennistoun.

His destination after 1908 when he left Ireland is impossible to find currently. We have come across a passage for himself and his wife from New Zealand in 1924 although what he was doing there we do not currently know. However he then went to Australia in 1925 and that is where he stayed until his death in 1956.

There is no record of him on the golf course when he went to Australia as he is designed as a painter and in subsequent electoral rolls he is shown as living in 18 Kerr Avenue, Camberwell in Victoria and as late as 1933 he is still living in Tooreak and described as a painter. He died in Victoria, Australia in 1956 though we do not have exact information about that. We have not been able to trace his wife subsequent to that.

William Fairful(l)

1858 – 1943

For some reason there are a large number of Fairful(l)s in Fife mostly connected with the mining industry and coal. Our William Fairful was born on 24th March 1858 in Earlsferry – again the birth certificate does not identify the actual house but see later. His father was John and his mother Christina ms Jervis. By a process of elimination we conclude that between 1850 and 1890 his family lived next door to David Scott the father of Andrew and James Scott. That would have been Ferry Cottage which makes the Fairfuls as living in what is now Twoways in Earlsferry High Street. But then in the English census of 1891 we have a William Fairfiel (this is a misprint, it is clearly Fairful in the actual register) and he is shown as being a golf club maker and he is married to Jeannie living in Greenwich.

He is shown as having two children Francis and Christina both of whom are apparently born in Stirlingshire – Francis in 1887 and Christina in 1888 and the fact that they were born in Stirlingshire suggests that at that time he was resident in Stirlingshire where he was professional at Falkirk Tryst 1888-1890 and there is a newspaper report in 1892.

Only however for six months. He is also credited with being the professional at Dunfermline G.C. 1895-1900

He must have gone south after that and then returned in 1892. So by 1892 he was back in Scotland.

ELIE.
GOLF APPOINTMENT.— Mr Wm Fairfull, Elie, has been appointed greenkeeper and clubmaker to Dunfermline Golf Club.

We cannot find any reference to his golfing exploits during this period until his employment with Alloa. Indeed it is difficult to know where or if he was employed as a golf club maker in London. He may have worked in Army & Navy Stores under Braid's guidance. Since Alloa G.C. was established in 1892 we can assume that WF was employed to bring the course up to a standard that was fit for the people of Alloa. Later in 1930 James Braid redesigned the course.

WF remarried in 1903 and with Isabella Harvey they had three more children Magdelana 1905 and Wilhamina 1906 both born in Elie. They were living at that time in what from the census looks like Balhram Cottage but we have yet to pinpoint that property. They also had a son John born in 1909. By that time however he had taken up employment with Wm Gibson and Co the golf club makers in Kinghorn where he stayed for the rest of his life until he died in 1943.

So although we do not know where he may have done an apprenticeship he still qualifies as a member of this elite bunch by virtue of his positions in Alloa, Falkirk and Dunfermline* even although his golf professional career was relatively short.

*Post Hoc we are grateful to Dunfermline golf club who recently supplied some details of his tenure with that Club. At that time the golf club was at Halbeath and subsequently moved to Ferryhills near North Queensferry but the minute books of the club in 1897 show that WF was initially employed as greenkeeper/clubmaker and club steward.

> The terms of Fairful's engagement as Clubmaster were next considered, and the Secretary & Treasurer were appointed as a Sub-Committee to arrange with Fairful as to his engagement as Clubmaster, Greenkeeper & Clubmaker, at a salary of £45 per annum, giving 3 months' notice on either side and with free house, coal and light, and that he provide a competent servant.

February 1897

By March 1898 WF had sought a pay increase of £10 which was granted.

By September 1898 WF decided that the tripartite role of greenkeeper/clubmaker and club steward was too onerous so he resigned as clubmaster but offered to stay on as greenkeeper and clubmaker. This was accepted.

In April 1900 he tendered his resignation which was accepted in somewhat enigmatic circumstances. It is not known his misdemeanour but shortly after this he went to the States to visit his friend.

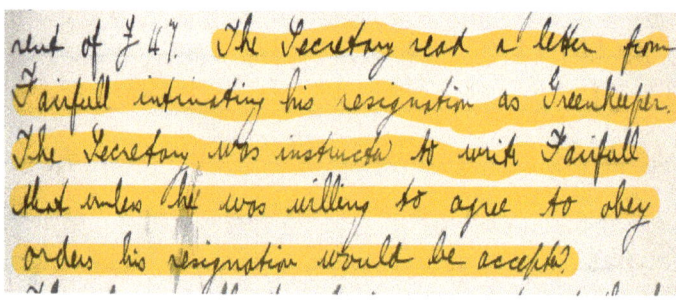

James Forrester

1879 – 1956

> **PLAN FOR WORKSHOP REJECTED.**
> A petition and plan for a shop and workshop to be erected at the top of Club Wynd was submitted from Mr James Forrester, Earlsferry. It was remarked that no sanitary accommodation was shown on the plan. The Provost considered it doubtful whether they could pass a plan for a workshop which showed no sanitary arrangements. The Clerk read a section from the Public Health Act, which stated that sufficient accommodation of sanitary conveniences must be provided according to the number of persons employed. Mr Foggo asked whether similar places to that proposed to be erected by Mr Forrester had sanitary accommodation, and, if not, why the medical officer had not reported the matter. The Provost said the shops were only used in the summer months, and when the medical officer visited the town in the winter they were closed. It was agreed to reject the plan as no provision was made for sanitary accommodation.

> **INTERESTING GOLF MATCH.**—An interesting four ball match was witnessed by a large crowd of spectators on Earlsferry Links on Tuesday, when Mr McKay (the well-known West of Scotland player) and James Forrester, Earlsferry's crack professional, opposed Mr Outhwaite of Craigforth and James Keddie. The play, both morning and afternoon, was of the closest nature, and although Keddie was not seen to advantage in the long game, Mr Outhwaite had only to acknowledge defeat on the home green each round. We understand there is a possibility of the match being replayed, when Mr Outhwaite will claim as his partner a player nearer the calibre of James Forrester perhaps A. H. Scott. Such a match would attract a large crowd.

James Forrester was the only son of George Forrester (q.v.). He was born in 1879. As was often the case in these days he was named after his grandfather, James, born in 1808 and who died in 1876. James senior was a merchant, grocer, etc (see George Forrester). James married Jessie Anne Mackenzie in 1900 and we know he had been apprenticed to his father George as a golf club maker. For some reason he and his father fell out and there was very little connection between them in the subsequent years. However James became a professional golfer and whilst he was not officially recognised as the professional to Earlsferry and Elie golf club or their successors the Golf House club and Earlsferry Thistle, he nevertheless advertised widely that he was available for golf lessons at Earlsferry. We do know that shortly after he had finished his apprenticeship with his father he was brought into the business and it became known as George Forrester and Son. His father apparently sent him off to London to set up a shop there but this must have been short lived and he was back in Earlsferry plying his trade as a professional golfer and clubmaker to some extent in competition to his father although by that time, 1920s, his father was getting to the end of his career. However it is significant that when George decided to retire he did not pass on the business to his son but advertised the sale of the machinery which he had collected to manufacture golf clubs and balls. Why he did not see fit to let his son take over is not known but there must have been a fairly serious rift between them. In any event James setup in business in Elie and he had a hut/premises at the top of

Golf Wynd leading up to the clubhouse of the GHC. We know for what it was worth that Jack Ballantyne (q.v.) succeeded him in that shop when he retired in 1950. His first plan for his workshop failed to pass the stringent requirements of the Dean of Guild Court of Earlsferry in 1910 (wonder if his father was provost at the time?)

He did succeed in 1925 !

James had built up a reputation as a very good golfer and many accounts exist of his matches at Elie especially with A.H. Scott and others. This report in 1902.

> THE PROFESSIONAL GOLF TOURNAMENT AT SUNNING DALE.—Play was begun in this match on Tuesday, the local players included being A. H. Scott and J. Forrester. In the first round Scott beat his opponent by 3 up and 2 to play, while Forrester beat him by 2 up and one to play. In the second round Forrester Thomson North Berwick, by 2 up and one to play, while Scott was beat by Herd by 4 up and 3 to play.

And the following year his exploits became sufficiently newsworthy.

James Keaddie (sic) is James Keddie (q.v.) Mr Outhwaite was a motor dealer and very good amateur golfer. He lived with his family in Craigforth prior to it being an emergency Hospital. He died during the first world war.

Even in his quasi amateur days he was successful and looking at the list of winners in this clip he seems to have been a better prospect than some more illustrious names in the prize list.

> **EARLSFERRY.**
> THISTLE GOLF CLUB.—The members of the Club competed for the Glover Cross and monthly medal on Saturday. A large number of players turned out. The game was greatly interrupted by a strong westerly gale blowing over the course. James Forrester won the medal and cross with a score of (84—6) 78. Other scores :—A. H. Scott (79 plus 2), 81 ; W. Mackie (88—6), 82 ; James Rowley (91—8), 83 ; John Mackie (90—7), 83.
>
> **ELIE.**
> VISIT OF THE CHAMPION PROFESSIONAL.—Arrangements have been concluded with Mr James Braid, the champion professional, to visit Elie on Saturday, and take part in an exhibition game with Mr James Forrester. The first round is likely to start at 10.30, and the second at 2.30 in the afternoon. The exhibition game has been arranged by the Joint Green Committee.

...and others.

> EARLSFERRY AND ELIE LINKS.—The professional match between D. A. Given, Elie, and James Forrester, Earlsferry, took place on Saturday, the latter winning by two up and one to play. The Balcaskie Medal (scratch) and Glover Cup (handicap), along with other prizes, were competed for on Saturday. The greens were keen, and a strong wind prevailed. The following are the prize-widners:—J. H. Outhwaite, 86; G. B. Key, (scratch), 89; J. W. Sime (92—2), 90; J. H. Outhwaite 86-6,) 92; J. Gemmel (103—10,), 93.

1903 a busy year for him,

> EARLSFERRY.
> GOLF MATCH.—Interesting foursomes were played on two nights by Messrs James Nelson and George Elder, two of the Ferry cracks, against Professor Hele Shaw and Mr James Forrester, the local professional. After very closely contested rounds the latter couple finished two and one. A third round was arranged when undoubtedly the Ferry players came to the front, and squared matters. Ferry pluck still shows itself in the rising golfers.

James Nelson (q.v.) and George Elder (q.v.) were also proteges of George Forrester.

1895

He retired in September 1950 with this send off.

LINKS WITH GUTTY BALL *DAYS Mr James Forrester, golf professional at Elie for over half a century, who on Wednesday celebrated his 72nd birthday, is to retire at the end of this week. James Forrester was one of the leading professionals in Scotland at the beginning of this century, and played with men like James Braid, Harry Vardon, Andra Kirkaldy, and Sandy Herd, but he gave up competitive golf to concentrate on teaching and golf club making. Among his pupils were Mrs E. C. Beddows, former Scottish champion; Ian Roberts. ex-Boy Champion; Donald Cameron and K. T. Thomson, the Walker Cup trialists. Mr Forrester is a member of an old Elie golfing family, his father was George Forrester, the man who invented the drill neck joint for golf clubs, which displaced the splice neck, and is* now adopted universally in clubmaking. James Forrester left school at the age of 12, and served his apprenticeship as a golf club maker with his father. .....Mr Forrester left his father's business to go into business on his own account. As a young man, he was a regular competitor in the Open Golf Championships, and played at St Andrews, Hoylake, Muirfield, and other famous centres. His most memorable money match was against another Earlsferry man, the great James Braid. They played 36 holes over their own course at Earlsferry. Forrester was round in 72, and was three up at the end of the first round, but Braid got in front in the second round, and finished the match two up. Forrester does not play with more than six clubs, and the last time he was out this season, he went round the Earlsferry course 72. He has gone round the course the days of the gutta ball in 65. His set consists of driver, spoon, three irons and a putter.

James owned a modest house at Devon Cottage in the High Street of Earlsferry.

David Affleck Given

(1ST November 1875 to 7th July 1928)

There were a number of Given families in Elie and Earlsferry at the end of the 19th Century. This article concentrates on David Affleck Given who was born on 1st November 1875 to David Given, a shoemaker and his wife, Jane. His younger brother was Douglas Given (q.v.) and his birth certificate gives his address as Elie, Bonnington House, Bank Street.

The 1901 census shows him as living with his wife Jessie at seaside Earlsferry. It is difficult to work out where exactly he was living at this time but if the census can be trusted they were neighbours of the Mackies who at that time were in Waldeve but he was described as a golf club maker so we can probably assume he was working with George Forrester or Scott. But he was not there long before he was appointed in 1902 to the professional position and golf club maker at Irvine Bogside golf course in Ayrshire. He had married Jessie Tarbat from Forfar in 1899 and is shown as living at Enfield Cottage in Elie. Enfield Cottage was just off Kirkpark Road and it seems it was demolished in 1970s to make way for social housing on the site.

David was an accomplished golfer having won a number of competitions at Earlsferry Thistle and playing alongside such luminaries as Isaac Mackie and Jamie Braid himself. Indeed his confidence was such that he could afford to advertise in the local press thus:

David A Given is prepared to play anyone resident in Earlsferry (A.H.Scott excluded) over 18 holes on Earlsferry Links for £1 over 36 holes for £5 within a fortnight of this date Elie 27th January 1898.

There is no record of any takers but it is of significance that he did not think he could beat A.H. Scott.

Like so many of his contemporaries there was little in the way of employment locally so he applied for and was given the professional job at Irvine Bogside in about 1900 which would have necessitated him moving through to the west. This was a young course setup in 1887 and his employment included green keeper, clubmaker and professional as was often the case in these days. A knowledge therefore of course management was expected. He had already played in a number of local professional tournaments and his appointment gave him a chance to spread the word of golf to the West of Scotland. He took part in a number of money matches, competitions and exhibitions during his time at Bogside. In 1903 he is noted: He left in 1908.

GOLF. PROFESSIONALS ELIE INTERESTING CONTEST. To-day the members the Scottish section the Professional Golfers' Association are competing at Elie for the four places allocated to them in contest Sunningdale next month for £200 prizes offered by the proprietors the "News of the World". The Association does not seem to have taken firm hold in Scotland, for only a dozen of the professionals turned to-day. Play started ten o'clock, which time heavy mist hung over the links, but the sun was making gallant struggle to force passage through. Considerable interest is being taken in the professionals' play, and a crowd assembled at the first tee, most of them waiting to follow Scott, the local man, who partnered Massey.

We should note that William (Willie) Fernie also took part in this and many other competitions in the professional arena at that time. May 1907

In 1903 he had a son Leonard George who was born in Rose Cottage in Earlsferry on December 6th. It is likely that by that time he was already established in Irvine but a home birth was obviously preferred. The Rose Cottage referred to here could either have been the Rose Cottage close to Chapel Green or the Rose Cottage which is still in Earlsferry High Street. The latter was the home of the Pearson family with whom the Givens seemed to be friendly and indeed in the 1901 census his next door neighbour is said to have been George Pearson a fellow golf club maker and subsequently professional (q.v.)

He had moved with his family to Irvine by 1905 and is shown as living at 5 High Street, Irvine and seems to have moved to Troon by 1911. He is shown as living at Wellbeck Crescent in Troon.

The following year however tragedy struck when his wife died of cancer. Her death certificate shows her usual residence as Golf Club House, Troon.

It seems strange that this would have been her normal residence unless by that time David was actually employed as a golf club maker at Troon. Which brings us back to Willie Fernie who was the head professional golfer at Troon at that time and with whom David was friendly.

Further tragedy was not far away when his son Leonard died aged 11 of tuberculosis in 1914. His address on that certificate is shown as Templehill in Troon which suggests he was living with his father there after his mother's death.

> **DEATH OF WELL-KNOWN FIFE GOLFER.**
>
> A well-known Fife golfer and clubmaker, David Givens, has died at his residence, High Street, Kinghorn. He was employed with Messrs Wm. Gibson & Co., Castlerig Works.
>
> He was for some time professional to the Barassie Club, Kilmarnock, and afterwards with the St Cloud Club, Paris. Deceased was 52 years of age, and a native of Elie.

Where he went after his son's death remains unclear until his death in 1928 in Kinghorn. That death certificate shows him as a golf club maker. Normally if it was a former golf club maker it would say so - we can assume he was employed. There was a large manufacturing plant of golf clubs in Kinghorn and Wm Gibson's golf clubs were being produced there at a commercial rate.

We can, we think, trace him firstly at Bogside and then perhaps at Barassie but certainly by 1911 he was at Troon. The introduction of St. Cloud in Paris is interesting because a number of professionals would spend their summer in Scotland at their club and then have a winter job on the continent. However mostly these jobs were in the warmer southern climes in the winter so his sojourns to Paris may have been latterly. Wm Gibson & Co was a large manufacturer of golf clubs in Kinghorn for many years – it came later on the scene than Forrester or Scott and initially their expertise was in the forging of metal cleeks and mashies before moving on to the whole set of golf clubs.

Douglas Pride (Pride/y) Given

2nd February 1883 – July 1931

Our particular concern here is Douglas PRIDE Given although it is referred to as Pridy as well. He was born on 2nd February 1883 and his father David and mother Jane then lived in Park Place in Elie. In 1901 however they are living at Kirk Road, Enfield Cottage.

They married in 1871 in Leven. He is described there as being a shoemaker but at Douglas' birth he is described as letter carrier and we assume he went on to become a postman. The other Given, David, seems also to have been the son of David and Jane and his birth certificate shows the address of Bonnington House in Bank Street. It is clear now that Douglas is the younger brother of David Affleck Given (q.v.) which conforms to the newspaper articles indicating that they had played together at Bogside when Douglas was pro at Barassie from 1904 -1914.

Douglas was proficient and active in Earlsferry Thistle at this time featuring often in reported results.

> In 1904 the Barassie Club appointed its first professional, Douglas Given, and the growing prestige of the course was recognised by its selection in 1905 as the venue of the "Evening Times" Trophy competition—the first competitive event of any consequence to be held there. During the next decade the Club went quietly on an even keel. The course was kept in excellent condition, alterations were made as these seemed desirable, and the clubhouse was improved.

By the following year he seems to have been considered a professional hence this from Montrose in 1904

He was trained as a golf club maker but we are not sure if it was under Forrester or Scott. However he seems to have been appointed pro etc at Barassie in 1904 rather at the same time as his elder brother was appointed to Bogside.

He then leaves Fife and goes south where he marries in 1912. Here he is described as a golf club maker and in 1912 in Surrey and his address is given as Sunningdale. We suppose it is highly likely that as a golf club maker he would have been in demand at Sunningdale and it is not unreasonable to assume that workers of this nature very often lived pretty close to their place of employment.

We have not managed to find any reference to his golfing prowess when in Surrey and it seems more likely that he was just employed as a golf club maker rather than as golf professional.

William Ramsay Graham

1906 – 196?

William Ramsay Graham ("Bill") was born in Williamsburgh on 1st June 1906. His father, George Graham, had the garage and coach hiring business in what is now Cavel Place.

He shared the premises with the Elie Hotel company who had stables alongside. The family also at one time owned Rotomahana in Ferry Road/Germans Wynd as the family home. As far as we know Bill went to the local school and no doubt learned to play golf on the golfing tract in Earlsferry. He did not appear to have set out to be a professional golfer since on his first visit across the pond to Canada in 1930 and then America he was described as a motor mechanic. We think therefore that he may not have served apprenticeship with Forrester or Scott. It was clear that he was a good golfer and had many promising results with Earlsferry Thistle including partnering Jock Smith as the top couple in winning the Ranken Todd trophy at Balcomie.

On the assumption that had he stayed in Scotland and would have featured in the prize lists for the Thistle for a number of years we conclude that he went over the Atlantic 1930 or so. Nor are we exactly certain when he crossed the Atlantic for the first time but he is shown as having crossed the border into USA in May 1930, although the border pass suggests that he arrived in Quebec on 4th May 1930.

We think he went initially to Canada but shortly thereafter became resident assistant professional at Broomfield Hills CC in Michigan. This at that time was a fledgling club but heavily subscribed by the motor industry moguls of Detroit so even today it's a very exclusive and private institution.

He seems to have been there for a number of years. He married a Canadian lady Leah Altretta Welsh in Highland Park Wayne Co. Michigan on 16th December 1932 but so far as we can see they had no children. It is highly probable then that he was already professional at that club.

Certainly in his registration of 1939 he is shown as being employed by Fred Lamb(q.v.) the golf professional at Bloomfield. So we can assume that he was assistant to Fred Lamb at that time.

He applied for and was naturalized as an American citizen in 1937.

He continued with moderate success in America. He was PGA Assistant champion of Michigan in 1935. His wife died in 1966 and he died in 1969.

The Keddie Family

There were a few Keddies in Fife, many associated with the mining industry, but George and his brother James were living with their aunt in Earlsferry. It is not clear where or why they were not living in family.

It might have been that their father, a miner, was semi itinerant. It might have been that their parents thought the environment of Earlsferry was preferrable to the polluted mining communities of that time. However there were a fair number of Keddies in Fife and George seems to have been a popular Christian name making it more difficult to track him.

George Duncan Keddie

1869 – 1937

George Keddie was born in Earlsferry on 4th October 1869.

It is more than likely that George became an apprentice to Forrester although he was slightly older and generally he would have been a proficient golfer honing his skills on the Earlsferry tract. He was a member of the Thistle club. He first surfaces as a professional in the early 1890s when he seems to have been a first professional at the fledging Chiswick Park golf club which received in-depth treatment in The Golfer in November 1894 thus:

One of the most pleasant little Golf courses in the near neighbourhood of London is that of the Chiswick Golf Club. About two years ago a small club was formed there, in a picturesque piece of ground adjoining the station of the London and South-Western Railway. ......A lease of the ground has been taken, and at present the club numbers, 185 members..... George Keddie, a name well-known in Elie and Earlsferry, is the green-keeper, and his sister*, bright and cheery, looks after the comforts of the members in the club-house, a fine, well-situated building, right in the middle of the course, with the first tee at the door. ....For the occasion [of the opening] the committee had arranged an exhibition professional match the players being Douglas Rolland (Rye) and George Keddie((Chiswick), against James Braid of Elie, and James Keddie((Hastings). The match was one of thirty-six holes, and contest was followed by a large and eager crowd of ladies and gentlemen anxious to see such a renowned player as Rolland. .... James Keddie ought to have his attention called to one circumstance, which, in our judgment, is not only a flagrant breach of etiquette on the part of a professional match player, but a gross want of respect to the members and committee of the club who invited him to play. He lighted and smoked his pipe several times while playing, even disdaining to take the pipe out of his mouth to play his tee shot, and this, too, in a serious match, with a gallery of onlookers. Keddie ought to know that this is not the game. ....The captain of the club, Mr. James T. Currie**, is a golfer who has learnt his game on the hither side of the Tweed. A better selection, for the difficult post could not have been made. Mr. Currie, has the advantage not only of knowing the game thoroughly and playing it well, but he has experience of many greens here and in Scotland; and it is out of the fulness of such experience that a young club like Chiswick will in all probability be prevented from going wrong at the most critical point of its career—the outset.

*His sister was presumably Nellie who lived in Elie latterly (see later).

** James T Currie was the son of James Currie of the Commissary office in Edinburgh and he was born in Edinburgh. He (at least one of the same name) competed in a boys competition in Earlsferry in 1881 coming 4th. He does not appear to have been related to the Currie family of builders of Elie but there is a strong Scottish connection.

We are not sure how long he stayed in Chiswick but he appears again in Berlin in 1899 when he is married to Jessie Margaret Oliver from the borders. At least that is what one entry in Ancestry says but there is another one suggesting it was in 1909. Since, as we will see, he later appears in the US census of 1900 along with his wife we have taken the 1899 date as the accurate one unless 10 years later to the day they decided to renew their vows in Germany. Since golf was very much in an embryonic state in Germany at that time it is highly likely that George was employed in setting out a golf course in Hamburg or thereabout since there is evidence that another Scot was also carrying out his trade there. (George Pearson q.v.).

Rolland G Keddie J Keddie and Braid at Chiswick

Shortly after he was married he and his new wife went to America where they arrived probably in 1900 and it seems he was immediately employed as a golf professional and is shown as living in New York State in the census of that year. His first club seems to have been Powelton GC in New York state and in 1900 he is shown as living in Newburgh which is close by.

He seems to have been there for about two years before he was offered and accepted the position at La Grange club in Illinois just to the north of Chicago. This must have been again as a recent development since the course itself was not fully operational until a year or two later.

In 1902 he was professional at Edgeworth Golf club. It seems that as professional he was merely engaged "for the season" and in most cases in northern aspects of USA that would have been starting in April. Hence during winter seasons the professional may well have to seek warmer climes and that is what George did because he was reported as being attached to Winter Park golf club in Florida which is near Orlando.

The players seemed to spend much time travelling to where the money was.

Then in 1903

> The Edgewood Golf club has signed as coach for the season George Keddie, who was last season with the Edgeworth club, of Sewickley. Nichol Thompson, the old coach of Edgewood, will, upon quitting his term with the Birmingham, Ala., club, return to the Hamilton Golf club, of Toronto, Can., which he left to come to Pittsburg.

It should however be noted that in some of these newspaper reports there is a suggestion that we are talking about George S Keddie but despite best searches we cannot find a golfer of that name. We are assuming therefore that Keddie was our Keddie in each of these reports.

However he or perhaps his wife, tired of the peripatetic existence in the States returned to Great Britain. He is seen to play in Earlsferry in 1905 before resurfacing again in 1909 at Whitstable where he was the professional.

And the census shows him there - Clare Road, Tankerton Whitstable.

> **EARLSFERRY.**
> GOLF APPOINTMENT.—Mr George D. Keddie has just been appointed greenkeeper to the golf course at Clackton-on-Sea in the Isle of Wight.

He moved in 1905 and later he is shown as the first professional at Lee on Solent. He then goes to Tankerton & Whitstable 1909-1911.

We then lose him in the South of England and he comes back to Elie in about 1912 where he is shown in the valuation roll as owning property in Earlsferry. It may be that he kept this property on after he went south but it seems more likely that he resumed occupation of it in 1910.

> **NEW TENANT FOR THE SHIP INN, ELIE.**
> Mr George Duncan Keddie, golf professional, Inglisfield, Earlsferry, applied for the public-house certificate for the Ship Inn, The Toft, Elie. The premises had been closed for the past two years, as owing to the war pleasure steamers had stopped coming and the potato trade at the Harbour had ceased. Mr Cook, solicitor, said Mr Keddie had been living abroad for the past 20 years, and had brought some ideas home with him. He wished to get the licence for the garden connected with the Inn as well as for the Inn as he desired to introduce the Continental system of drinking in the open.
> Several of the Justices saw a difficulty in including the garden in the licence, and on the motion of Mr Clement only the Inn itself was licensed.

Further research shows that he took over the Ship Inn in the Toft in about 1919. However he did seem to fall on hard times and was being sued thus:

ELIE PUBLICAN SUED Sued in Cupar Sheriff Court yesterday Low, Robertson, & Co., wine and spirit merchants, Leith, for an account amounting £14 17s 6d*, George Duncan Keddie, the Ship Inn, Toft, Elie said was unable to pay anything owing to illness and bad trade. Was only drawing £2 5s a week, and on Wednesday, his books would show, he only drew 4s 9d. With the season coming on he might be able to pay £1 a month. Mr A. H. Macdonald, Cupar, said he might accept £1 week. Sheriff Dudley gave decree for the amount sued for, payable at the rate of 10s per week. 1929 * current value £900

He died in 1937. There were no children of the union.

James Keddie

1862 – 1901

James was the elder brother of George Duncan Keddie (q.v.) and was born on 18th January 1862 which made him 7 years older than George but like George he was brought up in his aunt Duncan's home in Earlsferry.

> PROFESSIONAL FOURSOME.—Last Saturday Douglas Rolland and George Keddie essayed to beat James Braid and James Keddie over the links of the Chiswick Golf Club. Braid was playing a fine game, and Rolland, though driving well, was constantly at fault on the green, and this shortcoming may have had much to do with the loss of the match. It is almost unnecessary to say that the course was in a heavy state after the recent deluge. When the first round had been polished off Braid and his partner had the useful lead of three holes. After lunch the second round was started, and many ups and downs were seen. At one time Rolland and his partner were four holes to the bad, but sticking well to their work they managed to reduce this lead to two. However, Braid and James Keddie were not to be denied, and drawing away again the pair found themselves at the end of their day's work, when they were four up and three to play. The quartet had a large following of spectators, amongst whom were many ladies, who seemed to evince keen interest in the game.

He is given the occupation of mason in the census of 1881. However it is more than likely that he learnt to play golf along with many of his colleagues and became quite proficient at the game. We do not know whether he was trained by Forrester but he started in the business of golf club making in 1890s.

In the census of 1901 he is shown again as a mason which belies the accuracy of the census because we know that by 1894 he was the club professional at Hastings but featured with his brother at Chiswick, and reference to his play at Hastings - this article in 1894.

> THE GOLF CONTESTS.
>
> On Monday the first Week of Golf in connection with the Hastings Club was commenced on the East Hill Links, and terminated yesterday (Friday). Throughout beautiful weather prevailed, and considerable numbers of spectators witnessed the games. The greens were in excellent order. There were three competitions the first and principal one being for the challenge cup presented by the town. To become the property of a player the trophy must be won three times, not necessarily in succession. This competition lasted over two days. In the result Mr H. S. Colt won. After the decision of the contest on Tuesday the winner met the Club professional, James Keddie, who comes from Elie, Scotland, in a single match. Both players were in good form, and after a good and evenly contested game they finished tie, with eighteen holes.

In this article it is suggested that Keddie was with Royal Ashdown but we think that maybe erroneous since he was at Hastings by that time unless he had a part time position at Royal Ashdown.

He is shown as playing at Earlsferry in 1896 and we wonder if this was when he returned home at the end of season since he also challenged D.A. Given (q.v.) unsuccessfully in 1898.

Whilst he is shown being back in Earlsferry it is likely that he had given up the Hastings post perhaps in favour of C.R. Smith (q.v.) continuing the Fife connection, but in these days a professional golfer in addition to playing for money purses in competition might only be employed at a golf club for a season and it looks as if that is what may have happened with Keddie.

James never married but he died in 1901 at the age of 39 and the cause of death is shown as chronic epilepsy and alcoholism. A sad end to a good golfer but the family itself is not without tragedy because his younger brother David who was born in 1882 died as a result of falling though the ice of Kilconquhar loch whilst skating. He was 11 years old.

James died at Inglisfield in Earlsferry which was the home of his sister Nellie.

Frederick Lamb

1884 – 1942

Strictly speaking Frederick ("Fred") Lamb does not meet the precise criteria of this section. He was born in Edinburgh on 29th August 1884. His father, also Frederick, was a railway worker but by 1890 he had moved to Elie because he died there in 1890 as a result of a railway accident although it does not seem to have been reported in the newspapers of the time. It resulted in his wife having to bring up five children on her own. They were initially living in the Toft in Admiralty Square having moved from Edinburgh two years earlier. By 1901 they had moved to 5 Park Place where Frederick is noted as an apprentice golf club maker. It could have been either with Forrester or Scott. By 1911 he is still living at 5 Park Place but by this time he is noted as a professional golfer.

We cannot find any of his successes prior to his departure for USA in 1912 where he is described as a professional golfer but there does not seem to have been any particular destination in mind when he arrived other than New York. We know that fairly quickly he found employment because in 1912 he was named as professional at Detroit Golf Club and he must have been living in Michigan and this was the clubhouse in 1912.

In October 1913 he married Grace Evelyn Denly in York Ontario and in 1920 they were living at Moss Street in Wayne county Michigan and he was employed at Detroit golf course until he moved to Bloomfield Hills Country club in 1922 where he remained for the rest of his career.

This is one of his hand made clubs which came up on a Japanese website and seemed to be much sought after.

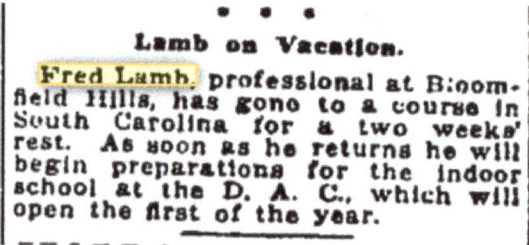

Lamb on Vacation.

Fred Lamb, professional at Bloomfield Hills, has gone to a course in South Carolina for a two weeks' rest. As soon as he returns he will begin preparations for the indoor school at the D. A. C., which will open the first of the year.

Master Brassie Shots, Lamb Advises Golfers

Form on Fairway Lie Is Best Way to Judge a Player's Ability, He Declares

By E. L. Warner, Jr.

Fred Lamb learned his golf at St. Andrews, the Scottish seaside links which is regarded as the game's sacred shrine. He has watched golfers on both sides of the Atlantic for many years and he has found a pretty good way to gauge a player's ability.

"Just let me watch a player hit a few shots with a brassie and I can tell you how good he is," asserts the veteran Bloomfield Hills professional. "A brassie shows up the weakness of a player better than any other club. If a player has mastered the brassie, he is pretty sure to be a good golfer."

A brassie will get the ball into the air providing the golfer swings correctly.

In a properly executed brassie shot, there will be a small divot taken after hitting the ball. Hitting in back of the ball before the point of impact will spoil the timing and generally result in a less efficient if not a dubbed shot.

Once the brassie is mastered, the player is sure to be an accurate driver. The tee shot is much easier in comparison because the ball is teed up and the player can get at the ball with ease. There is much less tendency to throw the body into the shot in order to attain loft.

He had a very successful career as pro at Bloomfield Hills CC which is a very exclusive club in Michigan. However he was also a public tutor via the newspapers as quite a few of his advices were published. and he was much admired as a teacher. However he had no pretensions of being a world class golfer but he did impart to his son the classic golf swing.

His exploits were sufficiently of interest to the golfing community that most of his ventures away from Michigan were published.

He died in 1942.

He must have been considered a success since in the 1939 census he was shown as earning in excess of $5000 per annum which equates to $100k today.

William Webster Latto

1873 – 1935

William Webster later to be called William Latto was born in Earlsferry on 27th February 1873. His father was actually Alexander Latto a merchant seaman but it is pretty certain his mother never married his father (but see later). However William assumed the name of Latto and he lived with the Webster** family in Ivy Cottage what was at that time Germans Wynd and is now, Ferry Road. In the 1901 census he is described as a green keeper. William attended Earlsferry school – he was living in the High Street in Earlsferry at this point and no doubt met and played golf with James Braid. In 1902 he took part in a professional golf competition at Elie where he was described as being a professional golfer playing out of Earlsferry. He was probably a member of Earlsferry Thistle. His first position seems to have been at Bearsden in 1891-1895. However he later became professional at Crieff golf club and it may have been as a result of his meeting Peter Rainsford the then Crieff professional in the 1902 competition.

He was there until 1910 where he was then professional and green keeper at Ardeer Golf Club in Ayrshire where he died on 19th July 1935. ** there was another William Webster of golfing renown (q.v.)

NOTES AND GAMES. *Wm. Latto, the new professional at Ardeer, comes with an excellent reputation as a greenkeeper and player. A native of Elie Latto, who by the way. was schoolfellow of Elie's greatest golfing product, James Braid, might be said to have been "teethed on golf clubs," and he knows the game from beginning to end. He has had a varied experience. He was at one time engaged at the Cathcart Castle Club's well known course, which he laid out and he has also had experience at a private English course, Kidderminster course, at Elie, at the West Chester (U.S.A.) County Club's course*, and Crieff, which he left to come to Ardeer after four years experience there. He holds the record for the latter course, which is a nine hole one, with the excellent score of 33. Latto is also a* splendid club-maker and repairer, and should give entire satisfaction to his new club. *Ardrossan and Saltcoats Herald October 1910*

*West Chester county golf course might well be Dunwoodie Golf course nowadays. If so there is a connection here between Latto and another Earlsferry man Chris Sunter who was professional there in 1920s. At this time West Chester county was the site of a few fledgling golf clubs in the Hudson Valley so it is difficult to know which Latto may have been at although it seems likely he was there a fairly short time. There would have been a Scottish connection with all these clubs in the Hudson valley.

In 1901 census he is shown as living in Germans Wynd with his grandmother, and he is described as a green keeper so we can probably assume that this was his primary function and the golf club making may have been a side job and when he moved to Ardeer he lived in the actual club house.

He died in 1935 at Ardeer golf club where he was still living.

The value of his estate in today's equivalent is £158,000. There seems to have been a good living made from the profession.

The Mackie family

Along with the Simpsons (q.v.) the Mackies were the most prolific of the Earlsferry golfers. Unlike the Simpsons, however, all four Mackie brothers William, Issac, Jack, and Dan emigrated to the United States and became pillars of the golfing fraternity there. Not only were they resident professionals at prestigious golf clubs but they took an active part in the early administration of the professional golf scene in the Eastern United States. Needless to say they were all very good golfers brought up and sharpened on the links at Earlsferry. The Mackies were at that time living in Waldeve on the shore which is almost adjacent to Earlsferry Town Hall. The house has undergone quite substantial renovations in the succeeding 50 years but it is still closely recognisable as the Mackies' house.

Daniel Sutherland Mackie

1886 – 1961

McLean Advanced.

George McLean, who was a clubmaker and a junior golf professional under Jack Mackie at the Dunwoodie Country Club, has been promoted to the rank of as- Forest Park links on Saturday, thevery merly occupied by Dan Mackie, who re- signed to accept the position of full- fledged professional of the Century Coun- try Club, of White Plains. McLean is an excellent golfer, having a record of 68 for the Dunwoodie course. He is a promising young homebred and the mem- bers of the Dunwoodie Club feel that good home talent should be appreciated and encouraged.

Daniel Sutherland Mackie was the youngest of the four Mackie brothers. He was born in Earlsferry in September 1886. We are not entirely sure of his early days in Earlsferry but it is highly likely that in addition to becoming proficient at golf on the golfing tract was also apprentice to either Forrester or Scott. However he initially trained as a mason and that was his profession in his first sojourn to the United States in 1907. It is likely that he was encouraged by his elder brother Jack (q.v.) who had gone to USA in 1900. Dan seems to have joined Jack at Dunwoodie prior to 1914. In 1914 he married Adelle Galatius whose father was originally Danish, in New York, with whom he had a daughter, also Adelle. He is described in the marriage certificate as "golf expert" but no work address. He appears as the professional at Winged Foot

Head professionals at Winged Foot

Name	Years
Dan Mackie	1923
Mike Brady	1924–1939
Craig Wood	1939–1945
Claude Harmon	1945–1978
Tom Nieporte	1978–2006

but later he joined Century Country club of White Plains.

In 1938, Ben Hogan joined Century as assistant to Dan Mackie. His "letter of recommendation", written by a Century member, stated that "he made a nice appearance".When Mackie left for neighbouring Old Oaks Country Club in 1940, Hogan became the Head Pro and remained at Century for two years.

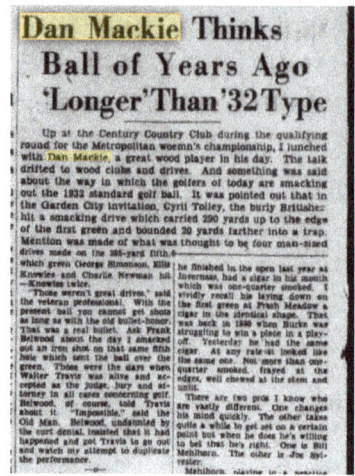

He was a proficient golfer as evidenced by this :

and as usual often sought after for his opinions.. then became heavily involved in the administration of professional golf.

In addition he became involved in the affairs of the PGA and was chairman of Westchester branch. He died in 1961 survived by his wife - she died in 1977 - and daughter.

Isaac Mackie

(23 September 1880 – 22 June 1963)

Isaac S. Mackie was apprenticed as a club maker under George Forrester. He was born in 1880. He grew to be a tall man of stout build. While in his early 20s he married Annie Schacht, a native-born New Yorker. Following his brother Jack—who had emigrated to the United States in 1899—Mackie also made the trans-Atlantic journey in 1901.

Jack Mackie, (q.v.) was one of the early pioneers in American golf being one of the founders of the PGA of America. He accepted a job as professional at the Fox Hills Golf Club on Staten Island soon after his arrival and remained in that post until 1914. On 13 July 1905 he won an Open Tournament at the Van Cortlandt Park links by shooting 152 on a course that had been soaked with rain. He held off joint second-place finishers Willie Anderson and Bernard Nicholls who finished at 157. It was the first ever professional tournament held on a public links golf course in the United States and had various other successes from Foxhills.

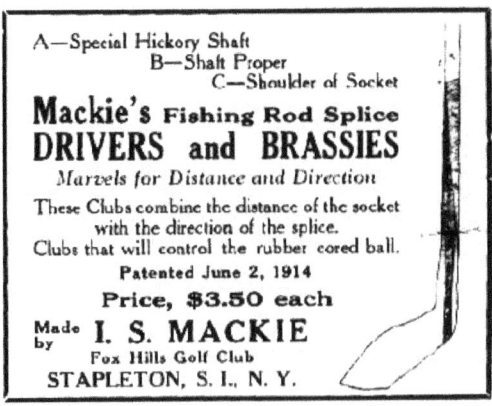

In a $500 four-ball match held on 26 August 1905 at Hollywood Golf Club in Deal, New Jersey, Mackie partnered with Willie Anderson of the Apawamis Club went on to defeat George Low and Bernard Nicholls. The winners were described as being "at the top of their game" as they played before a large gallery. The play was described by a writer for the *New York Tribune as* "the finest exhibition of golf that has ever been seen upon the course, and the match was greatly enjoyed". Mackie was runner-up to George Low Sr. in the 1906 Metropolitan Open and was victorious in the 1914 Shawnee Open which was contested at The Shawnee Inn & Golf Resort in Smithfield Township, Monroe County, Pennsylvania.

He patented a fixing method for clubheads, as can be seen in his 1914 advertisement, which attempted to combine the strength of the socket head with the 'direction' of the splice, by minimising the rotation of the clubhead on impact.

He came back to Britain in 1910 to play in an Anglo-American tournament at Walton Heath 'to create a more friendly union between the professionals in this country and those in the States' according to the Manchester Courier which was rather odd given that most of the participating US professionals, like Mackie, were expats.

He was a regular in the US Open between 1901 and 1921 and won the Eastern PGA Championship in 1908 over his home course at Fox Hills.

Walter White and Isaac Mackie (leaning on his club in background) at Foxhills in 1905

He remained there until 1914 with some winter sabbaticals, from 1903 he was the "winter pro" at the Lakewood Country Club in New Jersey and he spent the winter of 1910-11 at Cape Fear in Fox Hills GC Wilmington NC. He designed the Hollywood course in Deal, NJ.

"Isaac Mackie (left) at the 1904 U.S. Open with Jack Hobens, Alex Ross, and George Thomson"

Lakewood Country Club *The new links were laid out over 100 gently rolling acres, and were ready for play by the spring of 1903. The Golf Club's old course was used in the interim, after which the Laurel-in-the-Pines Hotel ran it as the Pine Forest Country Club. Isaac Mackie of Fox Hills served the club as "winter pro". Lakewood Country Club's new course measured 5,810 yards, and did not have a single cop bunker, which was unusual for those days. The second and third holes were side-by-side par 3's that played back and forth across the creek. In 1916, he was appointed the head professional at Canoe Brook Country Club, replacing Louis Tellier. Following the 1915 season, the club found itself in a difficult situation. The unsatisfactory revision of the course had become a source of discontent, and even embarrassment after Canoe Brook head professional Louis Tellier shot the course in 63 that summer. Some members questioned whether Canoe Brook was really a "championship course." The Board moved quickly to alleviate the concern. The following is taken from an article in the New York Times on January 30, 1916: "Simultaneously with the announcement of the securing of Isaac Mackie as professional at Canoe Brook Country Club to succeed Louis Tellier, the former French champion, the officers of the club have announced some revolutionary changes in the golf course at that institution which will, according to the expressed opinion of the famous Walter J. Travis, place the Canoe Brook course 'second to none in the Metropolitan district'." Canoe Brook's original course was designed by Jack Vickery and the first nine holes opened for play in 1902 and the second nine followed in 1905. He left Canoe Brook in 1926. We are not certain where he went but not long after he acquired Netherwood Golf Course himself and set about establishing a golf club.*

He continued until...

1955

After leaving Netherwood with a pretty good fortune behind him he probably continued the occasional teaching and visiting of a golf professional but he eventually retired to Scotch Plains which is very close to Netherwood and lived in Colonial Drive.

He died childless in 1963. And his will provided for substantial sum of money to be used for the benefit of people in Earlsferry/Elie. This generous gesture led to the establishing of Isaac Mackie House in Bank Street in Elie.

His widow died in 1965. His ashes were brought across to Elie and scattered in Elie/Earlsferry Bay from a local boat - a fitting tribute to one of Earlsferry's most famous sons.

John Bruce Mackie (Jack)

1878 - 1953

John Bruce Mackie (Jack) was the second youngest of the four Mackie brothers who had a huge influence on the development of the game in USA. He was born in Earlsferry. His father was a journeyman mason and they lived in Waldeve on the shore at Earlsferry. Whilst all four Mackie brothers were successful in the USA it was Jack who pioneered the way by arriving in New York in 1899 although we cannot find a record of his arrival. He was the first professional and involved in the layout of Roseville N.J.

> Jack Mackie has been engaged as professional of the Yountakah Country Club. He will take charge of the Nutley greens on March 15. He has been the professional at the Roseville Golf Club for several years.

1906

And later George Pearson (q.v.) was professional there. He then moved to Dinwoodie and in 1916 he moved to Inwood. This is from the Inwood website

.... Jack Mackie, whose tenure began in 1917. Mackie improved the course further, bringing it to championship calibre. An important figure in American golf, he was vice president of the PGA for two years, and treasurer for ten. He retired from Inwood in 1950

He was also heavily involved in golf administration in the New York area. 1952 and famous story of the moving oak tree.....

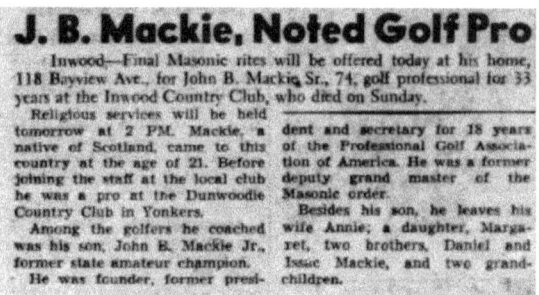

Inwood was where Bobby Jones won his first major, the 1923 US Open, but it was Jack Mackie's instant architecture at the USPGA in 1921 which springs to mind when Inwood is mentioned, Walter Hagen had found a strategy to play the 17th by driving up the parallel fairway on the 18th. The evening before the championship began Mackie and a greenkeeper dug up a fifteen foot weeping willow in the woods by the 16th fairway and replanted it to divide the fairways. On arriving at the tee Hagen remarked that he had never seen such fast-growing trees. Two minutes later the wind caught the supporting wires and the tree fell leaving the 18th fairway open to Hagen.

He died three years later in 1953.

William Leishman Mackie

1876 – 1941

William was the eldest of the four Mackie brothers. He was actually born in Glasgow but his family moved to Waldeve in Earlsferry shortly after his birth so we are treating him as an Earlsferry son.

We are not too sure of where or if he served an apprenticeship with Forrester or Scott and he may have been a mason as was his father. He first emerges in 1898 when he seems to have been appointed professional at Banstead Park Golf club from which club he entered the 1899 open at Sandwich. He then moved to Barnehurst near Crayford in Kent. And his address is shown as the Golf Club Lodge at the club suggesting he was also a sort of caretaker/manager.

This is an interesting golf club and ties in with Earlsferry. It was one of the very early Ladies clubs and Alexa Glover (q.v.) played a couple of exhibition matches there so we assume that they connected in some way. He married Emma Sparrow in Romford which makes us think there might have been some connection with Braid who by that time was in his prime at Romford before his move to Walton Heath. He may well have set off with the golfing skills acquired as usual on the Earlsferry tract with the reputation as being a good golfer and joined Braid. By that time Braid was very famous and would have attracted many young men from his former bailiwick.

English census in 1911 where he is shown as a golf club maker and living in Bexley Heath

By this time his brothers had all gone to America and it seems that he decided in 1915 to follow them.

> William L. Mackie, golf professional who has been with the Wingfoot Golf Club for the past two years, and has been a resident of Union avenue with Mrs. Mackie for that time, has severed his relations with the Wingfoot Club, and has taken a position on a private course at Port Washington, L. I. Mr. and Mrs. Mackie and their son, William will start in a week or two for that town.

There is a reference to him as being at Winged Foot and we suspect that he may have also been involved with some or all of his brothers who at that time were prominent in New York. In 1924 and he was employed by Guggenheim (Isaac) at his private estate both in laying out the private course and to give lessons. He stayed the rest of his career with the Guggenheims in a managerial capacity for the estate. This was Carola Farm which was very private but he obviously had earned a lot of respect since on the future occasions when he sailed back to Earlsferry he usually travelled first class. We stumbled across this thread looking for information on Isaac Guggenheim's Private Course on Long Island. *The course is noted on a map of Metro Area Courses in the July 1917 edition of Golf Illustrated, but like many of the estate courses from back then there is little to no coverage of its design and construction in the various periodicals and guides.*

Guggenheim built "Villa Carola" around 1916-17, a project that took several years to complete. At the same time work was started on a 9 hole course. The story is that Guggenheim was denied entry to the local club and decided to build his own course. Isaac would pass away in 1922, with the estate being taken over by his brother Edward who renamed it "Trillora." From what we can gather the estate and the course were maintained by Edward and later Solomon Guggenheim up until Solomon's death in 1950.

By all accounts, the Guggenheims had a passion for the game. They hired a slew of professionals, including Willie MacFarlane, Francis Gallet and one or two of the Mackies. The course itself was considered to be a good test, containing two par 3's and three par 5's and measuring out to around 3,600 yards.

By 1940 Bill was living in the estate with his family which by then consisted of William, born in 1908, Evelyn born in 1909 and Janet in 1913. During our research we made contact with Joseph Caserelli who is a "docent" *as he put it for the Guggenheim estate and we were able to get some sort of insight into WL's life and a report of what he said is above. He became a professional golfer etc. to Guggenheim (both Isaac, Edward and probably Solomon) but he must have earned a lot of faith since he was also Guggenheim's personal assistant and manager of the estate. It is said that he played a game of golf almost every day with Guggenheim and they were obviously firm friends.

*According to the Merriam Webster this a term for a teacher/lecturer.

He died in 1941.

James Laing Melville

1866 -1909

James Laing Melville (Jim) was born in Earlsferry on 2nd March 1866. At that time probably because it was in Earlsferry Parish Rotten Row Williamsburgh was considered to be Earlsferry. He was the youngest of 8 children having two elder brothers William and John. We believe he went to USA in 1881 at the relatively young age of 16. We do not know much about his golfing ability whilst in Earlsferry and we cannot find any reference to his exploits on Earlsferry golf course. His oldest brother William emigrated in 1873 and it may have been this stimulus that made Jim make the trip. We cannot find the actual arrival details so cannot confirm that he was destined to stay with his brother in Kansas. He seems to have been a caddy in Earlsferry where he would learn much and he may well have done a form of apprenticeship with Forrester. In 1885 census he is shown as living with his brother and being employed as a farmer which was his brother's profession. At the same time the census shows that the second brother John was also there. By the next census in 1890 he is no longer shown as living with his brother. And whilst we cannot track him then he next appears as pro at Monterrey in 1899 and where he apparently was an instructor.

> until this tournament takes place the matter must still be a question of opinion. Dave Stephenson, Willie Anderson and Jim Melville are the three most likely candidates for first honors. Anderson is at present at Oakland and Melville is at Monterey.
> Between the showers during the week

He moved to Monterey in 1899 and was instructor at Hotel del Monte. *"The property extended south and southeast of the hotel and included gardens, parkland, polo grounds, a race track, and a golf course. Originally used for hunting and other outdoor activities, the hotel's property became Pebble Beach, an unincorporated resort community, and the world-famous Pebble Beach Golf Links. The famous 17-Mile Drive was originally designed as a local excursion for visitors to the Del Monte to take in the historic sights of Monterey and Pacific Grove and the scenery of what would become Pebble Beach. The hotel became popular with the wealthy and influential of the day, and guests included Theodore Roosevelt and Ernest Hemingway, as well as many early Hollywood stars.* Wikipedia

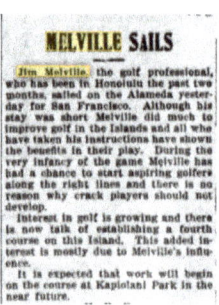

In 1905 he was appointed to Sacramento Golf Club. That was where he died of pneumonia in 1909 said in one obituary to be 47. Although there is some doubt to that statement because if the Jim Melville who died in 1909 was our Jim Melville he was actually 43 years of age.

The Antique Golfers website says that in 1897 he was appointed as instructor at Oakland GC and in 1898 went to Hotel Del Monte in Monterey. It seems in these days that a pro teacher might well have a number of contemporaneous appointments at golf clubs. Furthermore there was a migration of professional golfers to better climes during the "off" season. That is what our Jim Melville did since he was a frequent visitor to Hawaii from San Francisco.

He spent a number of seasons in Hawaii and seems to have been well regarded.

Died at Sacramento

We were informed last week that Jim Melville, who is well known to many of the people of this vicinity and readers of the SUN, died at his home in Sacramento, California, on November 17th. His brothers Wm and John knew nothing about his death until last Friday when a postal card arrived from Santa Cruz, California, stating that a telegram had been received there announcing the death of Jim, but does not give the cause of his death.

He was the youngest of the Melville boys, was born in Scotland 43 years ago, and at the age of 17 years, came to America. He leaves a wife and children to mourn his loss.

And this certainly seems to be him and the death notices give a further clue. This from a Kansas newspaper.

This looks much more like our Jim. He certainly had the brothers William and John who stayed in Kansas.

He married Cristina Malarin in 1900.

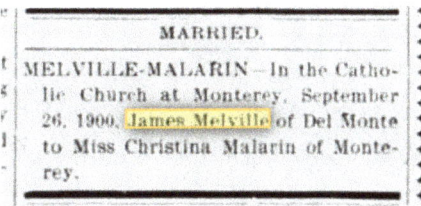

MARRIED.

MELVILLE-MALARIN — In the Catholic Church at Monterey, September 26, 1900, James Melville of Del Monte to Miss Christina Malarin of Monterey.

This lady had a very interesting back story. She was the grand daughter of Juan Malarin who was one of the last 49ers in the Californian gold rush. He had a large ranch establishment and land holdings all in his wife's name!! He owned considerable interest in banking and railroads and was a descendant of the Mexican royal Family that once ruled California. Jim and she had one child Myrtle who died in 1982. Christina remarried and lived her whole life in Monterey. His death was also announced in the East of Fife newspapers but merely as the youngest son of the late David Melville.

James Nelson

1871 - 1951

James Nelson was born on 29th July 1871 to Thomas Nelson a Surfaceman and Helen Mcgregor or Nelson who had been married in January 1860. It is significant that he was born a little later than Jamie Braid (1870) but they were obviously contemporaries in Earlsferry.

The family lived in Links House in Links Road which is substantially different now but it is fronted by Cleek Cottage which was A.H. Scott's workshop at one time. This property seemed to have belonged to A.H. Scott (q.v.) at one time. Scott also had a cast iron shed two doors along which contained most of his manufacturing equipment.

We have a note of him as a golf club maker although along with many others in his profession seem to have started as a mason. Again we surmise that he played a lot of golf in Earlsferry and was indeed almost an exact contemporary of Jamie Braid.

In 1891 he was living in Edinburgh again as mason but by 1901 he was back with his parents in Earlsferry at Links House. For some reason he must have given up mason's work and we suspect he did a training of sorts either with Forrester or even Scott. His parents lived behind Scott's workshop so it was perhaps the latter albeit that Forrester's workshop was two doors farther east. In any event, in 1903 he was appointed to Peebles Golf Club as professional/greenkeeper so we must assume that part of his training would have been in keeping the course in good condition. He would certainly have obtained that training whilst working for Forrester because Forrester at that time was also the green keeper for the Earlsferry golf course.

We are most grateful to Peebles Golf club who have given us details from their Centenary Book of his exploits.

> In November 1903 J. Nelson was engaged as professional and greenkeeper in place of R. Brewster who had left the club in October 1902. Allan Smith had again looked after the course during the playing season of 1903. James Nelson was to figure prominently in the affairs of the club for some years to come and he must have been a competent golfer. There seems to be no doubt that he was a popular figure and a great attribute to the club. We should probably regard him as the Peebles club's first true professional rather than greenkeeper cum professional. Nevertheless, he was responsible for maintaining and improving the course under the direction of the club committee.

His career as greenkeeper professional at Peebles seems to have been a success judging from the extracts from Peebles Centenary book.

The highlight, as it were, of his time at Peebles was a match arranged in August 1910. Jamie Braid had recently won the Open Championship at St Andrews and was obviously a prime catch for Peebles but it may have been his friendship of long standing with Nelson and his expertise that was being employed in doing some remodelling of the course. The occasion merited much publicity in the newspapers of the time. The Scotsman reported:

GOLF THE OPEN CHAMPION AT PEEBLES . • THREE ROUNDS AT KIRKLAND . Thanks to the enterprise of the Executive of the Peebles Golf

Club, golfers in the Borders and the many visitors who at the present time are seeking that pleasure for which Peebles has long been famous, were afforded an opportunity yesterday of seeing James Braid, the open golf champion, play three rounds of the new course at Kirkland. About two years have elapsed since this course was laid out in a delightful situation over-looking the town and the wooded hills and dales beyond. In the interval the course has come on splendidly. A firm body of turf gives an excellent fairway from the first tee right round to the last hole, and so carefully has Nelson nursed the greens that to-day it might be said their quality is unsurpassed by that of any in the Borders of Scotland. Braid....... in his first round with Nelson in the forenoon of yesterday, his approximate score was 70, and in the evening in the four-ball foursome, he again had a total of 70. Braid played in the forenoon a match with James Nelson, the local professional, whom he defeated by five up and three to play; in the afternoon, with Sir Henry Ballantyne as his partner, the champion had a halved match with Mr Lyon, the secretary, and Nelson; and in a four-ball foursome, played in the evening. Braid and Mr Ruckbie were defeated by Mr T. Ballantyne and Nelson by two holes. The pleasure of the forenoon game was somewhat marred by heavy showers or rain but otherwise the conditions for good golf were by no means unfavourable. Each game was witnessed by a large and interested gathering, especially the one played in the evening after work at the mills had ceased for the day .. BRAID V . NELSON. Braid started on his three matches by playing a single with James Nelson, the local professional, who, like Braid, is an old Elie and Earlsferry-player. ....he had a total of 70 against 76 recorded by Nelson . At the conclusion of play [in the evening] Sir Henry Ballantyne called for three cheers for Braid for the magnificent exhibition of golf which had had given. The champion responded by assuring the club that it had given him great pleasure to play over that course, which, he said, must be a great asset to the town of Peebles. The course was a splendid one, and when a few bunkers were added, it would be difficult to be beaten by any other course in the Borders.

Nelson reduced the professional record to 66 in June 1911 and by 1912 had further reduced the record to 65.

He played in the Scottish Professional championship at Cruden Bay in 1913 where he finished 11th and was rewarded with the prize of £1. Peebles Golf Club under the patronage of Sir Henry Ballantyne of the tweed and knitwear fame offered a prize of £2 for the best round in a match between Edward Ray, Open champion, and George Duncan (later an Open champion) to play an exhibition match at Peebles. It was quite an event and both went round in 65 so each received £2 but James Nelson seems to have been a bit "pit oot" so he then went out and broke the course record in August of that year lowering it to 62. He must have been well ensconced at Peebles because he had the effrontery to seek an increase in his salary in 1915 to 30 shillings per week. His request was granted. But he must have been tempted away the following year.

However not long after that in 1917 he left and he shows up again living in Nairn, described as a golf professional and living at 15 Albert Street in 1917. He had been appointed professional at Nairn.

James continued in his position as professional/greenkeeper and was responsible for extending and remodelling the course in 1924.

He left Nairn in April 1927. He was back living in Earlsferry in Links House where there was also a workshop. His wife died in 1947 and her death certificate shows that she died in Salisbury Cottage in Elie. We originally thought that James Nelson may have owned Salisbury

Cottage as well but the valuation roll for 1940 shows the proprietor as James **B** Nelson. However if you consult the voters roll you find that James Nelson (our one) was registered as voting from Elie but giving an address in Nairn which was his known abode. Pure speculation but we wonder whether after the tragic death of their daughter, Janet came back to live in Elie at Salisbury Cottage and that both she and James(our one) lived there and on her death in 1947 he sold Salisbury Cottage and moved to Links House where he was found dead in his house in March 1951 aged 79. That would certainly account for two James Nelsons but not the B.

James Paterson

1886 – 1941

James Paterson (shown on right above alongside his son) although he does not fit into the specific category having been born in Elie or Earlsferry he was a significant player in the profile of Earlsferry professionals in that he devoted his life and professional career mostly to the one golf club. He was born in Strathkinness on 10th September 1886. His father was a house painter by trade. But the family must have moved to Earlsferry fairly shortly after his birth since he is shown in the 1891 census and living in Chapel Green – this was the generic area for anything west of Earlsferry House at that time which makes it sometimes difficult to determine the exact house. The house in which the family lived was probably Rose Cottage which is in the valuation roll close to Earlsferry House between Elphin cottage and Craigview. In the 1901 census he is shown aged 15 as a golf club maker and I think we can assume that he was apprenticed to Forrester. He went down south and is shown as having married Isabel Harriet White in 1910 in Barnet where he is shown in the 1911 census as living in Middlesex at Friern Barnet and he is described as assistant golf professional and club maker although it is noted that he was then resident in Hastings. We are not sure where he started his professional career but it looks likely, if the club still exists, that it would have been Mill Hill or Hendon both of which were established shortly before Paterson arrived in England. Indeed James Braid with whom we assume Paterson was friendly having both come from Earlsferry was one of 50 players who opened the Hendon club in 1900 or so. It might have been Stanmore club which was established about the same time. Although the nearest club to where he lived in 1911 at Alexandra Villa Oakleigh Road Friern Barnet is actually North Middlesex golf club and that may give us a clue since one of the other Earlsferry people was professional at that club round about this time. He became the professional at Hastings St. Leonards in 1925 where he stayed until he died in 1941.

We are fortunate to have a very comprehensive summary of this golf club.

Hastings & St Leonards/Hastings Downs Golf Club, Sussex. (1893 - WW2)

Originally known as Hastings & St Leonards Golf Club it became Hastings following WW1, it eventually became Hastings Downs Golf Club prior to WW2 until closure.

Founded 1893. From the Manchester Courier and Lancs General Advertiser, Saturday 11 March 1893 "A club is likely to be formed on an excellent tract of ground on East Hill at Hastings. The course will be without a "tame hole".

The formal opening of the 18 hole course took place in fine weather a couple of days earlier on Friday 16th May 1902 with a 36 hole match between James Braid, Romford, and Harry Vardon, Ganton. There was a large crowd in attendance when the players teed off at 11am. At the end of the first round Vardon was 4up.

The Golf Clubhouse. Throughout the 1930s the secretary was C L Taylor MBE VD,....... The professional was J Paterson and the greenkeeper E C Bumstead (early 1930s) C White (from about 1935). 18 holes with a membership of about 360. Course records were, amateur A Winter 68, professional J Paterson 69.

> In 1940 the club was listed as Hastings Downs Golf Club, Barley Lane. The secretary was G W Foxon, 147 Edmund Road, Hastings, telephone 2422. The professional was J Paterson and the greenkeeper J Barkess. The 18 holes had a S.S.S of 74 and a membership of 200. Course records were, amateur W H Mee 70 and professional J Paterson 68

Whilst there during the darker winter months he set upon a novel idea of earning his living as a teacher.

GOLF LEARNING TO PLAY INDOORS James Paterson, the popular Hastings Downs Golf professional, has opened golf school at the Metropole Hotel, Robertson-street, Hastings, where lessons will be given daily from 10 a.m. to 10 p.m. Beginners will find lessons more interesting than ever because the new practice golf net makes it possible to play a complete round indoor golf under something approaching actual conditions. The net itself diverted into five pockets, each one set at a suitable height for particular shot* that unless the ball is struck with complete accuracy it will not enter the pocket intended. Mr. Paterson, who was formerly assistant to Harry Vardon**, will be in attendance during the evenings and by appointment and at other times careful attention will be given by his son, Mr. J. A. Paterson. assistant at Hastings Downs Club, who has done exceptionally well in competitive golf recently. 1936 *Novel we suppose but difficult to master!

** probably Ganton

He died in 1941 somewhat suddenly and the members opened a subscription for the family.

> **DEATH OF MR. JAMES PATERSON**
>
> Members of the Hastings Downs Golf Club and many other local golfers will learn with great regret of the death in a Middlesex hospital on Monday, of Mr. James Paterson, aged 54, for 18 years the professional at the Hastings Club.
>
> "Pat," as he was known to everyone, devoted his life to golf and its teaching. He came to Hastings from the job of assistant to the great Harry Vardon. He was popular among every class of player, and he gained a considerable reputation as a maker of clubs.
>
> Mr. Paterson left the Hastings Downs Club three months ago to take up war work, similar to that on which he was engaged in the last war.
>
> His son, Jimmy, who is now on military service, was professional at Brooklands Park Club, and is himself a golfer of brilliant promise.

SUBSCRIPTION LIST FOR PROFESSIONAL'S WIDOW The directors of Hastings Downs Golf Club have decided to open subscription list for the benefit of the widow of Mr. James Paterson ("Pat"), until recently professional at the club, whose death was recently reported in the "Observer". The directors' action is in tribute to Pat's memory, and they feel that his widow can scarcely have been left other than somewhat straitened circumstances. There is to be no limit to the amount of individual subscriptions, either upwards or downwards, but the directors wish to emphasise that, in these difficult times, none can be considered too small. They wish the list to be lengthy as possible. It is not proposed to keep the list open for long, and those who would like to subscribe should send their contributions to Mr. G. W. Poxon (hon. secretary), at the club house, Barley-lane, without delay. 1942

The death of Mr. James Paterson—"Pat" to his friends—until recently professional at the Hastings Downs Golf Club, was announced in last week's issue of the "Observer". Pat's gone! The news gets round. And members of the club are shocked to think They'll ne'er see Pat again. Nor with him play another round. Kit's gone! The genial, optimistic Pat, A man who always played the game; Who sometimes lost and some- times won. But when he lost 'twas often by single stroke or putt. And now he's gone, And we shall miss him. Farewell, Pat! But over yonder may you roam on some Elysian course, And find at least A friendly comrade at a nineteenth hole. Bon voyage..[sic] 1941

It is of a little interest that his son James Anderson Paterson (Anderson was his grandmother's name) was also a professional golfer and he started as assistant to his father at Hastings and then at Brooklands before the outbreak of war. After the war he became professional at Northbourne Golf club in Sussex but in 1949 there was an inquiry into the financial records of the club which he and his wife ran as stewards. He emigrated to New Zealand where he became the professional in Bay of Plenty and from his residence at Sinclair Street in Tauranga it seems probable that he was professional at Tauranga G.C. and died in New Zealand after 1981.

The Pearson Family

There were a large number of Pearsons indigenous to Elie/Earlsferry and it has been difficult to track them down. There were in the 1891 census 5 families of Pearsons living in Elie and Earlsferry. The golfers we are concerned with were John otherwise J.S., Andrew and George.

David Pearson who married Anne Tulloch and they had 11 children of whom George was born in 1870 They lived in Rose Cottage in Earlsferry High Street and we think it was the house two along from Cadgers Wynd rather than the Rose Cottage at Chapel Green Road – since the former was much larger for a family of 13.

Then there was Andrew who married Catherine and they had four children the youngest was John Stewart who was born in 1864 but he was born in the Isle of Skye. His parents (his father Andrew was an estate worker) eventually moved to Elie and they were living at 21 High Street in 1891.

Then there was Robert who married Susan and had three children one of whom was Andrew born in 1881 and the family lived in 4 the Vennel, Elie.

Andrew Pearson

1881 – 1949

Andrew Pearson comes to this list as a result of a passing remark in a newspaper article of 1902 which was discussing the various "Ferry" men who had a current influence on the golf scene. The writer mentions various names of which we are now familiar but one sentence finished "Andrew Pearson represents the Ferry at Deal". In Jackson's book on the professional golfers at this time he is shown to have been assistant at Deal (Royal Cinque Ports)

He was born on 24th April 1881 the son of Robert Pearson and Susan.

The address given was 4 The Vennel which house belonged to his mother and father. He features in the 1901 census as living there with his parents and his sister. The newspaper article above suggests that he was in Deal in 1902. We cannot trace his presence there but the next time we come across him is in the 1911 census in England where he is shown as living in Wanstead in Essex and his profession is professional golfer. Initially we could find little reference to him then…

Wanstead G.C. We had made for the George Hotel, just ran Acme a little village green kind of space, flanked with very nice new houses, turned up a private road, drove through a very fine old brick archway, and there we were, with the car's nose a foot from the door of Andrew Pearson's modest little shop. The clubhouse is evidently a converted private residence, long, low, roomy, and seasoned by years of being a meet inspiring place, and as one looks down from the lawn in front of the dining room there in a very gem of a course stretching away to the infinite. A grip of the fist from Andrew, a word to the caddy master, an assurance that goloshes were something of which no thought could be necessary, and we were out on No. 1.

> Wanstead Park Club.—The junior monthly medal was won by H. S. Casselton (14), 72 net. Andrew Pearson, the club professional, playing with Mr. J. Turner, did the eighth hole—a distance of 150 yards—in one stroke.

1913

It's at that point the references dry up and we assume that because of World War 1 activities at Wanstead Golf Club were in abeyance. After the armistice it seems that Andrew did not return to Wanstead and the next professional there was the famous Percy Aliss. It is not unreasonable to suppose that he was called up and the fact (see later) that he was in the British Legion suggests he served but it is difficult to ascertain where and for how long. After the war he worked at Daventry until 1927 and he returned to Elie. We know he died unmarried in 1949.

His obituary in the newspapers of the time said *"The Elie Branch of the British Legion lost one of its best members by the passing of Mr Andrew Pearson. He was one of the original members of the branch* and was undoubtedly one of its finest members. For some years he was honorary secretary, and during the whole of the 15 years of his membership he helped in every way to make it one of the best branches in the area. His keen humour and his most obliging nature endeared him to all the members and if anything was required they could rely on Andrew being the man to lend a hand They have lost a great friend, and one who will be missed.*

*This per se suggests he was in the armed forces and if the article is accurate he must have joined in 1934 which would accord with his return to Elie to the Vennel but where he was meantime we do not know. We have reason to believe that he joined up for the first world war via the Sportsman regiment. He features in the roll of Honour compiled by Alan Provan of the History Society.

He died in Elie on 1st December 1949.

George Pearson

1870 -1955

George was born in Earlsferry on 14th November 1870 and so far as can be told he was born in Rose Cottage in Earlsferry High Street. We can find no trace of any of his exploits locally. We know he married Emily Smith in 1894 at Higham Oxtead when we assume he was at Rochester Cobham golf club in Kent. He was professional at Rochester Golf club in Kent prior to his move to the USA and preceded Robert F Walker(q.v.). *Rochester Golf Club (Oakleigh Course), Higham. The professionals were; C Crawford 1891/2, G Pearson* 1892 -96, R F Walker 1896 – 1912, E N Kettley 1913 and A R Andrews 1914.*

We know that he crossed the Atlantic to USA and from the New York census of 1915 he was supposed to have emigrated in 1896.

1905 census shows him at New Jersey.

In 1915 New York census he is shown as having been in US for 18 years which means he must have emigrated in 1896 shortly after leaving Rochester. In 1897 he played in a tournament attached to Rockaway Hunt Club which has an interesting history. It was originally a polo club but in 1896 they built a golf course and it looks very much as if George Pearson may have been instrumental in bringing on the fledgling golf course. In 1897 he entered for the US Open. We have information that he entered for the US Open on four occasions. 1897,1898, 1905 and 1907.

> zation. Robert Marshall, also of Chicago, will be stationed at Kissimmee, George Pearson, of the Albany Country Club, at Ocala, and J. M. Watson, of Minneapolis, at Winter Park.

And by 1900 he seems to be at the Albany Country Club and it is noticable that he would be wintering in Ocala (see J.S. Pearson) probably recruited by J.D.Dunn.

In 1906 he moved to Forest Hill Golf club NJ which was very much in its infancy having recently been started and he is shown as being there for a professional tournament. In 1909 he took part in tournament at Nassau.

In 1910 he was shown as living in Nutley ward 2 Essex New Jersey where he is described as a "Clerk maker" but the manuscript clearly says "club", and there is reference to his wife and daughter living in Lynchburg VA but no sign of him. He is described as a golf instructor and his entry in newspapers about that time refer to him as being the pro at Lynchburg Country Club although that no longer seems to exist. We cannot find him exactly in the 1920 census and he may have been on tour. But that entry is interesting as it shows that there is new baby under a year old, living there ostensibly being the daughter of Emily but we are pretty clear that George K Pearson was his grand son - Jessie's, son. Emily and child are shown going back to Scotland in 1927 but George and Emily appear to have stayed on for a year or two before 1928 when he resigned from Oakwood Oakwood CC.

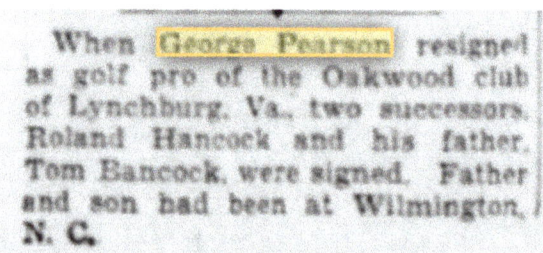

> When George Pearson resigned as golf pro of the Oakwood club of Lynchburg, Va., two successors, Roland Hancock and his father, Tom Bancock, were signed. Father and son had been at Wilmington, N. C.

He returned to Scotland in 1929.

Emily died in 1942 and she is described as married to George Pearson Golf professional retired. Whilst there may have, in the 1940s, been more than one George Pearson in Earlsferry he seemed at that time to be the proprietor of a number of houses. Fairview and Ampersand were two of them but of course they are built on the extended feu of Rose Cottage from Earlsferry High Steet. He died in Rose Cottage Earlsferry on 29th January 1955 and is buried in Kilconquhar churchyard.

J.S.Pearson

1864-1923

A J.S. Pearson figures considerably in the American Newspapers especially in Florida at Ocala and he is buried there having died in New York in 1923. Whilst we know that a man of that name became a professional golfer we are also aware that this John Stewart Pearson was born in 1867 or 1868. His gravestone in Florida indicated that he was aged 55 and died in 1923. We know that a J.S.Pearson golf professional died in 1923 in New York, was buried in Ocala in Florida and had a cottage in Pittenweem which he called Ocala Cottage. That would make his date of birth 1868/7 which we think is an error. He was born in Isle of Skye in 1864. His father who was a farm worker eventually lived in Elie at 21 High Street and we think that JS spent his early school days here and learnt his golf in Elie.

We first pick him up as a joiner aged 15 in 1881 census. In 1894 he was in Elie because he competed in the Elie Athletic games in the summer of that year where he was second in the long driving contest and he is noted there as a professional from West Middlesex. In 1898 he competed in a tournament in Carnoustie and there he is said to be from Southall GC which actually is West Middlesex Golf Club and there he may well have been assistant to the then professional, also from Elie, C. Ralph Smith (q.v.). He seemed regularly to play in tournaments. It is difficult to get information about the West Middlesex club now as it has just been sold in administration. However we know that he went across to USA and seemed to spend his time in Florida in the winter and New York or thereby in the summer. So far as we can see he went to America probably 1899. There is a John Stewart Pearson golf professional commuting between Florida and Cuba between 1915 and 1917.

> Ealing is one of the newest of London's golf clubs. The links, however, at Twyford Abbey are by no means new, in the sense that they have only recently been devoted to the game. The links are already, so far as the frost allows, in excellent condition, and the engagement of John Pearson, a professional from Bournemouth, to look after the greens as well as to coach members, ought to be a further attraction to intending members. Pearson, who was four years at the golf links at Brockenhurst, is a first-rate player, and holds the record of the Brockenhurst links with the fine score of 74 strokes. The club is being properly organised, and the first monthly medal competition will be held on Saturday, March 30, at Twyford Abbey.

What we also know from 1895

So tracking that back he must have joined Brockenhurst in 1890 or so. He certainly played in a number of exhibition games and tournaments between 1890 and 1900 being attached to West Middlesex golf club which was the forerunner of West Middlesex and Southall golf Clubs.

NEW GOLF LINKS OPENED.

FORMAL DEDICATION OF HOMEWOOD CLUB'S COURSE.

Match Play Between J. S. Pearson, the Club's Professional, and Alex. Smith of the Washington Park Club Is the Feature of the Day, Smith Winning by Five Up and Four to Play—Many Social Features Enliven the Occasion.

The Homewood Country club formally opened its new golf course and clubhouse to the golfing world yesterday. Five hundred people were in attendance, this number being increased by the late afternoon trains. The principal golf fixture of the day was an eighteen-hole match between the club's professional, J. S. Pearson, formerly of the West Middlesex club of London, and Alex. Smith, the Washington Park professional, which was won by Smith after an excellent exhibition of golf by the score of 5 up with 4 to play.

We next find him in America having travelled there probably about 1899 although we cannot find his entry. He appears in an article in 1900 at the opening of a golf Club in Illinois called Homewood. There are two clubs in this area now Calumet CC and Ravisloe but no sign of the original Homewood. He seems to be the first professional and his previous history ties in with our research.

Since Homewood and most of the courses north of New York were only playable in the summer most professionals "wintered" in sunnier climes. JS started going to Ocala in Florida in about 1900 and every year until his death he spent time there as a golf professional. He became a bit of a local personality his every (almost) move being chronicled in the newspapers. It does however give a clear insight as to his comings and goings. He stayed with Homewood for only two years we think before he joined Richmond County Golf Club.

This from 1902.

GOLF AT AMPERSAND.

Special to The New York Times.

AMPERSAND, N. Y., Aug. 20.—There have been some interesting events on the Ampersand golf course this week, including a contest for a handsome cup presented by Frederick I. Pearsall, a match between professionals, and the breaking of the records for the course by John S. Pearson of the Ampersand Club, and later the lowering of Mr. Pearson's record by one stroke by George Bouse.

The qualifying round for the Pearsall Cup was held on Saturday, when H. B. Reynolds, Otis L. Williams, Harold Naylor, Mrs. Milton Work, Mr. Lawrence, W. D. Gordon, Dr. Gibney, and H. Schmelzel were successful. The finals brought Harold Naylor and H. B. Reynolds together, and Mr. Naylor won by 3 up and 2 to play.

John S. Pearson of the Ampersand Club made a new professional record for the course Saturday. He made the first round in 34 and two rounds in 72.

There was a match for professionals on Monday, when George Bouse of Lake Placid and Jack Jolly of New York met G. V. Keddie of the Stevens House and John S. Pearson of the Ampersand in a thirty-six-hole match. Bouse and Jolly won by four holes. The features of the day were the playing of Bouse and Pearson. Bouse established a new record for eighteen holes, making the distance in 71. His second eighteen holes were not as well played by eleven strokes. Pearson played a remarkably steady game, covering the eighteen holes twice in 73 strokes each time.

GOLFERS WILL FOLLOW THE BIRDS.

Many Local Professionals Plan to Winter on Florida Links.

Chicago golf professionals will be well represented on the Florida links through the winter. Herbert Tweedie, who returned yesterday from Dayton, closed an agreement with the Plant system, which controls a number of the Southern courses, by which Lawrence Auchterlonie will go to Belleair, Jim Foulis to Tampa, William Marshall to Kissimmee, James Watson to Winter Park, and James Pearson to Ocala. John Dunn, the New York professional, will go immediately to Florida to inspect and alter most of the courses. George Low and Arthur Fenn, the two Eastern professionals, will both be located through the winter on Florida courses.

Richmond County golf club is in Staten Island in N.Y and we also know that he was playing in a tournament in New York in 1904 where he is said to be attached to Ampersand Golf club which was also on Staten Island. We think he probably had appointments at both. He still wintered in Ocala and seems to have been part of a syndicate called the Plant System. This was a syndicate organised and managed by J.D.Dunn originally from North Berwick who promoted a number of tournaments and also assigned various professionals to their winter quarters.

In 1910 he seemed to move north to Illinois and was establishing the Lake Shore County Club which is on the shore of the Lake Michigan 15 miles north of Chicago. He came back across the Atlantic in 1909 and returned in 1910 and significantly his destination in the ship manifest was Glencoe Illinois which is slightly south of Lake Shore. In 1912 he was leaving Ocala and going back to Chicago. Whilst in Florida he was wont to travel between Florida and Cuba on a number of occasions between 1912 and 1921. He seemed to have interests also in New York and often his return heralded from Florida to New York and on one occasion to West Orange County in New Jersey. In effect he had a fairly peripatetic existence.

In 1921 he returned to Elie in April of that year which may have been significant because his mother died in early 1922. But that event may well also have precipitated him making a will which he did in Edinburgh in October 1921 very shortly before he returned to the United States.

He was not married and had a stroke in New York in 1923 from which he subsequently died. His wish to be buried in Ocala was carried out. He actually was quite a wealthy man and at a rough estimate his estate was worth about $10000 in 1923 which equates to about $160,000 today.

The Peebles Family

Robert Peebles senior was a fisherman and indeed one of the founding members of Earlsferry Thistle G.C. (q.v.) He and he was married to Elizabeth Thomson. She was of the Thomson stock of fishermen from the Toft. He had two sons Robert and William. He and his brother and two sisters actually lived with his maternal grandparents at the Toft Mount Pleasant. His father was drowned in Elie bay in 1886 and before that they lived in Williamsburgh. There were three Peebles families and three Robert Peebles all born within 5 years of each other but we are fairly certain that Robert Senior was the father of Robert Brown Peebles and William Thomson Peebles. (q.v)

MELANCHOLY OCCURRENCE AT ELIE. TWO MEN DROWNED. *Elie Bay was the scene of a terrible affair on Saturday. The little Yarmouth smack, Friends, was descried making for the harbour about 1 p.m., when two boats were promptly manned race for the pilotage*. The smack was scudding before the breeze, but one of the boats, the Evely o Emily, attempted to snatch the prize. The next moment the little craft was crashing under the bow of the smack, and sank like a stone. One of four men, Alexander Thomson, leaped to the deck of the vessel. The second, John Thomson, a youth of fifteen, seized hold of spar, but the third and fourth were left struggling in the waves. Captain Stanard and his mate were no idle spectators, and the comrade threw a rope that one of the men was seen to clutch as the other hung to his waist. But almost within an arm's length of help the strong hand relaxed its hold, and both rolled, as it were, into watery grave. Meanwhile the second boat was hastening to the spot, only in time, however,[to] save the youth floating on the spar. The two [who] perished are the Earlsferry fishermen, Robert Peebles, aged about 37, who leaves a widow and two children, and his half-brother, Henry Tullis, fine young man within month of twenty—the stay a widow mother, who, we believe, has lost three sons by the cruel sea. No time was lost by the neighbours in trying to recover the bodies, but the search was in vain till next forenoon, when both were discovered within a few yards of each other, about half a mile in the offing. The boat was likewise raised and brought to the pier. It is impossible to describe the agitation into which the villages of Elie and Earlsferry were plunged by the catastrophe especially on Sunday, when the procession passed with the melancholy burdens to the house of mourning.* [Dundee Courier May 1886]

- *When a ship was intending to reach harbour it would invariably need someone with local knowledge to guide it though the sea to the harbour. It seems that local fishermen often offered their services to incoming ships and obviously would be entitled to demand a fee for safely guiding the boat in. From this article is seems that when a boat appeared to be making for Elie Harbour there would be a scramble of boats trying to get to the incoming vessel first to offer its pilotage service. However as time went on often these fishing boats were engaged in their trade and professional trained pilots were later used. In this case there would have been a scramble to pilot the boat in but in addition if the boat got into difficulties if any of the local boats manage to save the ship, cargo and crew they were entitled to a fee for salvage. A ship in trouble was often a magnet for these sort of bounty hunters.*

Robert Brown Peebles

1882 – 1959

Robert Brown Peebles was born in Elie on 22nd September 1882. Whilst we have no evidence to the contrary it is reasonable to assume that Robert did an apprenticeship with George Forrester learning to make golf clubs and he was a proficient golfer himself as were many of his contemporaries in Elie and Earlsferry.

Robert was schooled in Elie, he had spent time at Mount Pleasant in the Toft where his grandparents had lived. His early career seemed to have taken him to Glasgow

> He is a native of Scotland, having been born near one of the most famous golf courses in that country, and he practically grew up on the links. He started his professional career with the Pollok Golf club, of Glasgow, Scotland, with which he was connected for five years.

And he left these shores to cross the Atlantic to America aged 19 where he initially was employed as a golf professional in Fox Hills NY.

> Fox Hills Golf Course opened in 1900 in Clifton. The property consisted of a clubhouse on the Vanderbilt Avenue side, which at the time was considered the largest clubhouse in the country.
>
> Many newsworthy tournaments were held there and many significant awards were presented.
>
> The golf course closed in 1920 when the land was taken over by the government. It was later used for military barracks for American soldiers during World War II as well Italian prisoners of war.

He travelled via Columbia and arrived on 28th April 1904 and from a look at the ship's manifest for that journey also on board were – James Mackie, George Pearson, James Crowley who was bound for Chestnut Hill in Pennsylvania but a few yards from Pennsylvania Cricket Club where he was employed as a golf professional. Another golf club maker was on board Henry Waters from St. Andrews so no doubt they had a lot to talk about. There he married Hannah Martha Graham who was originally from Glasgow. By co-incidence she travelled on the same ship but a later sailing arriving in New York in October 1904 shortly after which she seems to have married RBP.

He was said to be a golf professional at South Orange County in New Jersey when he married in 1904 and there is evidence that he was professional/teacher at Tuckahoe. If there was a course at Tuckahoe it may have changed its name or location. However, New Jersey was in the forefront of the development of golf and golf courses at the turn of the century and many famous courses would have been within easy reach of Bob when he lived in New Jersey including Baltusrol where George Low was the professional for many years and it may be that Bob was employed by him as a clubmaker/teacher. He played in a number of tournaments between then and 1910 when he is found in Dallas, Texas. In addition in these days golf professionals/teachers/clubmakers were fairly peripatetic moving during the off season in the north to winter in the south to some of the other courses being set up and developed so it was not unusual to find a professional/teacher being attached to a number of golf clubs on a freelance basis. In 1908 for example he was shown as having competed in a tournament out of Fairview wherever that was. In 1909 he was shown to be playing in a tournament out of St. Joseph's Valley which seems to be in Missouri.

In 1912 he and his wife were hired as club managers for Emporia Golf and Country club in Kentucky but I venture to suggest that did not last long since he was shown in 1913 as being at Topeka. And he travelled around various clubs giving tuition and playing in exhibition and money games.

Mr. Robert Peebles of the Topeka Golf club, was in Lawrence today and gave a number of people lessons He is to be here every Wednesday to teach all that come to learn.

In 1914 winning a golf prize in Texas. In 1915 when completing his registration for call up card he said he was working at Idle Hour Golf Club Lexington, Kentucky but by 1921 he was in Peoria Ill. And yet by 1922 he was said to be playing out of Louisville Kentucky. He was reported as being employed at Wichita and further that he had affiliations with Sound Beach (this may have been in NY), and with Shawnee Heights in Kansas where there are a number of golf clubs now. Latterly he was also teaching pro at Mexico City Golf Club. There is no doubt that golf professionals/teachers in these days had to travel around to get the business and very often with the north USA clubs being winter bound the pros would often have affiliations to clubs further south with which they would spend the winter. As can be seen from a number of contemporaries this was very much the norm and it became rather difficult to settle in the one place.

In the census of 1910 he is shown as living with his wife, Hannah, two children and his mother Elizabeth Thomson in Dallas but ten years later his two children Barbara and Robert G were living in Illinois with his mother and they were at school and it seems likely that his wife was living there in 1916 when he completed the registration card for his call up for world war 1. In his registration card for world war 1 in 1916 he is shown as working as a golf professional at Idle House Country Club which is in Lexington.

His next of kin is shown as his wife who is then living at 217 Court Street Pekin Tazewell Ill. The children were both at Pekin Community High school in Illinois and Barbara appears in a yearbook for 1921.

> **SECOND DAY'S PLAY FOR WESTERN CHAMPIONSHIPS**
>
> (By United Press Leased Wire)
> Oakland Country Club, Cleveland, O., Aug. 25.—Low scores featured the early half of the second day's play in the Western Open Golf championships today.
> Robert Peebles, veteran pro of Peoria, Ill., who had second lowest score in the first day of 69, came right back with a 73 today, making his totals for the first 36 holes 142.
> Scores of 73 were not uncommon and indications were that there would be numbers of scores under par, which is 71.
> Scores for 36 holes, included: Robert Peebles, Peoria, Ill., 69-73-142; Fred Ford, Kansas City, 78-73-151; Alex Ayton, Evanston, Ill., 77-79-156; John Long, Peoria, Ill., 85-78-158.

But there is no sign of her living with her father and mother at that point, only her grandmother. In 1931 his son is at University in Illinois. In 1940 census he is living in Pickaway Washington NJ with Edith Newbauer who eventually becomes his second wife. His first wife is shown as living with the Slabys in Washington so it looks certain that they were separated at that time if not before. There was a disparity of age here - he was 54 and she was 20. His first wife Hannah died in 1945 and it seems from that census that he was separated from her and living with Edith Newbauer who became his second wife after the death of his first wife. Obviously in his later years he did not compete on the circuit but confined himself to a number of teaching jobs. Latterly he moved to Greenville in Ohio which was the home area of his second wife and he died there aged 76 in March 1959. His second wife went on to marry again and she eventually died in 2008.

> Robert B. Peebles, 76, who came to US from Elie, Scotland, in 1900 died recently at his home near Greenville, O. . . . He had worked as teaching pro for L. E. Beavins at White Springs GC, Greenville, in 1951 and 1952, then went to the Bardstown (Ky.) CC for a brief period after which he retired . . . He was an excellent player and teacher and had an engaging personality . . . Mr. Peebles undoubtedly was in more good pro jobs than any other pro in the game . . . The USGA championship record book lists some of Bob's connections: South Orange, Fairview, Sound Beach, St. Joseph Valley, Dallas, Wichita, Topeka, Shawnee Heights, Louisville . . . He also served as pro at the Mexico City CC . . . He is survived by his widow, two daughters and a son.

This man was prolific in his activities. Not only was he constantly on the move playing and teaching golf, he also supervised many designs of courses. His influence on the game in America cannot be understated.

William Thomson Peebles

1884 – 1945

William was the eldest son of Robert Peebles(q.v.) For more background information see Robert Peebles his brother.

Although William was probably a very good golfer he did not, it seems, become a professional golfer but he did cross the Atlantic. He arrived in USA in 1909 and naturalised in 1919. He married Alice Watt in Chicago in August 1918. We find him in 1920 in Chicago and he is described as a "mechanic golf balls" which rather stimulates the imagination! In the 1930 census he is described as "Salesman Golf" and in 1940 census as a golf club inspector for Wilson Sporting Goods Co. He died in 1943 but I think we can claim him as an Earlsferry/Elie golfer who was loosely associated with golf as a career.

Alexander Philp

1885 – 1945

Although Alexander Philp does not meet the exact criteria for inclusion in this section he is so sufficiently identified with Earlsferry, as shall be seen, to warrant inclusion.

Alexander Philp (Snr) his grand father was born in 1857 and Alexander Snr (his father) was the son of Mary Harris later to marry Jamie Braid's father. She and his father John Philp a ploughman were not married. He was assumed into the household at the Grange farm as grandson of Alexander Harris and his wife. AP senior was therefore the half brother of Jamie Braid although rather older than him. He lived with the Harris family and his mother at Grange Farm initially but he moved to Edinburgh where in 1884 he married at Newington.

Then in 1885 his son Alexander (Jnr) was born in Edinburgh.

The census of 1901 shows Alex Jnr as living with the Harris family in Earlsferry High Street in Linmara aged 16 and employed as a golf club maker. It looks as if Alex Jnr was sent off back to Earlsferry for his education and his apprenticeship. By that time his grand mother Mary Harris had married and was living with James Braid Snr., Jamie Braid having been born in 1870. Whether he was with Scott or Forrester we do not currently know but his friendship with Braid suggests it might have been Forrester. Thereafter he joined Jamie Braid at Walton Heath as evidenced by this excerpt from Walton Heath history.

> Notable artisans include, Alex Philp one of Braid's early helpers and club makers, who during the winter of 1909 went off Argentina to ply his trade. He must have been a fine golfer because on the afternoon of Wednesday 21st September 1910 he won the Argentine Open at the Golf Club Argentino in Buenos Aires where he was the resident professional. He won again in 1913 at the San Andres GC. Another member was Fred Dudley,

CANTEGRIL GOLF CLUB

Cantegril Golf Club is considered the best golf course in Punta del Este, Uruguay. This course has 18 holes and the first nine were designed by Alex Philp, started in 1929 and the second by Luther H Koontz in 1947. Located 5 km from Punta del Este and one mile from the seashore.

Then he seemed to have gone to Argentina and been a professional at Golf Club Argentino in Buenos Aires. In addition to his duties as a club professional he also took a hand in designing courses in South America - see this from Uruguay. We are not sure when he moved clubs but spent most of his career at Miramar.

Miramar Buenos Aires - This golf club was built in 1930 and it seems likely that Alexander Philp was one of the first professionals. It coincided with his purchasing Jamieson Place in Leith.

He was permanently at Miramar Links in Buenos Aires since the valuation and electors roll for Edinburgh from 1930 onwards show him as retaining 8 Jamieson Place as his abode but citing the Dormy House in Miramar as his residence.

The hotel Dormy House was built adjacent to the golf course by the Buenos Aires Great Southern Railway, and later a tunnel was built to provide access to the sea from the hotel.

He travelled fairly frequently back and forth to Buenos Aires. We are reasonably certain that he died in Edinburgh and was cremated in 1945.

It is interesting to speculate as to why he should have chosen South America for his career. A pure guess but it is likely that by his association with James Braid he could have been selected to go to Buenos Aires. At that time Braid (1909) was the colossus of golf and much in demand but he did not travel (at least not by boat and little by train and less by car – he suffered from motion sickness).

It is possible therefore that Braid may have been courted by people in South America to plan and lay out their course and delegated the job to his half brother. Who knows?

Tom Reekie & John Reekie

1880 – 1958   1923 - 2007

There cannot be anyone who has visited Elie in the last 100 years who has not heard the name Reekie. Father Tom and son John were stalwarts of the Elie golfing scene from 1918 when Tom came back from World War 1 and 2007 when John, who took over the business, died.

Tom was actually born in St. Monans on 20th May 1880. His father was one of a number of Reekies in the area who earned their living from the sea. It was a hard and hazardous life and Tom made it clear at an early age that he disliked the sea which rather ruled out his succession to the family boat.

However, aged 15, he was taken on as an apprentice with George Forrester in 1895. Initially he commuted from St. Monans (which he could do by train) although he may have had some sort of temporary lodgings in Earlsferry. On his return from World War 1 he set up his own plate as a golf club maker and professional. By that time Forrester was still in business but his son James and he did not see eye to eye and there was a lack of successor to the business which eventually was wound up in 1926 and the machinery, devised in the main and built by Forrester, was put up for sale. Tom probably acquired some of the machinery and stock in trade from the auction. He certainly acquired the brass mould which was used for the gutty ball making.

By that time Andrew Scott (q.v.) was the pre-eminent golf club maker in Earlsferry but his market was more international than local. Tom decided to set up as a professional as well teaching and making golf clubs. When James Maclean Sunter (q.v.) the appointed professional at Elie Golf House club moved to Edinburgh in 1930 one would have thought it would have been natural that Tom or Andrew Scott would be appointed the resident professional for the club in his place. However it was not to be and it may have had something to do with the competition that was provided by Crowley (who by then was in Glasgow) Scott, Reekie and James Forrester. All four had a shed/shop up against the wall of the car park area at the sports club. He also established a workshop in his house in Viewforth in the High Street of Earlsferry and for a time in 1921 he was the tenant of Forrester at Moonzie Cottage in Links Road which he may have used as a workshop. Viewforth had been owned by Mrs Catherine Sime the mother of Willie Sime (q.v.) and the Reekie family originally living in the Cross merely crossed to the other side of Earlsferry High Street in 1923 or thereabouts.

He became a renowned teacher and many an aspiring youngster was taught by Tom Reekie in the sports club area beside the Pavilion. His shop in addition to selling golf equipment also served at one time as the ticket supplier for those playing the Ladies' Course (Baird Course now). Tom married Katie in 1919 and moved to the Cross before moving to Viewforth.

It was the norm in these days for Earlsferry and Elie residents to move out of their homes during the summer "season" and live in a shed or cottage in the garden. The newspapers of the time would report which eminent families from which metropolis were spending the season renting the Earlsferry residents' houses. The Reekie family was no exception and the author of these articles has fond memories of living in Viewforth for two or three "seasons". Tom and family lived in a small cottage in the garden during the "season" but he often came into the back garden of an evening and watched the author develop his golfing skills (aged 4). His future success owes much to Tom's sage advice.

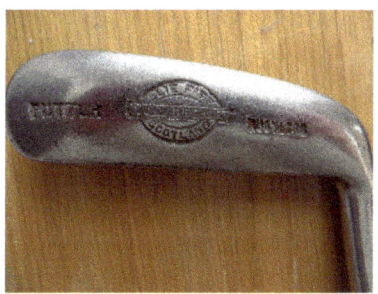

Tom initially made his own clubs from wood blanks he had prepared. Sometimes they were laminated, other times solid beech or persimmon. The shafts of course were initially hickory but that soon gave way to steel shafts. His first foray into iron clubs would have been the manufacture by Anderson in Anstruther – the blacksmith – who forged iron clubs and would pass them on to Tom. He ran his own brand of golf clubs which latterly were made by Nicoll in Leven but always contained his signature. He must have sold many thousands of clubs from the cut down smaller ones for children through to ladies' sets and then the men's sets. He also had a range of Tom Reekie putters.

Here is an example of one purchased from caddy earnings during holiday.

On the golf course Tom and John were canny players – not perhaps the full bloodied slash and hope brigade but the measured stylish swingers. It was teaching really however that was their strength.

Tom handed over to his son John in 1945 and it became Tom Reekie & Son and John was to continue the business until his retirement in 2000 or so and he died in 2007.

Andrew Rolland

1818 -1901

It would be easy to dismiss Andrew Rolland as no more than Dougie Rolland's father which in itself would be an accolade but along with one or two others he must rank as one of the progenitors of the Earlsferry Golfers. Although he was a miner by trade he obviously earned a good living by challenging others to golf. This would be at a time when golf was not really the common pastime as it later became but he was a frequent winner in Earlsferry competitions.

He and his family lived in the Chapel green area of Earlsferry probably in Rose Cottage which was situated in Chapel Green Road between Elphin Cottage and Craigview.

In 1864 or thereby he played a famous match against Mungo Park which is referred to in an article about the coming match between Dougy Rolland and Mungo Park's son thus - *In connection with the match between Douglas Rolland and Willie Park, it may be interesting to recall what was considered a great match in those days, nearly 30 years ago, when Andrew Rolland Duggy's father and Mungo Park* Willie's father, played old Tom Morris and Mr Proudfoot, then of Kilconquhar. Tom and his partner gained the match by one putt, which Rolland should have easily taken, but which he did not, much to the disgust of Park, who, turning round told Rolland he 'couldna play.' Times have changed, and those who thought themselves cracks then could not hold the candle now.1894*

*Mungo Park won the open in 1884 so Andrew was up there with the best.

His obituary perhaps speaks for itself.

EARLSFERRY. DEATH OF AN OLD FERRY GOLFER AND COUNCILLOR. —*At the ripe old age of 84, Mr Andrew Rolland, Earlsferry, passed away last Thursday. With him is gone another link to the golfing days of the middle of last century. In those days his tall spare form was familiar and respected on all Fife links. He held a foremost place amongst the golfing professionals and did much by his prowess to establish the golfing reputation of the Ferry. Few of his compeers are now spared, since he was in his prime as a golfer three or four generations of leading lights have succeeded and gone. Amongst these must be ranked his own son, Douglas Rolland, whose best days may now be said to be past; but Ferry folk are proud to think that his nephew, James Braid, is still in the very forefront. Mr Rolland saw many changes in the tools and balls, as well as in the personnel of the players and the development of the game, to which he was to the last devoted. Several years ago he was a member of Earlsferry Council. He was a miner at one time, and engaged at the now deserted Balklivie near Kenoway. Miners were scarce in the district, and he travelled backwards and forwards to the Ferry by the train; it was in his interest and that of a few other workmen that the late Mr Andrew*

Wilkie granted the privilege tickets to tradesmen, special terms which were in force until the end of last year. Mr Rolland is survived by his wife, several children and grandchildren. 1901

1877 Thistle GOLF CLUB. This promising young Club*, which though only in the third year of its existence already numbers nearly 70 and of which Mr A. H. Browning is captain, held a competition for the Mason medal Saturday afternoon. At the close of two rounds of the Links, it was found that Douglas Rolland and Charles Simpson had tied for the medal with a score of 89, and having elected to play off the tie by another round the former proved the victor by a majority of ten strokes. In addition to these two, David Simpson and Andrew Rolland were winners of sweepstakes. * it had been established for 2 years.

EARLSFERRY. GOLF.—A number of money prizes were played for last Saturday afternoon, open to all local players. As the day was fine (though the wind was high), there was a large number of competitors. The usual two rounds of the links-22 holes—were played, and the successful competitors stood in the following order: Ist prize won by Andrew Rolland in 104 strokes; 2d won by David Simpson in 112; 3rd won by David Sime in 115; Bob Mackie and Thomas Davidson tied for the 4th and 5th at 118; James Forrester and David Melville tied for the 8th and 7th at 120; James Rolland won the 9th in 122; Robert Peebles the 10th in 123; and James Paterson the 11th in 124. 1871

John Erskine Douglas Stewart Rolland

1861 - 1914

John Erskine Douglas Stewart Rolland – "Dougie" was probably one of the most promising of the Earlsferry men who became professional golfers. His career was cut short by injury to his wrists which resulted in him giving up the game. However at the time he was considered to be one of the longest hitters of all time and his prowess and indeed bravado on the links were legendary. His career was described in an obituary in the newspapers in 1914 which started. "

> The death of Douglas Rolland, writes "R.B.M.," in "The Golf Monthly" for September, at Farnborough, removes from the arena of golf a figure around whose name there was a perfect cluster of romance, and concerning whose deeds on the links professionals of the older school have a liberal hank of yarns. There is a deeply pathetic touch in Rolland's life, for when thirty-four years of age, and at the very height of his golfing power, he was stricken with an affliction in his wrists which prevented him freely swinging his club, and cut short, as if with a knife, the promise of his brilliant career.

He was born in Earlsferry is 1861 one of several children of Andrew Rolland(q.v.) and Isabella Harris. His father who died in 1901 at the ripe age of 84 was also a professional golfer. He was in addition a mason's labourer at a time when a lot of the Earlsferry young men were employed as masons.

Whilst Dougie trained as a mason he, also along with the usual coterie of Earlsferry boys, played golf on the golfing tract of Earlsferry. Physically he was a large man for his era and his original training as a mason obviously gave rise to extremely strong forearms and hands which he put to good use on the golf course. *"In his prime he stood just over 6 feet weighed 13 stones erect as a dart he measured 42 inches round the chest, had a right forearm of 12 and half inches; indeed his physique was admirable, the very type of an athlete in whom a sculptor would rejoice. (same source as above)*

Open Golf Championship

In 1884 Open at Prestwick Jack Simpson (Earlsferry) won but Dougie and Willie Fernie were joint second. In the 1894 open at St. Georges Sandwich again Rolland was runner up this time to J H Taylor and in 1882 and 1883 he was tied 13th and 10th.

After his second place in 1884 it is reported that Dougie went to USA but we have only been able to find this reference to his exploits.

> When Andrew Kirkaldy was in America a few years ago he played in a foursome with his brothers, Hugh and Jack Kirkaldy and Douglas Rolland. Andrew and his partner lost, and he was loud in his expressions of disgust. A few professionals anxious to see a repetition of his anger asked him who played in the foursome, and he replied: "Me and masel, my brother Hugh and I, Jack, Duggie Rolland and me."

It is reported that when he returned a few years later he was but a physical shadow of himself although his lack of physique was at that time not attributed to anything. However he continued playing golf and took up a position initially as professional in 1901, he is reported as living in Hastings. He certainly was back in England in 1898 where he married Anna Emily Edmunds. Anna had a child before she married and it not clear whether Dougie was the father but Dorothy (Dollie) Phoebe Edmunds (later Rolland) was born in 1889. Subsequent to his marriage he had two other children, Mary Elizabeth Anna Rolland born in 1900 and Douglas Andrew Rolland born in 1901. In 1903 he was noted as being the professional at Tottenbeck although this was a misprint for Tooting Bec. A course which no longer exists. Again in 1894 he was reported to be the professional at Rye where he stayed for a short period of time. Before that it is reported that he was at Limpsfield Chart. The website of that club notes:

"[in] 1890, a small but picturesque club-house was built the cost being generously defrayed by two members. The same year saw Douglas Rolland engaged as professional. Rolland remained at Limpsfield for four years, the course rapidly improving under his care."

He was at the time famous for having played in money matches and challenges. Indeed it is recorded that the first exhibition in which gate money was charged was "....... at a match between Douglas Rolland and Jack White at Cambridge. The practice of paying for matches through private betting, rather than gate receipts and sponsorships, survives well into the 20th Century as a "Calcutta," but increasingly gate receipts are the source of legitimate prize purses."

His other exploits were his famous tussle with J.D Ball over Hoylake and Earlsferry and also against two of the St Andrews best players. It was reported thus

"Some eight or nine years or so have elapsed since Mr Douglas Rolland came into general notice, although, as a matter of course, his merits were well known in the village of Elie, or Earlsferry, his native place. It so happened that about that time Jack Simpson, also native of Elie, and a subsequent winner of the open championship, was at the height of his game, and Rolland and he were in the habit of playing together continually. Nothing much, however, was known of either of them away from their own green, and the first notice strangers had was the intimation that the two would be glad to play any two amateurs of the Royal and Ancient at St Andrews. Accordingly a foursome was got together with Messrs Leslie

Balfour and Horace Hutchinson who were the selected champions of the latter Club. The play exhibited by its challengers was a revelation. Jack Simpson was to the full as fine a player as Rolland himself, even if he was not, as the latter inclined to think, a trifle better, and the driving shown by them too simply pulverised their opponents, who never had a chance from start to finish. It happened to be blowing a heavy gale of wind, which exactly suited the play of the strangers, and, as so instance of their great power, an episode may be given which occurred at the very first hole. The gale was of such strength that Mr Balfour and his partner could not cross the burn at the third shot, although they had three very good drives, and it fell to Jack Simpson to play the like. He called for his cleek, whereupon a spectator, himself a first-rate player, and excellent judge of the game, remarked—" I should have thought a man who can drive like that would have risked the burn." With but a three-quarter shot with his cleek, he laid the ball within a few feet of the hole. This particular round was finished in 89, which, considering the day, was extraordinarily fine performance, but it should be added that their putting was scandalously bad. Neither the one nor the other appeared to have the most rudimentary idea of how to hole a ball out, and time after time, after reaching the green by magnificent driving and approaching, an extra stroke was almost sure to be required, unless the ball was absolutely dead. But, as the late Mr James Mansfield remarked in the course of the play, "with driving of that description you can afford a deal of slackness in the short game." 1891

His tussle with Ball in 1883 was legendary.

> **AMATEUR GOLF MATCH.**
>
> The great amateur golf match between Mr. John Ball, of Hoylake, the crack player of the Royal Liverpool Golf Club, who has carried off repeatedly the medals of his club, and Mr. Douglas Rolland, Earlsferry, Fifeshire, and of the Leith Golf Club, was continued yesterday at the Hoylake Links. The match, which was the outcome of an announcement in the *Field* that more than one Scotch amateur would be backed to play Mr. Ball over more than one links for a stake sufficient to cover the expenses of the contest, has excited much attention in golfing circles on both sides of the border, the players being the representatives of a Scotch and an English green. The numbers who witnessed yesterday's play show how popular this open-air game is now becoming in England. The first part of the match was played on November 29, on the links at Earlsferry, and was witnessed by a large company, including many from St. Andrews. The game here consisted of 36 holes, and resulted in Mr. Rolland winning by the very large number of nine holes on his home green. Yesterday the match was completed at Hoylake, Mr. Ball's home green; and in consequence of the fine play exhibited last week by Mr. Rolland several hundred golfers, many having come from Scotland and London as well as from Manchester, were present to witness the contest. The day was bright and fine, but windy, and the green was in excellent order. The game here also consisted of 36 holes, and at the end of the first round Mr. Ball was one up, completing the round in 90 to his opponent's 91. In the second round Mr. Rolland, playing a brilliant game, succeeded in completing the round in 85 to Mr. Ball's 90, being four up on the day's play, and winning the match by 13 holes

He had some affiliation with Leith Links. At that time of course he was still an amateur although the exact distinction was rather amorphous. On the other hand Leith Links and various clubs associated with it was a very active club. The Honourable Company of Edinburgh Golfers originated in Leith before moving to Muirfield. A "J Rolland" is shown as playing in a match for Leith Golf Club against Edinburgh Thistle. It is probable that this was Dougie since his first initial is J. He was an ordinary member of Leith Links and of course Earlsferry. It is clear that the match at St. Andrews and at Hoylake and Earlsferry referred to amateur golfers. As noted above he was also associated with Limpsfield golf club, Rye and a few others. There was some controversy in relation to Dougie's application to play in the Amateur championship at Westward Ho! in 1885. Horace Hutchison then the doyen of golf writers noted thus:

"It may be remembered—or it may not—that at the last meeting of the delegates for the amateur championship, held when that great competition was decided at Westward Ho!, they had before them, for discussion. The delegates are appointed to have general charge of the arrangements for

the amateur championship, but it is tolerably certain that they would not care to come to a decision touching the very fundamental conditions of the competition without definite instructions on this particular subject from the clubs which give them their office. It is to the energy and initiative of the Royal Liverpool Golf Club that the championship owes its existence. In 1885 that famous club instituted a tournament, open to all amateur golfers. The tournament, as its very name implies, was to be decided by match play, ………to be confined to amateurs, but seeing that no definition of an amateur golfer was at that time in existence, there was no recognised guidance for the committee in charge of the competition as to who should be included and who debarred. The point came up in an acute personal form for me on the reception of the name of Douglas Rolland, submitted as a competitor. I happened to be a member of the committee, and finding myself in a minority of one in their deliberations about the acceptance of Rolland's entry, I retired, quite amicably, from the committee, because I did not wish to be one of a body which voted for his exclusion. At that time I had visions of possibly being the winner of the proposed tournament, and, under these circumstances, did not wish to be associated with an action which ruled out of the lists one of the most formidable of the competitors. Rolland, whom I do not think our present definition would have excluded, was denied right of entry, and immediately removed all future trouble on his behalf by taking up the game as his profession the very same year. "1885

So we can be sure that he became a professional in 1885 and we can assume that that definition probably meant that you derived your main income from the game. His father Alexander Rolland who died at the age of 84 in 1901 was described as a professional golfer although he had other employment.

There is also a reference to Tooting Bec and Bexhill on Sea where he is credited with having redesigned the course prior to its move elsewhere. He is also associated with Malvern Green golf club and Aldershot Army golf course - he died in the club house of that course in 1914. He played exhibition matches very often at the opening of a new course designed by some of his friends. Jackson suggests that he joined the Marchant Navy while in USA and if so, it must have been short. Perhaps he was injured in the Merchant Navy.

> The Rye Golf Club has done well in engaging Douglas Rolland's services. Lately Rolland has been playing several matches in Sussex. Twice at Hastings he was beaten by the best ball of Mr. H. S. Colt and James Keddie, the local professional. On the nice little links at Bexhill, Mr. Colt and Keddie did well in halving a match with Rolland and Yeoman, the professional resident at Eastbourne,

*Keddie was an Earlsferry man too.

The East of Fife Record reported on his death in 1914 and quoted from an extensive article in Golf Monthly about him. It is worth looking in detail at that article.

His First Open Championship.

Rolland was still an amateur, and it was in the following year,1884 that he first essayed success in the Open Championship. The amateur contest was then merely a possibility, and Rolland at Prestwick, was beaten by his chum. Jack Simpson, tying with Willie Fernie for second place, Fernie being the holder of the championship at the time. On the eve of that event Rolland, Jack Simpson and another professional, who is prominent even to-day although older than Rolland were staying in the same house at Prestwick. Rolland had had a very merry evening, in fact, far too merry. He drew a ring on the floor, and said the championship medal must be there to-morrow night. He was correct in his prophecy. Simpson won. After that championship. Rolland immediately turned professional. He first competed as a professional at Hoylake, in 1884. And in 1887 he accepted the charge of the Malvern Green. At the tournament played in connection with the opening of the Sandwich Course he ran through to the final, in which, however, he was vanquished by Archie Simpson by the narrow margin of one hole, the driving in this match on both sides being something to he remembered. He was successful, however, in winning the prize for the aggregate the professional tournament in Westward Ho! In June 1889 he was singularly successful winning over £30 in virtue of a double victory one being a competition by holes, and the other an aggregate score of two rounds. These two rounds he holed 83 and 85, total of 168 being one stroke in front of Sayers.

His Second Championship.

In those days the English did not encourage their professionals in the same way as they do now, and Rolland had to leave the Open Championship alone. In 1890 he went from Malvern to Limpsfield Chart where remained for three years, and he then went to Rye. In 1894 his chance came, for it was that year that an English green was first included in the Open Championship rota. Sandwich was the venue, and Rolland had no difficulty in raising the funds and getting the time for the journey from the old Sussex Cinque Port to one in Kent. That Championship is historical, for there the great division of English professionals first hoisted the flag of victors, a flag which by the aid of Harry Vardon and J. H. Taylor, they have kept aloft with little interruption for twenty years. Rolland in that championship took second place, and the poor old fellow, when I had my last chat with him, had a tale to tell, nothing more or less than that his favourite driver had been damaged at the end of the first day's play, with the result that at the second hole in the third round the head flew off. It is worth recording now that at the end of the first day's play Taylor was leading by a stroke, and at the ninth hole in the third round the positions were unaltered. From that point however, Taylor steadily drew away, and finished in against Rolland's 331

The End of His Career.

At that championship, Rolland was in almost rampant form. On the Saturday to the big event Willie Park issued a challenge for a thirty-six holes match for £100. Rolland was backed, and won by three and two. After the championship, he also won the professional and amateur tournament, defeating in succession Mr Horace Hutchinson by three and one, Willie Auchterlonie, by two and one, Freddie Tait at the nineteenth hole, and in the final Taylor by two and one. Rolland's career almost ended with that meeting, although he subsequently played a match partnered by Ben Sayers against Taylor and Hugh Kirkaldy over Tooting Bec. The former couple won by a hole, and the circumstances are somewhat remarkable. They were all level, with one to play, and driving to the last hole, Rolland's tee shot went over a clump of tress and ran to 250 yards. This was with a gutta ball.

The Old Pro's Methods.

Rolland essentially belonged to the old school. The hard-living type which hung the border-land of the caddie. In dress and manner he was of the type which has long been superseded by the more prosperous professional. In the championship at Prestwick, some of the competitors walked from Musselburgh with an equipment of three or four clubs and a couple of gutta halls which had long lost a vestige of paint. In dilapidated boots and raiment burst at a variety of corners, and whisky their chief sustenance, they formed a ragged crew. Rolland was in the better-living division, but he had his curious ways. He told me that present-day golfers did not feed themselves properly and had a firm belief in big steak for breakfast. In this connection, he told an incident of the Sandwich championship. The feeding arrangements then, as now, were faulty. Rolland and one of the Simpsons- - he thought Bob—got into the little refreshment tent first. Four-pound steak with potatoes were laid out, and the two worthies consumed the lot, to the intense annoyance of the caterer, who intended to feed the lot off the one steak. The other pro's went hungry. Money was not plentiful, and this is illustrated by the match with Sayers and old Davie Grant for £20 a-side. Grant could not get up his corner of the stake. His wife refused to risk any of the family savings and it was only by a surreptitious visit and a "break open" of the home bank that Grant tabled his money.

Big Driving.

His power of driving, and especially against the wind was almost phenomenal and it was not an uncommon occurrence to see him forty or fifty yards in front of a shot which would in ordinary circumstances be considered an excellent one, and he could probably drive as far with his cleek as the majority young drivers could with a play club. In the short game however, he was not often seen to such advantage and he sometimes failed to hole out his short putts with precision. Looking at his play, as a whole, it was remarked by a not wholly incompetent critic of that time, that "the strongest part of his game is his temper," - and there was considerable justice in the observation.

His Secret of Big Hitting.

Rolland always carried a very heavy iron and he could use this with tremendous power. In an article he contributed to the Golf Monthly in April last, Rolland said, "I have often been asked the secret of long driving. But all I can say is that it is a combination of forces. A big man has a greater chance of hitting a longer hall than the small man, by reason of his physical advantages but you can hit as hard as you can and the golf ball will not take it. I have hit a ball as hard as my cousin Jimmy Braid, and I could not get the ball to stop in the air any more than 250 yards. Golf is a right-handed game, and I think the secret of my success as a long driver was the strength which I possessed in my right arm. The greatest drive was in the match I played against Lieut. Freddie Tait at Sandwich in 1884. In that year Tait and Mr Edward Blackwell were regarded as the longest drivers amongst amateurs, but off every tee I beat Tait in the semi-final. Often I was twenty yards better than him; I consistently outdrove him at every hole. In my biggest drive that day I felt that I had put every ounce behind my grips, and that I had caught the ball at the psychological moment.

Rolland's Influence on Golf.

Strangely, after Rolland left Earlsferry for Malvern he never revisited his native village*. His influence on the game of which he was such a master may be dismissed as nothing. He was a thrilling player, a dashing, daring fellow, but his light went out before his time. In the years between

1884 and 1900, he might have held the fort for Scotland until Braid came along but he passed out suddenly. All that remains is the regret that the success which was possible to him he never achieved and the memory of a picturesque personality.

*there is a suggestion that Dougie was not welcome in Scotland by virtue of a court action in which a lady claimed he was the father of her child and she wanted him to maintain it!

"THEN AND NOW At Eastertime of this year, after an absence of some twelve years or so, I revisited my old favourite resort, the Bexhill Golf Club, where, in the MacDougall-cum-Rolland days, I was a constant visitor, and temporary member. We find, too, a practically new course, with new ground taken in here and there, and a new punch bowl '* green in the added far country; new bunkers and hammocks galore, and some right good ones, too, amongst them; and lastly, old Penland Wood very much thinned off and opened out. ....Though very fond of the old course, laid out by Douglas Rolland, I am certainly of opinion that, as a whole, the course as now arranged, with the new ground in the far country, the additional length at the 2nd hole, well the portion taken into use at the 13th is far more sporting and attractive as well as being more difficult to negotiate."

It is his immense driving capabilities that were still remembered long after his death.

Anecdotes also abounded.

There is a story told of Douglas Rolland, the celebrated British professional, who died very recently. He had given a glowing testimonial of a new brand of golf ball, and one of his friends in a spirit of fun, asked him how much he had received for his endorsement.

Rolland frankly admitted that he had received five sovereigns. "And does the ball really fly further than the others?" The inquiry was a natural one, but Rolland's reply was startling.

"About ten yards *short*, I'm thinkin'."

Dougie died at the relatively young age of 53 in 1914 and perhaps fittingly it was in the Golf Club House Farnborough where he was the professional at the time. This is now the Army Golf Course at Aldershot.

It is said that Dougie never returned to his native Earlsferry after he went south (vide supra). But there is little doubt he was an endearing character and an immensely powerful golfer in his day. It was a pity he suffered from injury to his wrists preventing him from playing more golf. Without that he might have been a third Open Champion from Earlsferry.

The Scott Family

James and Andrew Scott's father was a stone mason (not much surprise here) and his mother's maiden name was Herd. They were married in 1872 but the marriage certificate merely gives their addresses as Earlsferry and Williamsburgh respectively. It is not clear from the census and valuation rolls exactly where the Scotts were living but it looks very much as if it was next door to the grocer's shop in Earlsferry High street which would means that it was Ferry Cottage. This ties in with the ground lying to the north of the High Street which extended up to Links Road and latterly Scott had a small factory on this site.

Andrew Scott

1875-1934

Andrew Herd Scott was born in Kilconquhar Earlsferry on 29th September 1875. Andrew was a cousin of George Forrester and information suggests that he started out on his own in 1894/5 when just 19. There is information that he also worked for a time – must have been short – for Charlie Hunter of Prestwick. (For golf club making pedigree see the chapter 10 on golf clubmakers.)

He was also a very good golfer again having learnt his skills on the Earlsferry golf course and being contemporary with many of the other young men who succeeded at the sport. He was a few years younger than James Braid but no doubt pitted his skills against him before Braid moved south. It is likely that his achievements were eclipsed by Braid but he came a little later than Rolland, Smith and others of that era. He did however compete in the Open Championship and his best placed finish was 6th.

Teaching

He made much of the fact that he was a skilled teacher and it was probably as a result of this that he was invited to play with, chaperone and no doubt teach Princess Patricia and the Duchess of Connaught on their visits to Elie (see also section on Royalty) although the Royals also patronised Ben Sayers in North Berwick.

That experience obviously did no end of good to Scott's business and his further tuition of more accomplished players was recognised.

> **The Ladies at Play.**
>
> Though the open and amateur championships have this year been relegated to England, Scotland will not be altogether poverty-stricken in the matter of big gatherings on the links which will have an international flavour. In the West of Scotland the ladies will hold high carnival. Ladies' golf may or may not be fitted for the St Louis Exposition, according to the temper and the will of the management; there is no doubt whatever about its suitability for the development of the maidens of Caledonia; and the American calendar will be all the leaner without the attractive presence of May Hezlett, Rhona Adair, and the lassie from Elie, who has been trained by that master of the art, Andrew H. Scott, of Earlsferry. With

The "lassie from Elie" was probably Alexa Glover (q.v.) there is reference also to his tutoring Madge Maitland and some other prominent amateurs of the day.

Course Design

Another string to his bow seems to have been course design if we go by this report in the papers

EXTENSION of Balcomie - Crail Golfing Society has with considerable enterprise lost no time in carrying out the extension of the nine-hole course to the orthodox 18 holes. The new greens are in course of formation, although rough should be in moderate condition by the 4th July, when it is proposed to formally open the course with an amateur tournament. Members of Anstruther, Elie, Lundin Links, Leven, Ladybank, Cupar, and St Andrews golf are to be invited to take part for a series of valuable prizes. A gentleman has also presented the Crail club with a gold medal, to be competed for by members on the same day, the winner to be the champion of the club for the year and get a small medal or charm

along with the large prize. The Society is also arranging the details of a bazaar, to be held at the back end of summer. Mr A. H. Scott, Elie, planned the course, which he says is not only a very fine eighteen-hole course for ordinary play, but affords scope for a really good test of first-class golf.
1902

Competitive golf

Being a professional at that time meant that he would compete for prizes offered by various clubs and also competitive games for purses among the better players. Scott was no exception and seems to have been quite successful

> A Professional's Challenge.—Peter Rainford, the professional to the Crieff Golf Club, who gave Herd, the open champion, so hard a match at Crieff and Carnoustie last month, has issued a challenge to Andrew H. Scott or James Forrester, professionals at Elie and Earlsferry, to play a home-and-home match of 36 holes for £20 to £50 a-side.

Feb 1902

> **DYSART.**
> GOLF MATCH —A. H. Scott, Earlsferry, and J. Fowlis, ex-champion of America, played a two-round match over the nine-hole course here on Wednesday. After an excellent display of "class" golf, the match finished all square.

March 1902

> A professional exhibition match was played on Saturday week at Bathgate between James Kinnell and Andrew H Scott, Elie. The course is one of nine holes, and Kinnell had two 39's—78—to Scott's 40 and 39—79. Kinnell had one fine tee shot measured at 223 yards.

1897

> ANDREW KIRKALDY (ST. ANDREWS) v. A. H. SCOTT (ELIE).— These professionals played a 36-holes match on the Baberton Club's Links at Juniper Green, near Edinburgh, on Saturday, the occasion being the formal opening of the extended course. At the end of the first round the men were square both as regards holes and strokes; but Scott played the better game in the afternoon, and, going round in 75 strokes—the lowest score on record—beat Kirkcaldy by two holes up.

1899

He took part in many professional engagements over the years when attention to his business would permit. He was in an exhibition match with Willie Fernie of Troon in 1908 which he won. He challenged Andrew Kirkcaldy for a £50 match which he lost over 36 holes by 3 and 1 but he got his revenge in another match against him at Baberton in 1903.

Andrew H died in 1934 leaving quite a portfolio of property in Earlsferry. Abbotsford which is at the top of the bottom half of Ferry Road was built for him by the Currie family of Elie with the distinctive astragal type windows. This remained in the family until the death of his widow in 1956. Waverley which is 4 Earlsferry High Street and in which Marjory Scott lived until her death and after that his youngest son Andrew H Scott had it. Ferry Cottage opposite the town hall in Earlsferry High Steet which was Andrew (Sen)H Scott's father's house and he took over on his father's death. David, Andrew's eldest son took over Ferry Cottage along with the workshop at the north end of the plot bordering on Links Road. He died in 1967 after which the ground was taken over for a development of houses. David also took over Andrew's business on his death in 1934 and continued until he retired which would have been in the late 50s.

Andrew was a pillar of the community but he had the occasional brush with authority. See this

> Andrew Herd Scott, Earlsferry, the well-known golf club maker and golfer, whose trial for failing to report for military service on 2d September was fixed for yesterday at Cupar, has got a protection certificate, as he is working at an aerodrome. The Fiscal deserted the diet on the understanding that Mr Scott paid the expenses of the Court.

Subsequently the charge was withdrawn when Andrew proved that he was employed in the defence of the realm by working at an airfield – the report did not identify the airfield but it may well have been Crail. On his death his confirmation showed assets of £1314 which is modern day equivalent of £77,000 and one wonders if he had advice in reducing his estate.

James Scott

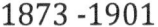

1873 -1901

James Scott on left

James Scott was the elder brother of Andrew Herd Scott (q.v.) and he was born in Kilconquhar parish i.e. Earlsferry on 14th June 1873. He was living in Ferry Cottage with his father, David and mother.

He seems to have been a good amateur golfer having entered amateur competitions locally when aged 12 but at some point he must have become a professional because he entered as a professional in the Open Championship at Prestwick in 1893. This was a championship marred by very bad weather and James withdrew after a first round 93 which was by no means at the end of the field. He served an apprenticeship with Forrester like his younger brother but he was appointed to the professional position at Royal Sydney Golf Club in 1896 although at that time he was designed as "caretaker", the club being in its infancy. Indeed his caretaking included discovering a fire at the Sydney club house *"Royal Sydney's current Clubhouse contains a wide range of facilities including bars, restaurants, function rooms, bridge rooms, billiards room, a bottle shop, sport shop, reading lounges and accommodation rooms. ....The second Clubhouse was built in 1897, erected on a freehold site acquired from the Cooper estate at the southern end of O'Sullivan Road (on the corner of Birriga Road), near Old South Head Road. The Clubhouse was a substantially constructed, picturesque building in the bungalow style. The building was occupied in August, 1897. A month later, at the official opening by the Governor, Lord Hampden, His Excellency announced that Her Majesty had agreed to the prefix "Royal". The first of the Club's four fires was in September, 1899. It began in the Clubhouse pantry but was "opportunely discovered and extinguished by the Ebsworth children" and by the Club's first professional, James Scott. From RSGC website.*

In what turned out to be a very short time with RSGC he acquired a name for himself as a good golfer. But on the morning in April 1901 he and two of his friends set off from Sydney to Bondi beach for a spot of fishing.......what happened is carefully chronicled....

DEATH OF A WELL KNOWN EARLSFERRY GOLFER. (By "Fader" in " The Sydney Mail" of 11th April 1902). Last week I wrote of the remarkable " record " score of 67 accomplished by the Royal Sydney professional, James Scott, of Bondi, and the player's characteristic remark that it might have been five less, as he missed that number of short putts. Poor Scott never read that paragraph. His score was made on March 30th, and on the morning of April 3rd, his dead body was being carried hither and yon by the ocean currents off the links. Scott went out with J. Clarke and T. Coonan, at 6 a.m., to fish from the cliff foot at Hierrivery, near the main sewer outfall. It is a popular fishing ground, reached by a stiff descent down a steep path to a rock wall, which is safe in fine weather, is sometimes 20 feet under waves in storms, and is dangerous in such a north-east swell as was rolling. This time he was clearing his line from the rocks after landing a fish, when a big wave was seen coming. All three abandoned their lines and ran higher, but Scott slipped and was washed into the sea and slowly drifted seawards. A schnapper line was thrown to him, and on the second attempt lodged on his arm, but he did not seem able to grasp it, and in about 10 minutes he disappeared about 40 yards from the cliffs. Scott was an excellent type of the Scotch professional golfer, race sui generic, unlike the professional in any other game, or the man in any other calling. He was tall, athletic, loosely knit, broad-shouldered, with speech as broad as himself, and the quiet independence of the class. He was born at Earlsferry, Fife, where his parents still reside, learnt his club making in Forrester's shop at Earlsferry, and his golf on the Ferry links, where his brother, A. H. Scott, the well-known clubmaker and player, has his headquarter. He was a good teacher and a good player, rising at times to absolute brilliancy, as on the Saturday before his death, and had the easy " classic " Scotch style. All our best men have been through his hands, and he was the first professional golfer in Sydney, and had been with the Royal Sydney since the club brought him out in 1896. His death is keenly regretted by all golfers. Besides teaching and clubmaking at Bondi, he had been to most of the suburban links, visited West Maitland and Tainworth, and assisted in laying out many of the courses. The last was the new Lindfield Club course, which he laid out in conjunction with Hunter, the S.G.C. professional, who left the other day for the United States. Scott was looking forward to the coming season as the busiest he would have had, and a week before his death showed me big trunks of balls which he had remade and seasoned, and his plentiful stock of finished and unfinished clubs. As soon as the news reached the R.S.G.C. committee they very properly postponed the important fixtures arranged for Easter Saturday and Monday. Scott was unmarried, and had no relatives nearer than Scotland. 1901

A sad end to what might have been a promising career.

William Brown Sime

1877 – 1949

Of all the many golfers and professional clubmakers that Earlsferry produced high among the rankings must be Sime (Bill). Not that he was in the same class of golfer as Braid or some of the other Earlsferry men but he was without doubt one of the most productive designers of golf clubs in the United States if not at the time in the world. We are fortunate in being able to make contact with his relatives and especially his granddaughter, Annie Welborn who not only has visited Earlsferry on two occasions but she has provided us with a wealth of information about Bill Sime both personal and commercial. It was Bill Sime's story that began this lengthy trek over the 50 plus golfers who originated in Earlsferry and subsequently went all over the world to promote the game. The wealth of material we have on Bill Sime does not do justice to this somewhat truncated biography but we retain with thanks the original documents provided by the family as a tribute to him.

Bill was born in Earlsferry on 17th November 1877 in Viewforth which was the family home. This house is immediately to the east of the Town Hall in Earlsferry High Street and its significance increased after his mother's death because Tom Reekie (q.v.) another of the golfing pioneers took over residence in Viewforth but Mrs. Sime retained a small cottage in the garden and indeed the feu extended from the High Street down to the high water mark. At one time therefore she also owned the house built on that area (Beachmont).

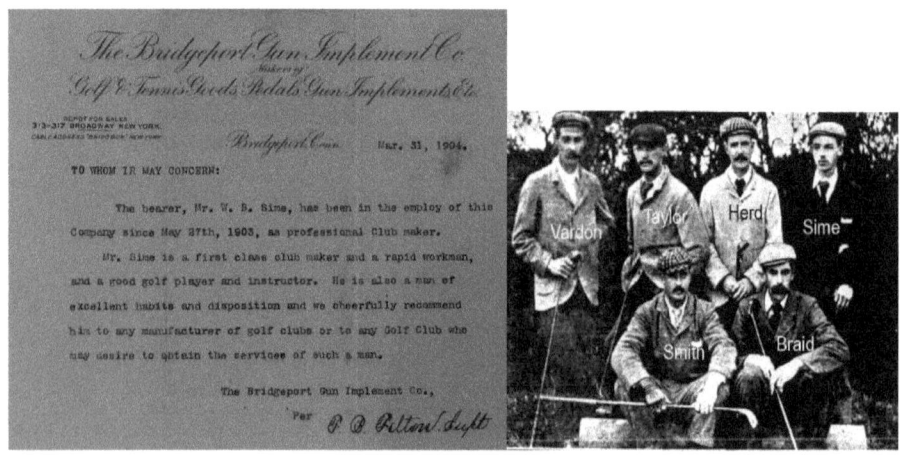

His father was a mason but died when Bill was three years old. Again he grew up in the optimistic golf environment of Earlsferry golfing tract, became proficient as a golfer and did his apprentice almost certainly with Forrester although there is a thought that he may have spent time with Braid at Romford. Of course he was a friend and contemporary of James Braid, Dougie Rolland and the other pioneering stars of that era. Bill perhaps was not such a good golfer as his contemporaries but his skills in engineering and design were very soon put to the fore in America. He mixed with the best of them and there is a photograph of him alongside some of the greats dated 1898 taken we think at the professional tournament at Carnoustie of that year.

He was one of the many who went to the United States almost on spec without a firm position to go to but he was armed with a holograph letter from James Braid extolling his virtues as a club maker. The original survives and we are lucky to have a copy.

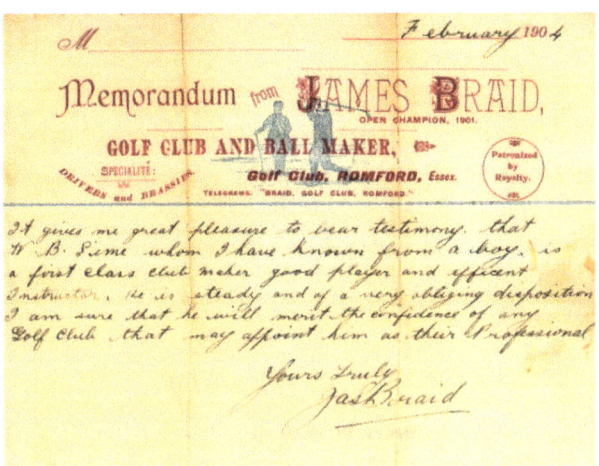

He arrived in America in 1903 although it will be noticed that the date on Braid's letter is the following year which suggests that it was not Braid's letter that got him his first job with Bridgeport Gun Implement Co of Connecticut but he worked there from 27th May 1903 and left in 1904. Putting two and two together it looks as if he worked for this company and then decided to take up professional golf and clubmaking.

He received this testimonial for his time there. There is evidence that he came back to England and was at Wimbledon Park for a short time in 1904.

He must have decided to seek different pastures and it looks as if he received the letter from Braid after he left Bridgeport since he left in May 1904 and Braid's letter is February 1904.

The story goes that he set off for America 1904 armed with lots of ambition and a letter from Jamie Braid commending his skill as a golf club maker. So the conclusion is that he did not do an apprenticeship with Forrester but joined Braid initially at Romford and it was there that he was given the recommendation of Jamie Braid which he took to America with him. By 1904 Braid was the pro at Romford and it is possible WBS learnt his trade with him there. He was relatively older than many of the others who made the trip across the Atlantic but he must have found work quite quickly. It seems that he would teach golf at the country clubs in the summer and then set out to design and make clubs in the winter. One winter he went to a company called Crawford McGregor & Canby in Dayton Ohio. This company originally made lasts for shoes but the owner at the turn of the century decide to start making golf clubs. The history of this company is interesting.

"In the early 1880s, two Daytonians, John McGregor and Edward Canby, became major investors in the Dayton Shoe Last Company, which now became known as Crawford, McGregor and Canby. Of the two new partners, Canby was the more dynamic businessman, but McGregor had a not insignificant role in the company's move into the golf industry. A native Scot, he talked Canby into trying the game of golf, which at the time — near the turn of the 19th century — was practically brand new to the United States. An avid sports enthusiast, Canby liked the game. A visionary as well, he became convinced that golf would become a major sport — and business — in America. He soon began to play a pivotal role in those developments.

By 1910, MacGregor was recognised as the pre-eminent manufacturer of wood clubs. The reputation was further enhanced when Will Sime was hired, in 1912. A Scot who had made clubs for Harry Vardon, J.H. Taylor and James Braid (the famed British Triumvirate of champions), Sime was signed on as MacGregor's chief club designer. He may have been the first in the industry to ever hold that specific title.

The shape of wood heads for almost as long as golf had been played was long-nosed. They looked much like a hockey stick, not surprising in that the origins of the game have been traced to a form of hockey played by the Dutch. This shape, called "long nose," was gradually being transformed, and Sime completed the transition with a shape inspired by the shape of a biscuit (probably roll) his mother baked, called a bap, which was blocky in configuration.

The idea behind Sime's MacGregor "Bap" driver and brassie was that a more compact head could deliver a more solid and powerful blow. The "Bap" was introduced in 1921, and proved extremely successful. For 15 years it was the best selling wood in the MacGregor line, and owing to this success the rest of industry developed similarly shaped heads. The MacGregor "Bap" effectively revised the basic design of the wooden clubhead."

The bap was supposed to have been modelled on the local bread rolls that were available in Earlsferry.

He boarded during this time with the Ullery family at Campbell street Dayton Ohio and it was there that he met his future wife Nellie and they married in June 1916. She was born in 1892 and thus 15 years his junior. They had one child Catherine born in 1919.

MacGregor golf company went through some troubled times and WBS was laid off but he started designing and making his own clubs. That venture did not seem very successful. He joined Wilson in 1917 to 1920 and then rejoined MacGregor in 1920 - when with Wilson he lived in Chicago.

He went back to MacGregors and became the chief designer of clubs and much valued by the company. He was instrumental in founding the McGregor golf course and here he is driving off the first tee at the start of that golf course.

He was with MacGregors until 1938. MacGregor became extremely well known and his imprimatur made a huge difference to sales.

Golf Course Expert Dies

William B. Sime, former Dayton golf club designer and golf course architect, died Tuesday at his residence in San Luis Obispo, Cal., where he had lived the past two years.

He planned several golf courses during 30 years' residence in this area. He was an employe of the Crawford, McGregor and Canby golf equipment company here.

He was a native of Scotland and a member of the Shiloh Congregational church and the Dayton Masonic lodge.

Surviving are his wife, the former Nellie Ullery of Dayton, and a daughter, Mrs. Catherine Hoover of San Luis Obispo.

Funeral services and burial will be conducted Thursday in San Luis Obispo.

He had another period on his own before rejoining MacGregors in 1940 until 1942 with the title of Head of Experimental and Model Design Department. He worked in Tucson Arizona during world war 2 then rejoining MacGregors for a couple years and he found time despite some illness to design the Piqua golf course in Ohio although the website does not credit him with doing so but his family indicated as such. He then retired from MacGregors before they moved the operation to Cincinnati and went to live in California. Where he died in 1949 and here was his obituary.

His daughter Catherine also became a well known lady golfer in the States.

In 1926 he patented a design of a golf club which he assigned to MacGregors.

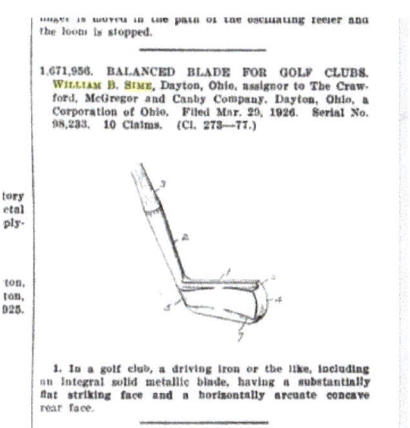

The Simpson Family

Along with the Mackie family (q.v.) the Simpson family probably had a huge influence in the development of golf and the making of golf clubs more locally. There were five Simpson boys and all bar one became professional golfers. Alex (1853), David (1855), Jack (1859), Robert – Bob – (1862) and Archie (1866). Robert became world renowned as a golf club maker in Carnoustie. The Family lived in Grangeview which was a house facing the golf course towards the west end of Earlsferry.

Alexander Stewart Simpson

1853 - 1927

Alexander Simpson was the eldest in the Simpson family of Earlsferry. He was born in 1853 and whilst along with his siblings was a good golfer it was only later in life that he turned his hand to making golf clubs. Initially he was trained as a ship's carpenter and lived in Leith – presumably servicing ships in Leith. However it was not until 1893 at the age of 40 that he joined his brother Jack (John) 6 years his junior in setting up a golf club making business in Edinburgh. The business was in Morningside Road. Currently the address is a shop unit but it is likely that in 1893 it would have been a workshop of sorts. In 1901 he was living in 4 Belhaven Terrace which is about 200 yds from the premises at Morningside Road. His brother Jack (q.v.) went to become professional at Mortonhall Golf club about a mile up the road from Morningside and presumably Alexander continued making the clubs. He was living at 12 Morningside Drive in Edinburgh and died in 1927.

His son, also Alexander, was born in 1880 and probably also worked in the workshop in Morningside as he is shown as living at 1 Maxwell Street in Morningside again close to the workshop. But he went off to America and is shown in 1912 census as living in Brooklyn. He had married Nell in 1907 and he became a golf teacher. They settled in Poughkeepsie but it is not possible to find out which golf course he worked at. However he became a naturalised American citizen in 1922 and his wife Nell followed fairly quickly to be an adopted American – he died in 1968 and Nell in 1962. He is also shown in one census as a golf professional working in a Department Store but it is not clear what exactly was meant by this.

Archie Simpson

1866 - 1955

Archie was the youngest of the Simpson brothers and arguably the best golfer. He certainly probably had the most success as a golfer whilst his eldest brother Robert was the businessman. It is not clear whether he was apprentice to Forrester but it seems certain that he had some training as a young man in Earlsferry. By 1883 Robert was already established as a golf club maker in Carnoustie so it is certain he would have spent some time there with his brothers. However he was a professional in so far as he played high stakes games for money. His cousin was James Braid although there were a number of cousins of James Braid who were competent golfers having been brought up in Earlsferry. He married Isabell Low whose father was carpenter in Carnoustie and made clubs for Robert Simpson. He was married in a sense by order of the Sheriff in Edinburgh – at this time a form of marriage could be undertaken by declarations on oath that they were essential a couple. This is probably the position with this marriage. It saved having to publish banns etc and since at that time Archie was living in the Isle of Wight where he was at the Bembridge club it made sense.

He was runner up in the open championship in 1885 and 1890. He was at Bembridge G.C. in the Isle of Wight, 1890-91 at Prestwick, 1892-93, Carnoustie 91-92 and 93-94 and again 1921. He was professional at Royal Aberdeen, Balgownie between 1894 and 1911 and then he went off to the states in 1911 and was at the Detroit country club and came back in 1921. He went out with his eldest son who later became a professional golfer in USA (see later). He was back in the States in 1922 and laid out Vincennes Club in Indiana. He became an American citizen in 1920s.

His son became a professional golfer and had the pro job at Clovernook GC in Ohio. Meanwhile his father was the pro at Tam O'Shanter CC in Detroit and later in Mariemont in Ohio. His son Archie Jnr died suddenly in 1930 when he was pro at Clovernook and his father took over that job shortly afterwards. As a celebration of the Simpson family the club had (maybe still have) a Carnoustie day each year when they hold a competition and have various events in celebration of the Simpsons and their contribution to golf.

The Dundee Courier published the following obit in 1955 after Archie Snr's Death.

Oldest Link with "Open" is Broken (By Our Golf Writer) If Carnoustie Dalhousie Club had not appointed Bob Simpson of Earlsferry its professional in 1883, Carnoustie golf might never have got out of the rut. For not only did Bob Simpson come to the town; he brought with him his brothers Jack and Archie as assistants. Jack, who won the Open died a young man. But Archie, who moved to America in 1911, lived to become the aides link with the Open Championship. He died in Detroit, Michigan, on Saturday, and was buried there on Wednesday. Carnoustie never could repay the debt it owes to Archie Simpson. It was he who made golf the town's biggest industry. The perfect stylist, his swing was imitated and copied by scores of the young men of the town in the latter years of last century. This swing—"The Carnoustie swing" —became world famous. Local men took it to almost every country in the world and won titles with it. It made many a man's fortune. Its exponents made Carnoustie famous and they inspired the town's traditional belief that its players must always be in the forefront of the game. And it all goes back to the Old Archie, who has died at the ripe old age of 89. He was a great player in an era when professionals had few chances to make good. In 1885 he missed the Open title by one stroke, being second to Bob Martin at St Andrews. It was the same story at Prestwick in 1890, when he finished one stroke behind the redoubtable Mr John Ball. As a match player he was unrivalled. Brother Bob and he whipped the boots off that all-star St Andrews team, J. O. F. Morris and Open Champion Jack Bums. Archie gave Morris a 9 and

8 drubbing over Carnoustie and St Andrews to win a stake of £25, which was big money in these days. In 1887, ...he challenged the 22-years-old Open Champion, Willie Park. Over Carnoustie and Musselburgh Archie trimmed the champ to the tune of 8 and 7. One Carnoustie resident who still vividly recalls Archie in his heyday is Mr John C. Stuart, now, fortunately, recuperating from a severe illness. Archie left Carnoustie to be pro. at the Royal Isle of Wight Club, but came back to Scotland to take over Royal Aberdeen, whose course at Balgownie Bob Simpson had designed. While there, Archie fostered and encouraged a young man called George Duncan, later to become Open Champion. From 1894 until 1911 Archie was pro. at Balgownie, then packed up to go to America. After a spell at Grosse Point, Michigan, he was chosen for the famous Tam o' Shanter Club. He retired, and when his only son, Archie, Jnr., died while pro. at Cloversnook, Ohio, the club asked the old man to succeed the son. He was so popular there that the club instituted an annual golf, sports and social day which out of compliment to their pro. they called "A Carnoustie" worth remembering, for his brilliant play, his fascinating swing, his tremendous personality and his passionate love of the game which without doubt made Carnoustie the golfing town that it is.

David Simpson

1855 - 1943

David was the second son of Alexander and May Simpson. He was born in 1855 and so far as we can see he may have been a good golfer. He did not follow the rest of his siblings into golf club making but he was a player of some renown. He had been trained as a mason and worked all his life as one. However he had an impact even though he was not one of the Simpson professionals or club makers. It is more than likely he popped over to Carnoustie of a Saturday afternoon to help his younger brother Bob in his enterprise there. However when he lived in St Andrews he achieved much on the golf course and was well known as a very good amateur.

His claim to fame in Earlsferry comes from the following cutting from the newspapers of 1896.

> **EARLSFERRY.**
> DISPUTE ABOUT GOLF CLUB TROPHY.—The Earlsferry Thistle Golf Club sued Mr David Simpson, 22 Abbey Street, St Andrews, in the Small Debt Court, Cupar, yesterday for delivery of the gold cross known as the "Glover Cross." Mr J. E. Grosset, who appeared for the defender, said that Simpson had won it twice—in 1888 and 1889—and that it would be his absolute property if he won it three times. Defender had received no notice of any kind of the last competition at which the cross was allowed to be won, and was thus prevented from coming forward. It was averred that the Club was not the same as that in 1888, and it was held that defender had a right to retain this medal. The Sheriff suggested that the action take the form of a reduction. Mr W. T. Ketchen, W.S., appeared for pursuers, and agreed to produce the minute-book of the Club, and the case was adjourned for proof.

It was the tradition if not the rule that if any competitor of a club won the same trophy three times in a row it became his own absolute property. In this instance as can be seen from the report David won the Glover Medal/Cross twice and obviously had he won it on the next occasion he would have kept the trophy. His complaint was basically that the club had advertised the competition in such a way as to make it difficult for him to know of its proposed date and therefore enter. He obviously claimed that the actual competition was invalid because he had not been given an opportunity to take part in it. The court continued the case to enable minute books and regulations to be lodged and so far as we can see they were lodged a few days later, witness this notice.

There does not seem to be a report of what happened "on Tuesday" so we must assume that his claim was withdrawn or refused. However there is an interesting side story to the Glover Cross/Medal. On the Earlsferry Thistle Website there is a section which deals with the trophies and the winners. The Glovers Cross/Medal according to that website was only instituted in 1953 when it was donated by Thomas **T** Glover. We are fairly certain that such a trophy would have been donated by Thomas **C**raigie Glover of Earlsferry House. There are a number of other trophies both at the Thistle Club and the Golf House club which bear his name. Thomas Craigie Glover (he was known as

"Craigie") purchased Earlsferry House which had been built by Admiral William Duddingston in 1806 and took entry to the property in 1887. He died in 1904. Thus if the Glover Cross/medal was donated by TC Glover it must have been with reasonable certainty within his lifetime. The Thistle website mentions the winners from 1953 onwards. Glover was actually captain of the Golf House Club and his daughter Alexa was the first Scottish Ladies' Golf Champion in 1903 (q.v.). Again newspaper reports give the information that the Cross/Medal was won in 1899 so it would be reasonable to assume that David failed in his bid to cancel the competition for this trophy.

His death in 1943 elicited the following obituary.

PASSING OF A NOTED ARTISAN GOLFER.—St Andrews has lost one of its noted artisan golfers of the old school by the passing of Mr David Simpson, who died at his home, Abbey Street, on Tuesday evening. He was in his 88th year and had been confined to the house for a considerable time. Along with Mr Willie Greig he had the distinction of heading the list of veteran members of the St Andrews Golf Club. When they were in their prime they were the Joint-winners of the Glasgow Evening Times foursomes trophy. Mr Simpson won many competitions of this Club in his time and had quite a collection of medals and trophies. He was also one of the stalwarts of the St Andrews team in the inter-Club matches with Leven and Carnoustie, and also played in national championships. The Club several years ago honoured his prowess as a golfer and his services to the Club by electing him life member. Mr Simpson was born at Earlsferry in 1855, and as his home was on the margin of the golf course there it was no wonder that he became a keen golfer. When a boy he made a walking stick serve as a dub in his first efforts to learn the game. He came to St Andrews when quite a young man to be a mason with the late Mr Ness, builder, and he soon became a prominent figure in local golf. He had the temperament for the game and excelled in putting. When 80 years of age he was quite proud of doing hole in one at the Bruce Embankment Putting Green. Mr Simpson was a skilled tradesman and helped in the building of the Burgh School and the tower of St Leonards Church. For the last thirty years of his active life be was on the outdoor staff of the Town Council,- and was particularly good in the laying of pavement. When he retired on reaching the age of 77, the late Mr William Watson, Burgh Engineer gave him an appreciative testimonial for the valuable work he had done for the city. Simpson was the oldest stone mason in the city. A happy domestic event in his life was when he and his wife celebrated their golden wedding in June, 1939. They were married by the Rev. J. E. Houston, at St Clement's Manse, Dundee. Mr Simpson was of an unassuming and kindly nature, and this, along with his pawky humour made him a popular personality with all who came in contact with him. He is survived by his wife, one son, and two daughters, and nine grandchildren. The son, Mr Alexander Simpson, has, like his father, been a golfer from his earliest days, and has a green at Massachussets. His daughter is also in America. The funeral took place at the Western Cemetery to-day (Friday). 1943

His son Alex was the professional at Springfield Country Club in Massachusetts and according to the 1940 US census his son was also employed at the club as an assistant. He and his family lived in Springfield at 17 Southworth Street.

He died in 1956.

John "Jack" Simpson

(29 December 1859 – 9 July 1895)

John known as Jack Simpson was born on 29th December 1859 in Earlsferry. As a boy, Simpson was the favourite caddy of Sir Alexander Grant, principal of the University of Edinburgh, and a regular at Elie GHC where Simpson grew up.

> **The Golf Championship.**
>
> The annual competition for the golf championship was played yesterday over the Prestwick Links. The wind was very boisterous. A strong gale from the north-west blowing across the green made scoring difficult. There was a large field, no fewer than fourteen couples starting. John Simpson, of Eastferry, played a brilliant game, and won the cup in 160 strokes, 78 to the first round and 82 to the second, and was declared the champion for the coming year. The next best scores were W. Fernie and D. Rolland, 164 strokes; W. Campbell and J. Park, jun., 169 strokes; D. Sayers and J. Kirkcaldy, 170 strokes; Mat Allan, 171 strokes; Tom Dunn, 173; Tom Morris and J. O. F. Morris, 174.

He was a powerful but erratic player. He won the 1884 Open Championship at Prestwick with a score of 160 for 36 holes, despite taking a nine* at his second hole. He did not have any other high finishes at the Open and concentrated mainly on club making.

*That is what is said in Wikipedia but the actual score card shows a 7.

1884 Open championship. He managed to capitalise on this to some extent as a result of some widely publicised matches.

THE FIELD, THE COUNTRY GENTLEMAN'S NEWSPAPER. *This week saw a series of very interesting matches played over the links all of which drew after them a goodly following of spectators. On Monday, Mr Edward Blackwell had a single of two rounds with Jack Simpson (professional), Carnoustie. Mr Blackwell is a strong young player, who drives a loose ball. Recently he has been taking the links with remarkably low scores, ranging from 92 to 88 strokes, and it was thought that he would give a good account of himself with his professional rival, who was reckoned as one of the best professional players. The match was two rounds. In the first turn both players were unsteady, their driving being wild and their putting below average. Mr Blackwell stood one up at the end last but Simpson brought the match square at the burn, and the last was halved, the first round ended even. Scores Mr Blackwell 92, Simpson in the second round the play showed much improvement. Both went out in 43, Simpson, however, standing one hole up. Coming home, the professional added another to his lead, but Mr Blackwell afterwards pulled both from him, and at the burn all was level. Mr Blackwell, however, secured the last hole, and with it the game by one.*

E L I E. JACK Simpson —*Mr H. S. C. Everard, writing on "Eminent Golfers," tells the following story of Jack Simpson: — Some eight or nine years or so have elapsed since Mr. Douglas Rolland came into general notice, although, as a matter of course, his merits were well known in the village of Elie, or Earlsferry, his native place. It so happened that about that time Jack Simpson, also native of Elie, and a subsequent winner of the open championship, was at the height of his game, and Rolland and he were in the habit of playing together continually. Nothing much, however, was known of either of them away from their own green, and the first notice strangers had was the intimation that there were two would be glad to play any two amateurs of the Royal and Ancient at St Andrews. Accordingly a foursome was got and Messrs Leslie Balfour-Melville and Horace Hutchinson were the selected champions of the latter Club. The play exhibited by its challengers was a revelation. Jack Simpson was to the full as fine a player as Rolland himself, even if he was not, as the latter inclined to think, a trifle better, and the driving shown by them too simply pulverised their opponents, who never had a chance from start to finish. It happened to be blowing a heavy gale of wind, which exactly suited the play of the strangers, and, as so instance of their great power, an episode may be given which occurred at the very first hole. The gale was of such strength that Mr Balfour-Melville and his partner could not cross the burn at the third shot, although they had three very good drives, and it fell to Jack Simpson to play the like. He called for his cleek whereupon a spectator, himself a first-rate player, and excellent judge of the game, remarked—"I should have thought a man who can drive like that would have risked the burn." With but a three-quarter shot with his cleek, he laid the ball within a few feet at the hole. This particular round was finished in 89, which, considering the day, was extraordinarily fine performance, but it should be added that their putting was scandalously bad. .....Douglas [Rolland], while still an amateur, came very near winning the open championship in 1884. His friend Jack Simpson, however, proved too good for him; but he was in front of everybody else, excepting W. Fernie, with whom he tied at 164 over Prestwick on a very windy day. 1891*

He died of typhoid in 1895.

DEATH OF JACK SIMPSON, (EX-CHAMPION). It is with much regret that we notice the death of Jack Simpson, which occurred at Edinburgh on Tuesday, July 9th, at the early age of thirty-six. He was in his usual health up till two weeks previous to that date, when he was stricken down with typhoid fever which, in this brief space, proved fatal. .....He belonged to a well-known family of golfers. natives of Elie in Fifeshire, where he was born in 1860. Of the six brothers, four have followed the profession of golfers or of club makers, ...and among them Jack was perhaps the most successful of all, although of recent years his younger brother, Archie, has been more before the eyes of the public. ......In 1884 he was at the zenith of his fame, winning the Open Championship over Prestwick with a score of one of the lowest ever recorded over that green in a competition for the Championship Cup. For some years after that date his name is not so frequently found as an aspirant to golfing honours, but more recently he has played in numerous Championship meetings and golfing tournaments, always making creditable scores, though not reaching the prize list. The last occasion on which he played was at the Musselburgh Tournament, on 7th June; and the following week he attended the Championship meeting at St Andrews, but did not play owing to an omission to give in his name before the entries closed. About two years ago Jack came to Edinburgh, and started in business as a clubmaker at Morningside, in partnership with his brother Alick, under the firm of J. and A. Simpson. Shortly afterwards he was appointed professional to the Mortonhall Golf Club, a post which he occupied at the time of his death. Simpson's genial, kindly, undemonstrative nature secured him many friends, who deeply mourn his decease, occurring as it did in the prime of his life.

The address at which he and his brother set up a golf club making business was 128 Morningside Road in Edinburgh and whilst his brother Alexander (q.v.) spent some time at Mortonhall Golf club as the professional there which was just a mile or so away in addition to using the Morningside Road premises Jack seemed to have continued the business. When he died he was stated as living at 128a Morningside Road and there is a possibility that there was, attached to the shop, living accommodation because his brother lived in Morningside Drive 200 yards away. It is difficult to imagine why a former Open golf champion whose game for whatever reason seemed to deteriorate very quickly and who passed the Simpson mantle, as it were, to his bother Archie and his second eldest brother Robert [Bob] who was an eminent citizen of Carnoustie died in relative obscurity. His brothers all otherwise made a great success of their golfing prowess. On the other hand had he survived beyond his 36 years he may have brooked greater success but it seems unlikely. There may be another story here. Jack is shown in the most recent census before his death 1891 as living with his parents in Earlsferry probably in Grangeview although the census of that time was based more upon reported living than actual physical inspection. We hazard a guess therefore that Jack was something of a loner. He never married and it is of some significance that when the Open championship the year after his success at Prestwick was at Hoylake indisposition prevented him from taking part. Thus by 1885 or so he was probably not in the best of health. His death from Typhoid (enteric fever) may have been part of an epidemic in Edinburgh about this time which was a waterborne infection caused apparently by insanitary conditions in dairies producing milk.

Robert Simpson

1862 – 1923

Of all the Simpson brothers who were all proficient golfers it was Robert that perhaps made the most impact on golfers throughout the world. Whilst he never won a major championship he was a very successful golf club maker setting up business in Carnoustie after his apprenticeship with Forrester.

"Robert Simpson, the original owner of Simpson's Golf Shop of Carnoustie, was an all-round club maker, ball maker, course designer, tutor and professional golfer. He was born in Earlsferry in 1862 and was the fifth of six golfing brothers. By 1920 the family had become a great name in the world of golf. His elder brother Jack won the Open Championship in 1884 and Robert twice finished 4th in the Open and was joint runner up in 1893. His younger brother Archie came second twice in the Open and later assisted Robert in the original design of the world

famous Royal Aberdeen golf course. Robert is also famed for assisting Old Tom Morris in the redesign of the Carnoustie Championship Course. Archie went on to become a famous course designer in the U.S.A.

Today, the Simpson's Golf Shop is a testament to this great golfing family and to Robert's high stature in club making which earned him a global reputation for innovation and quality. The Simpson's Golf Shop, situated on the corner of Links Parade (across from the Carnoustie Golf Hotel) has been trading continuously as a golf shop since 1883 and is reckoned to be the 2nd oldest golf shop in the world.

He was keen to play golf from an early age. Living close to the renowned Earlsferry Links Golf Course was a tremendous asset and from an early age he wanted to follow in the steps of other great golfers from his home town. There were many including James Braid, the five times Open winner. Bob's older brothers Alex, Davie (David), Charlie (Charles) and Jack (John) were already keen on the sport, but at that time no one realised what a great star Bob would become. The Earlsferry Golf course was the Simpson brothers' first club which had already produced some of the great names of golf. Douglas Rolland and James Braid, a five times Open winner, had already gone before and inspired the Simpson brothers to perfect the sport.

At the age of 17, Bob Simpson took an apprenticeship with George Forrester whose workshop was close to his home and just across the road from the Elie Links. This was convenient for Bob who honed his golfing skills and when still 17 came second only to James Anderson in an all-comers match at Elie which propelled him forward as an accomplished golfer while still in his teens. His career then took a fast upward turn when he became apprentice to Robert Forgan at St Andrews and it was there his club making talents grew quite noticeably. He had already played many tournament matches with success. While his playing talent was growing, his club making talent was also being noticed having been well schooled by two of the greatest club makers of that time; George Forrester and Robert Forgan. Apart from his club making and golfing prowess, of particular note was his striking character and he was well known as a gentleman and being most polite in all his dealings. Only kind words have been spoken of Bob and even to his death he was regarded with respect as a kind and gentle person.

Such qualities were recognised first when in 1883, at the young age of 20 years, he was hired as a professional by the Dalhousie Club of Carnoustie. The Dalhousie Club founded in 1868 recorded in their minutes "... That after careful examination and conversation.... The Chairman stated that he had seen and played with both candidates and on his recommendation the meeting unanimously resolved to appoint R Simpson, St Andrews, for 12 months at a salary of £5 per annum with the full use of the club's workshop and fittings..."

He never left Carnoustie and the rest is history. Robert's good fortune in coming from a good family with strong golfing traditions and good work ethic, coupled with his polite disposition and self-confidence at such an early age would catapult Bob Simpson into worldwide fame and a prosperous future in Carnoustie.

Bob was well respected by his profession. He was given a portrait by the most famous of golfers, Old Tom Morris who became a good friend. They worked together to redesign the Carnoustie Links course around 1890 when Bob was superintendent of the courses. He may have gained his on-the-job training from Old Tom and is credited with designing course layouts at Royal Aberdeen, Crieff (Ferntower), Edzell, Oban, Moffat, Linlithgow, Alyth and Blair Atholl.

Bob was employed by the Dalhousie Club as ball maker, club maker, teacher and golf course superintendent giving lessons to Dalhousie members and generally overseeing the playing of golf at Carnoustie. During his forty years in Carnoustie he went on to achieve a great deal more. Bob's golf business prospered and at various times his brothers Charles, Jack and Archie worked with him in Carnoustie where they also learnt the skills of club making. At one time he employed around thirty making and repairing clubs and it is estimated he taught a great proportion of the 200 or so professional club makers who emigrated *from Carnoustie to become professional club-makers and coaches in the fast growing golf industry of North America. Bob however was known to have forsaken the alluring aspect of playing for the more practical task of manufacturing but this didn't stop him becoming amongst the best of players.*

He was well respected within his community and became a town Councillor (Baillie) as well as a senior magistrate. His prowess as club manufacturer elevated him to friendships with famous people of his time. Sir Winston Churchill, a well-known golfing enthusiast, and at that time Minister of Munitions stayed at Rockcliff (the Simpson's family residence) as guest of Bob Simpson and his family in 1918 (during a visit to Dundee).

It was widely acknowledged that Simpson's clubs were the new "pattern" welcomed universally by playing golfers. In the manufacture of iron clubs Bob Simpson claimed he had done golfers a service through the patents that bear his name and many commentators agreed with this claim.

A SCOTTISH CLUBMAKER. While fully recognising the enterprise of American makers and the merits of their goods (says a writer in the recent issue of Golf Illustrated), we are told not to believe that club-making is lost art in the old country, have any fear that our American friends are going to swamp an industry that had its cradle in Scotland. The traditions of Hugh Philp, whose clubs combined balance with excellence and beauty workmanship, are still kept alive by the best makers, and none is more keenly imbued with those traditions than Bob Simpson, the head of the famous Carnoustie family of golfers. Bob has just put two clubs on the market which will challenge comparison with any golf clubs that have ever been made, alike from their playing qualities and their finish. The first is the Premier putter, a weapon in shape and design like the creations, the immortal Philp, but made of an alloy malleable cast iron, cast steel, brass, &c. weight and balance of the club are alike admirable, and its finish is perfect. The other club which we have seen is an approaching mashie of entirely novel design. Simpson says he could never see the object of having all iron heads made about double the breadth at the point to what they are at the heel, and has gone upon the sensible principle of making the broadest and heaviest part in the centre with which the ball is struck. The centre of this mashie, accordingly, Simpson has left a diced circle about the size of a golf ball whose base touches the bottom, the face and whose apex surmounts the top by about a quarter inch. Behind this circle the metal is thicker, so that larger proportionate striking surface and greater weight behind the stroke are provided than in any other club with which we are acquainted. Like the putter this mashie beautifully balanced, and its lie is perfect. Its look inspires confidence and the desire to use it. 1903

After he became established in Carnoustie and opened his golf shop at one time or another he employed all his brothers but Archie and Jack cashed in on their success at the Open by going off to the States. But in about 1900 Robert commissioned John Currie and company, and Thomas Currie to build a substantial house for him in Earlsferry although it seems that it was his mother who lived there until her death. That property was Lyndhurst and was built in the front garden/beach area immediately to the south of his old family home at Grangeview cottage. The valuation roll in 1920 shortly before his death shows that he owned the house and garden at Lyndhurst, the house and garden at Grangeview and also a cottage designated as being at Chapel green A guess here is it is the small cottage which lies between Grangeview and Lyndhurst. His brother Charles is shown as living in Grangeview but he is shown as the proprietor of both Lyndhurst and the cottage and no tenant. His father died in 1901 but his death certificate suggests that his wife was still alive and there is a thought that she may have died in 1901 but there is no apparent record of her death.

(1923) DEATH OF PROMINENT CARNOUSTIE GOLFER. Bailie Robert Simpson. Carnoustie people learned with regret this afternoon of the sudden death of Bailie Robert Simpson. Bailie Simpson attended business as usual this morning, and feeling little tired he returned home. 1923 worth about £1m 2021

```
.state, £1848:14: -.

SIMPSON, Robert, Golf Club Manufacturer, Carnoustie, died 1 May 1923
    at Carnoustie, testate. Confirmation Dundee, 24 August, to
    Symon Flett Sutherland, S.S.C., Edinburgh, Adam Oliver, S.S.C.,
    Arbroath, and Robert Sutherland Simpson, Rockcliff, Carnoustie,
    Executors. Will dated 1 February recorded Dundee 22 August
    1923. Value of Estate, £3659:18: 7.
```

Charles Ralph Smith

1871 – 1953

C (Charles) Ralph Smith was actually born in Canada of English father and Scottish mother in Quebec in 1871 but he came to live in Elie aged about 8 where he went to the local school. He lived in 6 School Wynd and his mother was shown as a lodging house keeper. He also had a younger brother James A. Smith (q.v.). He went to school and became very friendly with many of the young golfers of the time including James Braid with whom he had a long lasting friendship. He was Braid's best man at his wedding and he played many exhibition and high stakes games with Braid when in England. He signed on as apprentice to George Forrester where he learnt his trade and indeed it is said he taught Braid how to make clubs because although Braid was a joiner to trade Braid did not actually serve under Forrester.

He started as a pro at Beverley in Yorkshire in 1891 but there is no record of his stay there – the professional at that time was George Sayers (Ben's brother) and it is possible that he was assistant to Sayers. He did not last long there but he came south to London to join the Army and Navy stores as a golf club maker. The story goes that he was back in Edinburgh 1893 for a holiday and happened to meet Jamie Braid in Princes Street where they had a chat and he convinced Braid to join him at Army and Navy stores in London as a golf club maker. They lived in Sydenham together. He left Army and Navy stores and became professional at Hastings club in 1896 - this may have been Hastings and Down Golf club with which Braid had an association too, and he remodelled the course.

Then in 1900 he moved to West Middlesex club until 1921. The West Middlesex club was a prestigious organisation being reasonably close to the centre of London and many exhibition and challenge matches were played there. Indeed there are frequent newspaper reports of himself and Braid playing exhibition matches at the opening of new golf courses and there was often a good purse at stake. He was extensively sought after as a teacher and seemed also to occupy his winters in department stores including Harrods.

He went off to America at the quite late age of 40. His departure itself seemed to have been newsworthy.

> Postman's Holiday Dept.: Professional C. Ralph Smith of Denver's Wilshire Country Club, in Austin on a vacation tour, played the Municipal layout Friday in 73. Mr. Smith, who is 75 years old, played with Jack Gratton of Denver, with him on the "tour," and Dudley Krueger and E. B. "Red" Gober . . . Bill Perkins, noting a 270-yard drive by Mr. Smith, said he'd back the Colorado pair (whose combined ages total 110) agin' any other similar combination in these United States.
>
> Here's One for the Book Dept.:

His first appointment seems to have been in Denver, Colorado where he was instrumental in setting up the Denver Golf Course but he was not there for very long before he was probably poached for a club in Long Island and then he was appointed pro at Canoe Brook G. C. in New

Jersey as immediate successor to Isaac Mackie (q.v.). Indeed this was frequently the case over these years that the Earlsferry "mafia" dictated who followed whom into what jobs. It may have been however that they were the only professional golfers and it seems to have been the height of success to have a Scottish and especially Earlsferry pro at your club.

Whilst at Denver he played in many professional championships and whilst advertising Denver as a golf venue his success was not conspicuous. He played well into his late 70s featuring in a tournament in 1947 in Denver. He retired shortly after this and returned to Great Britain where he lived in Hastings but his fame was such that visits even in his 70s attracted attention as is evidenced by this article.

He died in Hastings aged 81.

Addendum

For what it is worth Smith was a fairly regular pundit to the newspapers and below are some of the interviews he gave.

C. RALPH SMITH. I SHOULD fancy I am correct in saying that Ralph Smith is the best Canadian-born golfer now before the public. Although, however, Smith's early childhood was passed at Quebec, he comes of an English father and Scotch mother, and it is probably from the latter parent that he inherits his golfing skill. When only eight years old the West Middlesex professional was taken to Elie, and at fourteen became formally associated with golf, when apprenticed to that well-known club maker, Forrester. Three or four years were spent in learning all that Forrester could teach him, and then, with a fine knowledge of his business, he migrated to the Army and Navy Stores in Victoria-street. There his complete mastery of his trade was soon recognised, and in a very short time young Smith became manager of the club-making department, having under him such well-known men as Braid, James Allen, Yeoman, Wakerley, Fairful(q.v.), and Neaves. With his time more or less fully occupied, it was, of course, impossible for Smith to get any golf except in the immediate neighbourhood of London, but there he soon made his name known, playing in many foursomes with Braid as a partner, and doubtless deriving vast help from the future Champion. In those days Rolland was a power in the land and one of the early matches in which Smith and Braid engaged was against Rolland and T. Smith, on the Taplow links, the prize at issue being a purse given by the club. The Stores' couple won, but not without lowering the record for the course from 81 to 79. Shortly after this the same couple were opposed to R. B. Wilson and T. Smith, and once again they succeeded in breaking the record, as on this occasion their total for the round was only 77. Finding, as one can readily believe, that Braid was a rare man to have on his side, Smith, in conjunction with the ex-Champion played two money matches against Munroe and Duncan at Chiswick and Richmond, and on each occasion won easily. ......During his residence at Hastings Smith was frequently opposed to Rolland, and, on the whole, had none the worst of the several meetings. He was also busy winning prizes in the professional tournaments, which were held at Forest Rowe, Neasden, Musselburgh, and other places, and was thus constantly playing in first-class company, no mean advantage for a young golfer. ....Every golfer has his good and bad days, but naturally when a man is playing four or five times a week throughout the year on a certain green there comes a day when he can do practically nothing wrong. Such a day seems to have come to Smith when he succeeded in compassing the links of the West Middlesex Club in the extraordinary score of 69. To fully realise the magnitude and brilliancy of this work it is necessary to state that the "Bogey" score at Hanwell is fixed at 78, a proof that the course cannot be done without some hard hitting. I am ignorant of the name of the golfer who was playing with Smith on this memorable occasion, but be he amateur or professional, it is certain that he must have enjoyed his object lesson in the game.....Physically the West Middlesex man is all that one could wish for in a golfer, and he certainly turns his great strength to the fullest account, for it will hardly be disputed that he shines most in the long game. With his brassey he is most deadly, and the length of balls he obtains is at all times wonderful. As, however, he gets nearer to the hole he shows possibly a slight falling off, and he lacks, perhaps, to some extent the deadly earnestness which characterises such men as Harry Vardon.... As a club maker I happen to know that such a grand judge as Braid considers him quite at the top of the trade, and it may, without any fear of contradiction, be said that the ex-Champion's opinion is shared by every member of the West Middlesex Club. Niblick The Illustrated Dramatic and Sporting News January 1903

GOLF AT HARRODS. RALPH SMITH AND THE LADY Mr. Philip Gibbs had an amusing article on Parlour Golf: A Comedy in Old Brompton Road "in the " Daily Chronicle" on Thursday. In the course of it he said, there was one girl who stepped forward with a pretty boldness, which was the admiration of all of us, but I fancy that before she had finished her lesson she wished the floor of Harrods might open up and swallow her into the darkness of the deepest basement. It was Ralph Smith who dealt with her, and he has a masterful way with him, kind but firm, gentle but determined. The girl swung up her driver, glanced at a sister as much as to say "It's a child's game, my dear," and missed the ball by half a yard. 'How utterly absurd," she remarked to herself, the professional, and the world in general. Ralph Smith did not commit himself to an opinion upon the subject of absurdity. But in a strictly businesslike way he put his hands on the club while the girl still grasped it and made her swing to and fro until *her hat was all awry and her face was flushed. "That's better," he said, "have another go at it." She had another go, but before she hanged at the little white ball sitting up perkily on its india rubber tee the professional grasped the lady's hat firmly in his right hand—it was a delightful hat with two feathers which said "What T What?" and held her head down as though he were the executioner of Lady Jane Grey. Presently, after many efforts on the girl's part to hit the ball, always frustrated by the professional before she had time to evade his restraining hand, he raked her left knee in with the crook of a niblick, and proceeded to twist her into a picturesque and easy attitude as though she were a figure of plasticine. "Now!" he said, releasing her. For a moment she managed rigidly fixed in the attitude of a coloured poster on the Underground Railway. Then she came unstuck, as it were, gave a little squeal, and made a vicious whack at the ball. Said Mr. Ralph Smith, "Still, you're getting the idea of it." 1914*

James Albert Smith

1882 – 19??

> Pre-1914. Ralph Smith's younger brother—the late James A. Smith—was professional at the former Oakwood Park Golf Club, Conway.

James was C Ralph Smith's (q.v.) brother and was born in Edinburgh but qualifies for this section by virtue of his residence in Elie with his mother and siblings in 1891. There is a reference to him in an article about his brother and it says as below:

We think he may have been professional at Oakwood Park golf club (which was also a Hotel). However the 1911 census shows our James living in the Wirrel with his family and it says that he is the professional at Bromborough. We are indebted to Bromborough Golf Club and Charlie Abbott who advises,

"James Albert Smith was the Pro at Bromborough for one year..1910-11

He was a PGA member from 1902 ...in 1904-5 he was Assistant to C.R. Smith at West Middlesex ...Bromborough 1910-11....Handsworth 1911-22."

He travelled across the Atlantic in 1922 arriving in Halifax and then he sought entry to USA citing his destination as Denver where his brother happened to be. We guess therefore that his brother probably employed him initially. Thereafter we do not know what he was doing. There is a reference above to CRS having survived his brother but we cannot find his death in either USA or UK. One of the problems of having such a poplar name. He went back acros the Altlantic because in 1928 he arrived again in New York. Although he seems to have predeceased his brother we cannot find any further information on him.

John Nelson Smith

1893 – 1950

We set out the requirements for this research that the golfers who featured in this section should have been born and/or brought up in Earlsferry and become a golf club maker then professional golfer. We thought that this should be extended to include those who may not actually follow the exact criteria but whose golfing exploits nevertheless brought honour and recognition to the golfing ability of those who have learned their golf in Earlsferry. John Nelson Smith more affectionately known as "Jock" was one of these who brought distinction to the name of Earlsferry but in his case he never turned professional golfer but his exploits and name live well on both sides of the Atlantic.

He was actually born in Edinburgh. He joined Earlsferry Thistle and his exploits are best summed up by others below but he is heir to two historical items associated with him. When he lost to Cyril Tolley at Royal St. George's he was given a civic reception in Earlsferry on his return and clapped all the way from the station in Elie to Earlsferry Town hall. The second is that to this day the 18th hole at Elie has a way to play it known as "Jock Smith's line". This entails hitting down the left hand side of the fairway into a small fairway valley. The advantage that this gives is that there is no need to flirt with what is known as the "valley of sin" at the front centre of the 18th Green. He was variously described in these reports as an "artisan" – a peculiarly English trait.

April 1950 NOTED FIFE GOLFER DEAD Mr John Nelson Smith, the well-known Scottish golfer and former Walker Cup player, has died in an Edinburgh hospital. Mr Smith, whose home was at Nelson Cottage, Earlsferry, won the Eden Tournament at St Andrews in 1929 and was runnerup in 1923, 1928 and 1930. He was also British Amateur finalist. He was 57.

THE RUNNER-UP: JOHN NELSON SMITH, A CARPENTER FROM EARLSFERRY, FIFE.

WELL-KNOWN GOLFER DEAD Jock Smith, of Earlsferry John Nelson Smith, of Earlsferry, Fife, one of Scotland's best-known golfers between the wars, died on Saturday. He was 56. Smith, like his famous townsman, James Braid, in his early days, was a joiner, and in bringing his measure of glory to Earlsferry, the well-known amateur kept their native town in the public eye long after Braid had gone into his honourable and lucrative exile as professional at Walton Heath. Jock Smith was a personality quiet and unassuming, pawky, and economical of speech, but with a sense of humour, and the many in the game who knew him, whether as opponent or partner, will regret his passing. Though he never won either the Blue Riband of golf or the Scottish amateur title, he was worthy of either for, brought up on the famous golfing coast, he was a first-class striker of the ball. His favourite club was the cleek, and he had an undeniable mastery of the irons. His career was crowned by promotion to Britain's Walker Cup team in 1930, when the U.S.A. had Bobby Jones in their side. Smith was narrowly beaten by Dr Willing. That British cap followed Smith's bid in the Amateur Championship at Sandwich in 1929, when he excitingly knocked out Johnny Dawson, the fancied American, at the nineteenth in the semi-final, and was beaten by Cyril Tolley in the final. In the Scottish Amateur Championship he was twice a semi-finalist, and he won the Eden Tournament in 1929 and the Evening Telegraph Cup twice. He also on one occasion helped to take the "Evening Times" Foursomes Trophy to his club. From 1928 to 1934 he represented Scotland against other home countries, and played against England for six years without a break from 1929. The "Nelson" in his name he took from an uncle who was professional". (James Nelson q.v.)

March 1930

James Maclean Sunter

1894-1957

Born in Earlsferry in Kilconquhar parish 4th November 1894 and living in Durham Cottage Earlsferry High Street son of Alexander Sunter golf club maker (q.v.) and Jessie Sunter he died aged 62 in Edinburgh. Durham Cottage was so called because his grandmother's name was Durham as was his mother's Christian name and she was part of the Given Family. There were four Sunter families (see Chris Sunter). He was the first officially appointed golf professional at Elie Golf House club and had a shop behind the current clubhouse....it is still there - see photo above.

1921 Golf House Club (Elie).—The annual meeting was held yesterday afternoon, when the Earl Lindsay, Kilconquhar House, was re-elected captain and Mr James Sunter was appointed professional. A dinner was held in the evening, over 60 members being present.

He was active locally on the golf course and had a few triumphs:

1902 GOLF. PROFESSIONALS IN FIFE. ELIE GREEN RECORD EQUALLED. A professional tournament under the auspices of the Elie and Earlsferry Clubs was held yesterday over the fine Links at Earlsferry, which were in excellent order. The prize-money in the aggregate amounts to £60, ten prizes the value of £20 being competed for yesterday, and the remaining £40 falls to be disbursed to-day, when the four lowest scorers compete by holes, two rounds. The entry was disappointing, only 24 professionals entering, Sandy Herd, the open champion; J. H. Taylor, Mid-Surrey; A. Kirkaldy, St Andrews;…… Locally comparatively little interest was manifested in the tournament, and the "galleries" never interfered with the players. FIRST ROUND. ……James Sunter holed the home hole (3) off his mashie.

1920 SCOTS FOR WESTWARD HO! LOCAL YOUTH SHINES AT ELIE. The Scottish professionals' qualifying competition for the forthcoming big event at Westward Ho! which took place at Elie on Saturday brought to the front James Sunter, a local youth who has served under ex-Champion Braid, of Walton Heath. He took first position among the thirteen of the twenty-five entrants who came forward to fight for the six seats. Two rounds were played under perfect weather conditions. There was no wind until the late afternoon, when a southeasterly breeze militated to a slight extent against the homeward scoring. Apart from Sunter's success there was the fine golf of Ben Sayers, the sprightly North Berwick prof., who thirty years ago, in Douglas Rolland day, occupied third place in similar competition. Ben Sayers drove far and sure, and his was the score of the afternoon, and only one stroke behind Sunter's. Sunter gets away a long ball from the tee, has rare touch with his iron clubs, but, like the bulk of the competitors, his putting at times was palpably weak. ……Sunter's prize-money was £10, and the other five Anderson, Marling, Sayers, and Duncan who qualified, each received 17s. For the sixth place Smith, Forrester, and Kirkcaldy tied, and on playing off one hole Smith won in four, Forrester requiring five, and Andrew six. The record of the course is 72 and bogey 182. James Sunter has been round in 69.

We have unusually clear evidence that he was also part time professional in France where he went during the winter as is noted in this newspaper article.

Bruntsfield Links G.C.

James Sunter, professional to Elie Golf House Club, has just returned home after wintering in France, where he has acted as professional at Sospel Golf Course. The weather was cold and wet and one time the rain came down continuously for four days and four nights. The golf course, which is situated on either side of a river, had its three wooden bridges washed away. At other times the dazzling sun sparkled on the snow-clad mountain peaks. Many of the hotel visitors were driven home by the uncomfortable weather conditions. Among the notables Mr Sunter met while pursuing his work as "professional" were the young son of the Prince of Monaco; Mr Clark (and family), of cotton fame, who has interests in Sospel; and Lady Dering, wife of one of our Ambassadors. The " season " closes at the end of April, when hotel and golf course are closed. Mr Sunter was accompanied by Mr Shields, St Andrews, who was secretary for the club. 1925

He left Elie and went to Bruntsfield Links Golf club, Edinburgh in 1931. It may just be coincidence but the distinctive tee boxes of Elie GHC are identical to those at Bruntsfield links.

He married Jean Robertson Scott in Edinburgh 1931.

He gave up the shop at Bruntsfield at the start of world war 2 and it is not known what happened thereafter except that he lived in 30 March Road in Blackhall, Edinburgh until his death. He was still described as a golf professional but where he plied his trade after world war 2 we currently do not know.

Andrew (Alexander/Bowie) Sunter

1884 - 1916

This gentleman is an enigma which we have difficulty reconciling. There were at least two if not three Sunter families in Elie and Earlsferry. There were two Christopher Sunters (q.v.) and there were two Andrew Sunters. One is christened or at least on birth certificate as Andrew Alexander Sunter son of Christopher Sunter and Robina Sunter born on 21st March 1884. So far so good but there is another Andrew Sunter who was born in Leith in 1880 and christened as Andrew Bowie Sunter. His parents are said to be Alexander Sunter and Elizabeth Sunter who had been married in Elie. What confuses the issue is that in the 1891 census living with Christopher and Robina Sunter is Andrew B Sunter who is said to be their fourth son and his age tallies with the one born in 1884. There is a further reference in the card index kept by Cupar Library thus

```
SUNTER, ANDREW
                            Emigrants
Death:  The fourth son of Mr & Mrs.
Christopher Sunter, Elie; he served
his apprenticeship with Mr.A Scott,
clubmaker, Earlsferry and afterwards he
moved to Montrose.  In 1911, he emigrat
:ed to Canda and enlisted for active
service on the outbreak of the First
World War.  He was killed in action on
the Somme on 22 July aged about 30.
He was recommended for a D.C.M.
In East Fife Record:  10 Aug.1916,p.3
```

This card index is made from announcements in the newspapers of the time and its accuracy therefore depends upon the accuracy of the newspaper article. We can further search about his emigration to Canada in 1911. We pick him up as living with his brother in the Bronx in NY in 1910 and he is described as a cook club (whatever that means) but Christopher Sunter his brother is described as a bricklayer but we know that not long after this he started playing professional golf. In 1909 however Andrew Bowie Sunter is seen entering the USA at Boston and he is described as a professional golfer. We have no doubt that Andrew Alexander was not a professional golfer so we must assume for want of any other explanation that he adopted the middle name Bowie when he was living in Bassview with his parents. We believe that the actual, as it were, Andrew Bowie Sunter was a cousin of his.

Yet a further complication is that in the papers which Sunter completed to join the Manitoba expeditionary force in Canada all give his date of birth as 23rd March 1883. The correct information seems to be 21st March 1884. It is most unlikely that he would have made a mistake with his birth date or why we cannot guess – it was not as if he was too young to join up. Perhaps his marriage certificate clears up the ambiguity. He has signed the marriage registry as A. **Bowie** Sunter so it looks very much as if for whatever reason he adopted the Bowie bit later. So we have tracked down the right chap.

He had a fairly good amateur career with Earlsferry Thistle and as can be seen he was apprentice to Scott and moved to Montrose shortly before he was married – it seems that his wife never actually joined him in USA or Canada and he is remembered in both the Montrose and Elie Rolls of Honour. He is buried in Flanders. His wife died in 1971 never having seemingly remarried and they had no children.

Christopher Mitchell Sunter

1878 – 1934

There were four Sunter families in Elie and Earlsferry. The Sunters that lived in Durham Cottage Earlsferry High Street the home of James Maclean Sunter (q.v.); next door to them was Elizabeth Sunter in 1901 census aged 73 and her son David Sunter a mason, and moving to Liberty there were again two Sunter families in the 1901 census, Christopher Sunter Snr. aged 56 described as a builder (mason) and two doors down James Sunter, also a builder/mason. Our particular concern is with Christopher Sunter's family. It does not help that there was also another Christopher Mitchell Sunter of roughly the same vintage as this one although he finished up living in Elie in Woodside and was a prolific builder and developer of property. He outlived his namesake by many years.

Christopher Snr, CMS' father, a mason was born in 1845 and he married Robina Thomson Sunter, one year his junior. They had seven children - Amy, David, Christopher (Jnr), George, Andrew, William and

Jane. We are particularly interested in Christopher Jnr who was born on 13 March 1878 and lived at Bassview more of which in due course*. In the 1901 Census he is described as a mason's apprentice - obviously planning to follow the family tradition.

The work for masons was flagging and a few of Earlsferry's golfers had already made the journey across the Atlantic and on this occasion we think that Christopher Jnr having done some sort of golf club making apprenticeship (his brother Andrew had been apprentice to Scott) decided or was solicited by the senior (John/Jack) Mackie boy on one of his early return visits to Earlsferry in 1906 from USA, where he had gone to seek his luck. It is within the bounds of likelihood that Mackie tempted the young Sunter with the prospects of being employed by Mackie himself. The ship's list of passengers for the 1906 crossing on SS Caledonia to New York in February showed traveller John (Jack) Mackie and his wife and right next to him on the manifest is Chris Sunter who is described as a mason but whose address in USA is shown as being that of Jack Mackie's in Roseville.

He was throwing in his lot with the growth of the game in USA. His fiancée, shortly to become his wife, (she was born in Scoonie) arrived in New York and they were married on 21 August 1907 in Manhattan. They had their first and only child Isabell in 1908 and they are shown in the 1910 census as still living in the Bronx, but he is shown as being a bricklayer so he obviously did not immediately find employment as a golf professional. Although we have a suspicion that in addition to his work as a bricklayer/mason he also took part in professional golf matches and a bit of tuition although not affiliated to a golf club. He features in a few newspaper reports.

> **CHRISTOPHER M. SUNTER**
> Leading figures of the golfing world as well as a large number of other friends attended a funeral service for Christopher M. Sunter at his late residence, 120 Briggs Avenue, Sunday, at 2:30 P. M.
> The Rev. Ernest T. Houghton, pastor of the First Presbyterian Church of Mount Vernon, officiated. He was assisted by the Rev. W. P. Moody, pastor of the Bryn Mawr Park Presbyterian Church. Interment took place in Mount Hope Cemetery.
> Mr. Sunter, who for many years was professional at Dunwoodie Golf Club, died Thursday at his home after a brief illness.
> Delegations attended the funeral from A. G. Spalding and Weber and Heilbroner of New York, where Mr. Sunter had conducted golf instruction classes, and also from the Dunwoodie Club.
> Honorary pallbearers were Frank T. Methven of Rye, Frederick Keddie of Yonkers, Jack Mackie of Inwood, L. I., William Mackie of Port Washington, L. I., Isaac Mackie of Flushing, L. I., and Daniel Mackie of White Plains. Other golfers present were George McLean, Andrew Robertson and Jack Foley.
> Surviving besides his widow, Mrs. Agnes M. Sunter, is one daughter, Miss Isobel Sunter of Yonkers; his

However another significant entry in the census of 1910 is that his brother Andrew B (q.v.) was living with him and was described as a labourer.

The 1925 census shows him and his wife and daughter living at 120 Briggs Avenue, Yonkers but this census does not show his occupation. We know that when he registered for the 1914/18 war draft he was said to be in "sporting goods". And certainly by 1920 he was a golf instructor. Living in 120 Briggs Avenue Yonkers he would have been near Dunwoodie Golf Course. This was one of the pioneering golf courses of this area. The nearby St Andrews Golf Club is reckoned to be oldest formal club in USA but *"Dunwoodie Golf Course, is actually the [nearly] oldest, having been established in 1906 as a private club that claimed Mary Pickford and Douglas Fairbanks Jr. as members."*

This according to the history of Westchester Golf in NY State. So, if he was a golf instructor in 1920 at Dunwoodie and later to the Highland

Park Hotel in Aiken South Carolina where he was in 1934 this was where he ended his career when he died, he may well have counted Douglas Fairbanks Jnr as one of his pupils. By 1930 census he was still living in Briggs Avenue (below) with his wife and as yet unmarried daughter Isabell and he is said there to be a golf professional. He died in 1934 and it is interesting who his pall bearers were (see inset).

*The house in Liberty in which he and his family lived was called Bassview but also at one time Sunterville. It seems likely that this was the last house in Liberty on the south side before Siward Lane and Williamsburgh in that at that time until the house at the east bottom of Siward Lane was built this property would have had a view of the Bass Rock hence its name perhaps.

William Charles Bald Thomson

1910 -2001

William C.B. Thomson (Bill) was born in Earlsferry 5th May 1910

W. C. B. Thomson Wins Guildford Alliance Competition

W. C. B. Thomson, assistant professional to the Berkshire Golf Club, won the Guildford Alliance competition at Tyrrells Wood yesterday with a scratch score of 73. Thomson was formerly an Earlsferry club-maker and in 1931 won the Eden tournament at St Andrews. The field he beat yesterday included A. Perry, Gus Faulkner, W. M. Watt and H. B. Rhodes.

The best score in the qualifying round at Barnehurst yesterday for the Kent County women's foursomes tournament was 79 by Mrs. Patterson and Mrs. Smith.

He and his family lived in Links View Cottage. There is no doubt he served an apprenticeship as a golf club maker but we do not know whether it was with Scott or Forrester although he was a time served golf clubmaker at least by 1931. He was as usual a prominent golfer in Elie and Earlsferry and won a number of medals of the golf club. But he shot to prominence when he won the Eden Tournament at St Andrews in 1931 beating T. Rodger of St. Andrews in the final. By all reports this was not a classic final but it served to suggest to Bill Thomson that a career could be made as a professional golfer standing his experience as a club maker and no doubt reports from his contemporaries.

It looks as if he turned professional (although in these days the requirements were rather less stringent) and shortly thereafter joined Royal Berkshire at Ascot as an assistant. Then in 1933 this newspaper report appeared:

From this it is possible that he was firstly attached to Formby but we know that he turned professional in early 1932 after his Eden win. We have no reference to him having been at Formby or Beaconsfield although he certainly was at Ascot before Bradley Hall. There are at least two discrepancies in this report. Firstly in relation to Elie but he actually won the Eden tournament in 1931

W. B. Thomson Goes to Southport

W. B. Thomson, the Bradley Hall Golf Club's professional since November, 1933, has resigned from his position, and has gone to Southport. He followed Allan Dailey at Bradley Hall, and although he has never won a Yorkshire title he has made a name for himself as one of the most consistent professionals in the county. On several occasions he has been among the leading players in the Yorkshire open and professional championships. He learnt his golf in Scotland and won the Eden tournament in 1930. When he came to Bradley Hall he was assistant professional to the Berkshire Club, at Ascot, and previously had been assistant to Wm. McEwan at Formby, and before that at Beaconsfield.

and not 1930. He played in a number of professional tournaments out of Bradley Hall and lived in Elland in Yorkshire until 1940 when this report appeared.

We cannot find reference to anything he may have done at Southport. However in 1950 he and his family set off for Canada . Whether he left on spec is difficult to know but very soon he seems to have established himself first in Ontario at Port Arthur in Thunder Bay where he was professional for 5 or so years before moving to Southwood golf club in Winnipeg in Manitoba where he remained for 20 years eventually retiring as Professional emeritus in 1975. In the meantime his first wife Connie had died and he remarried Ida Thomson.

> WILLIAM CHARLES THOMSON Friends and family are saddened to announce the death of William (Bill) Thomson at Victoria General Hospital on Friday, May 25, 2001. Born in Eagles Ferry, Fyfeshire on May 5, 1920, Bill immigrated to Canada in 1950 following a career as a Professional Golfer in Scotland and later England. He resumed his golf career as Head Professional at Port Arthur Golf and Country Club in Thunder Bay, followed by 20 years as Head Professional at Southwood Golf & Country Club. Bill received the title of Professional Emeritus on his retirement in 1975 and participated in the Bill Thomson Invitational Golf Tournament which continued for some 25 years. Bill is survived by his daughter Susan of Naples, FL and was predeceased by his daughter Isabelle and his wife Connie, and second wife Ida. A service to commemorate his life will be held on Tuesday, May 29 at 10:30 a.m. at Neil Bardal Inc., 984 Portage Ave., entrance on Aubrey Street with Mrs. Catherine Kinsman officiating.

George Finnick Walker

1870 - ????

There are three Walker Brothers. Robert born 1864, George born 1870 and John (q.v.). George was born in Earlsferry 2nd January 1870. The family lived at almost the last house at the west end of Earlsferry High Street.

We was clearly a good golfer hence in 1896:

> **ELIE**
> ANOTHER GOLF CHALLENGE FOR KINNELL.—A correspondent, writing from Earlsferry on Wednesday, informs us that a second challenge has been issued from this nursery of golf to James Kinnell, who only last Saturday won the match with A. H. Scott for £10. This time the challenge is from Mr George Walker, for £15 a-side, and is to be played off within twenty-one days of this date. It is not likely there will be any hesitation on the part of Kinnell to accept. The match opens up the possibility of another splendid exhibition game. G. Walker has a record for steady play, and though seldom on strange greens can always be relied upon to give a good account of himself. The Ferry folk, like the Frenchman, are never beaten, it is only a reverse. The match will be welcomed at both Leven and the Ferry, though preferable a foursome. Kinnell and a partner say against Scott and Walker, would have been even better.

> Driving golf ball (professionals)—1 Isaac Mackie, Earlsferry, 237 yards; 2 George Walker, Earlsferry.

In 1900 he entered the Elie Games.

There would appear to have been two G Walkers one Earlsferry and one Elie and we are assuming that our George was the professional. He is referred to in a newspaper article as going to Chesterfield *"Jack Duncan is in Stirling, and George Walker goes to Chesterfield in the same line*."* We have found reference also to him being professional and holding the record at a golf club in Gravesend. There certainly was a golf club at Chesterfield but he does not feature in any of the published information about it. We think that if he was at Chesterfield he cannot have been long before moving to Gravesend. From that article it would seem that he was at Gravesend at least in 1905. The course was located between Great Clane Marshes and Filborough Marshes, the clubhouse was near the junction of Higham Road and Castle Lane.

Although the information compiled to do a 1905 year book might well have been out of date.

> The following is from the 1905 Nisbet's Golf Yearbook; Instituted 1903; Membership of 70; Hon. secretaries; F H Stevens, Milton Road, Gravesend; W C Fletcher, 180 Parrock Street, Gravesend; Captain, Robert C Fowle; Entrance Fee £1/1s and Subs, £2/2s; Nine-hole course; Professional, G Walker;

We think it is of some significance that his elder brother Robert Finnick Walker (q.v.) was nearby at Rochester (Oakleigh) golf club between 1896 and 1912. They are probably less than 2 miles apart. Whilst we cannot find any reference to George living in the area at that time he may well have stayed with his brother in Lower Higham. However after that we cannot trace him. Gravesend golf club went into demise after the first world war. The confusion is not helped by the fact that there is another George Walker born on exactly the same day as our George in Roxburgh. He went off to the States and became a gardener and we first thought that the quote above referred to* the "line" as a greenkeeper/gardener rather than a professional golfer. But we consider that they are two different people.

George would have been 45 at the outbreak of world war 1 and it may be that he served in some capacity but strangely we cannot find him in any of the census thereafter. The 1939 census or register was most comprehensive but there seems to be no trace of him. We will continue our inquiries in the hope that we find something more. His brother who was 9 years older died in 1954.

John Notman Walker

1874 - 1945

John Notman Walker is designed as a golf club maker. He was born in 1874 in Earlsferry and he became a golf club maker after initially being a fisherman. In 1901 he was living in Earlsferry High Street and working as a golf club maker. There is no record of him having married and he died in Earlsferry in 9th October 1945 where he was living in the last house in Earlsferry High Street North side. He was still designed as a golf club maker. He did not seem to feature as golfer of any note. He was an amateur and a member of Earlsferry Thistle where he had a handicap of 2 in the early 1900s. On this basis it seems likely that he worked for George Forrester at least to start with but he seems to have stuck to the job of golf club maker for the whole of his life and never moved far away from Earlsferry. Since George Forrester ceased business about 1927 and Walker was still a golf clubmaker in 1940 it is reasonable to suppose unless he was on his own which is doubtful he worked for Scott. We do not think there was any other business in Earlsferry of that nature since Reekie and James Forrester were professionals on their own account and probably did not have any workers. He could only have been employed in St. Andrews or Kinghorn (Gibson &Co) and it is doubtful he would have travelled to either place on a daily basis.

Robert Fenwick Walker

1864 – 1954

Robert was the eldest of the three Walker Brothers (golfers rather than crooners!) George (q.v.) born in 1870 and John Notman (q.v.).

Robert was born 21st May 1864 and we think the family home was the last or second last house on the north side of Earlsferry High Street.

We know nothing about his early days in Earlsferry and the first reference we can find for him is in 1895 when he seems to be at Northampton Golf Club and the fact that he went to his "workshop" suggest that he might have been a golf club maker as well. He seems to have been in charge of that club but we cannot find any other references to him. It seems an unusual middle name such as to suggest that this is one and same person but again we know that his eldest daughter was born in Lyndhurst which is the home area of his wife.

> Charge of Theft from the Golf House.—John Cannon and William Jones, both of no fixed residence, were charged with stealing a golf scorer, a pair of soles, a metal clock, a dozen bottles of beer, and other articles of the value of 25s., at Kingsthorpe, on July 28th, the property of Robert Fenwick Walker, of Kingsley Park, the keeper of the Golf House at Kingsthorpe, of the Northampton Golf Club. They were also charged with stealing two pairs of boots, two jackets, two shirts, a table cover, and some keys, valued at 50s., the property of the Golf Club, at the same

1895

In the census in England in 1901 we do, however, find him in Kent. It is significant that three of his children appear to have been born in Lyndhurst in Hampshire. This is the county from which his wife came originally and noticeably his brother-in-law also. It is possible therefore that between 1896 and say, 1899 he was working in that area. There is likely to be only one golf club that could use his services at that time and that is what is now known as The Forest course as part of Bramshaw golf club. Inquiries continue. By that time he had married Merriam (spelling varies) Purkess and has had four children. We know that they were married in 1892 in New Forest so we can say by that time he was firmly established in England. Interestingly Frank Purkess is listed as golf greenkeeper and living with them – we hazard a guess that he was his brother-in-law.

He was appointed professional at Rochester Golf club in 1896 where he remained according to this report until 1912. In the 1911 census he is shown as living at The Bungalow at Lower Higham and that his son Robert was an assistant golf professional presumably to his father. Rochester Golf Club (Oakleigh Course), Higham. (1891 - 1924) *The club was founded in 1891. Originally a 16-hole course at Oakleigh Farm, Higham. The course was extended to 18-holes in late 1892, it was reduced to nine-holes by its closure in the early 1920s. The club was occasionally referred to as the Oakleigh Golf Club.* The Rochester Club at Higham was listed in the 1924 Golfer's Handbook but it's probable that the course was closed by this time.

The professionals were; C Crawford 1891/2, G Pearson* 1892 -96, R F Walker 1896 – 1912, E N Kettley 1913 and A R Andrews 1914.*Again here it seems that he succeeded G Pearson as professional. If we are correct about his brother George being in the neighbouring golf course of Gravesend it is highly likely that they kept very much in touch.

Robert was attached to Rochester golf club until 1912 but we do not know where he went then. The outbreak of the first world war was likely to reduce the employment prospects. He would have been 48 at this point but he seems to have stayed in the Bungalow until his wife died in 1951 in Chatham and Robert himself died on 6th January 1954 at what appears to be the home of his daughter Janet Fenwick Taylor at 66 Parrock Street in Gravesend.

William Webster

1882 – 1950

He was born in Earlsferry on 18th November 1882, although of some significance is the fact that in the papers relating to his war service in Canada he stated his birth as 18th November 1883 – maybe a mistake, who knows? Anyway he was, we think, trained by Scott as a golf club maker and he lived in Ivy Cottage in Ferry Road. He was related to William Webster Latto so far as we can make out, probably a cousin. He was unmarried so far as we can see. He went across to USA firstly in 1912 and of interest is that his travelling companion was William

Brown Sime (q.v.)and then to Canada and eventually became a golf clubmaker at Interlachen CC in Minnesota.

Interlaken CC and it seems he was recruited from Chevy Chase Golf club (yes - there really is one !)

He is described as such in his application for war service in 1918 although by then he seems to have moved to Winnipeg for the purposes of volunteering for the world war 1. We think that he deliberately decided to join up for the first world war and hence his moving to Canada. He returned to Scotland in 1912 and then back in 1915 before he joined CEF in 1918.

By 1920 census he was back from the war. After discharge in 1918 he returned to Earlsferry and we assume he carried on making golf clubs with Scott until his death in 1950.

Chapter 12
The Ladies

During some festivities of Golf House Club in 1881 T. Anstruther the Member of Parliament for the area mentioned that whilst the men of Elie now had a splendid club it ought to turn their attention to providing something for the ladies. *"It may not be out of place[to] take this opportunity of suggesting to the office-bearers of the Club the propriety of setting aside portion of the Links for the ladies, who, we are informed, are desirous of instituting club. We are quite sure the suggestion has only to be made in order to be taken up and acted upon."*

At this time (late 1880s) ladies golf was competing earnestly with men for press space and the pressure on golf clubs to cater for the ladies increased as the game became more popular and of course later so far as Elie was concerned the involvement of the Duchess of Connaught and her daughter (see chapter 13 Royalty) highlighted that golf was not exclusively a male preserve.

Any initiative to start a ladies' golf club in Elie certainly did not come from the Golf House Club.

> **ELIE LADIES' GOLF CLUB.**
>
> This fashionable and rising watering-place has just added to its many other attractions that of a ladies' golf club. The ladies of St Andrews and North Berwick, Elie's two great rivals, have for many years each possessed both clubs and links of their own, and now a club has been formed for the ladies of Elie, with an influential committee, under the name of "The Elie and Earlsferry Ladies' Golf Club." The links have been laid out in the new recreation park, immediately behind the Marine Hotel, by the popular local golfer and club maker, George Forrester. In many respects the Elie ladies' links surpass those at St Andrews and North Berwick. They do not consist merely of putting greens, but allow room for the display of skill in both the long and the short game. Under the rules the club will consist of lady members, a limited number of gentlemen honorary members and associate members, consisting of boys and girls under the age of sixteen. Meetings are to be held for competitions in each of the months of April, May, June, July, August, and September, the first meeting being held on Friday the 18th April. Already the club has received from Messrs Hamilton & Inches a very handsome "Challenge Medal" to be competed for annually. Ladies or gentlemen desirous of joining the club should communicate with D. W. Marwick, W.S., 116 George Street, Edinburgh; or H. M. Ketchen, the Bank, Elie, the hon. secretaries.

Initially the club was formed with the intention of using what limited facilities there were in the area behind the Marine Hotel (the Recreation Park). This was the report in 1890. At this point the Recreation Park only had half of its subsequent land and the ladies golf course would therefore have been relatively short.

> **ELIE.**
>
> LADIES' GOLF TOURNAMENT. — The annual tournament of Elie Ladies' Golf Club took place on the new ladies' course on Monday. Twenty-seven players started, the play being two rounds of nine holes each. This is the first year of the new course, which was found to be a very good one.

In 1887 came this notice which does not make sense because we understood that the Recreation Park was not operational until 1889. Perhaps it is the area behind the Marine Hotel that was laid out as a golf course.

> **LADIES' GOLF TOURNAMENT AT ELIE.**—A tournament was held on Friday on the new nine hole course laid out in the recreation park. The putting greens have been much improved, and consequently there were a large number of entries. A large number of spectators turned out to follow the players on their rounds. Several competitors both in their driving and putting showed that they could give account of themselves on the " big" links and indeed the scores of the winners would be very difficult to beat. On Friday afternoon the singles were played off, two rounds which resulted in two ladies " tying" for the first and second places respectively, and three ladies tying for the fourth place, viz:—Miss Lizzie Prain. 35. 36—71 : Mrs Kirkwood. 39. 35—74 :

This raises an interesting proposition. We know that the sponsors of the Recreation Park approached the Council in 1889. Their approach was rebuffed but they went ahead and took a lease of the southern part of the park and then almost immediately held a golf competition on it.

> **LADIES' GOLF CLUB AT ELIE.**
> Elie, which is a rising watering place, has just added to its other attractions that of a ladies' golf club. The ladies of St Andrews and North Berwick, Elie's two great rivals, have for many years each possessed both clubs and links of their own, and now a club has been formed for the ladies of Elie with an influential committee under the name of "The Elie and Earlsferry Ladies Golf Club." The course has been laid out in the new Recreation Park immediately behind the Marine Hotel by the popular local golfer, George Forrester. In many respects, the Elie Ladies Links surpass those at St Andrews and North Berwick. They do not consist merely of putting greens, but allow room for the display of skill in both the long and the short game. Under the rules the club will consist of lady members, a limited number of gentlemen honorary members and associate members, consisting of boys and girls under the age of sixteen. Meetings are to be held for competitions in each of the months of April, May, June, July, August, and September, the first meeting being held on Friday, the 18th April.

We know that Elie and Earlsferry Ladies Golf club was formed in 1884. We do not know where they played their golf but it seems highly likely that in 1884 a ladies' golf club would probably only have had a putting green on which to play. There are various hints to that in the newspapers of the time. In this 1890 excerpt it says that the course laid out by George Forrester surpasses those of St. Andrews and North Berwick in that they do not consist of "merely putting greens" but allow room for the display of skill in both long and the short game. This suggests that in 1890 most ladies would be playing golf on ground on which the holes were not much longer than a modern putting green. Indeed this is where the St. Andrews Ladies' started to play their golf on the putting green alongside the first fairway of the Old Course which was originally known as the "caddies" course but was sort of acquired by the ladies golf (putting) club. This ground is known now as the Himalayas and is not more than a longish, in modern terms, putting green. There is a distinct possibility that this is what is referred to in the article quoted above. In other words the actual length of each hole was not much more than tens of yards at the very most in today's parlance. There is a suggestion that the ladies played initially on the main golf course on the Earlsferry side but this is unlikely since the length a lady could hit a golf ball standing the equipment and clothing she was expected to wear would have made a full 18 holes on the Elie Links beyond her. This came later (see below). It is significant also that the Elie Ladies' club also had a number of men members. Why should men become members of the ladies' club if they were actually playing over the same course? The suggestion is that they were not. They were actually only putting and a wee bit more. If you look at some of the results of the ladies and gentlemen in the newspapers you realise that the course on which they made these scores must have been very short by today's standards. In 1887 the winner of the Ladies golf competition managed 18 holes in 71 shots. As an example, when the Melon Park - at least the south side - was assimilated into the Elie golf course there was enough room according to the layout for three holes in an area bordered by a fence drawn from the quarry to the GHC and the wall of the houses of Willliamsburgh. The first hole was played from a tee just to the south of the current 18th green to a green close to the then gas works. This hole would have measured almost 100 yards and the second hole from a tee beside the gas works to a green on the Elie side of the wall measures only just over 100 yards. Not only that if you look at the original golfing tract in Earlsferry it was said to be 1500 yards long and consisted of 11 holes. The holes cannot have been longer than 200 yards on average.

This then raises further questions. In 1884 at least until 1900 it looks as if the ladies of Elie Ladies' Club may have only been putting. But where were they putting? It is not thought that there was any such facility at the Golf House Club. Latterly in the Recreation Park in 1912 there was a putting green but the Recreation Park, the forerunner of the Sports Club and Ladies' Course, was not established until 1890 after a series of meetings about it, which resulted in some of the citizens of the village taking a lease from the farmer of part of what became the Recreation Park. There is a statement in these newspaper articles that the area laid out by George Forrester for the ladies was just behind the Marine Hotel. Whilst this also is a relatively accurate description of where the ultimate Recreation Park was it suggests that the area eventually used was much smaller than the southern half of that park. There is another hint in the article of 1891 that anyone wanting to join the ladies club should apply to D.W. Marwick in Edinburgh who is the secretary. Mr Marwick, an Edinburgh solicitor, was also the secretary of the Marine Hotel Company of Elie which suggests that the Hotel may have had some involvement in the ground of the ladies' course at that stage. Indeed in an article of 1889 (note before the Recreation Park was up and running) it says that the hotel stands….in front of …. "what used to be known as the Ladies Links and which, we hear, are again to be given up to fair golfers." This is a very strong hint that before the Recreation Park and the official ladies' golf course there was a ladies' links available behind the Marine Hotel. It is therefore safe to conclude that from 1884 at least until the turn of the century when the ladies' course was up and running there was an area known as the Ladies' Links on which the Elie ladies' golf club were able to play golf. We also conclude that the length of the holes were not much more than a few tens of yards.

This might explain why there seemed to have been an Elie Ladies' Golf Club in 1887 and yet the Recreation Park was not constituted until 1889. It is highly unlikely that they would be able to play on the main GHC course at that early stage of its existence.

> The first competition for this season of the Elie and Earlsferry Ladies' Golf Club was held on Friday. In the ladies' singles competition the first scratch prize was won by Miss Pearson, with a score of 116 for the twenty-seven holes. Miss

This calculates at an average of 4 per hole. We very much doubt that this would have been on a golf course measured by modern standards and most certainly would not have been in the extended course.

However the first competition on the main course was reported thus.

1897 ELIE AND EARLSFERRY LADIES' GOLF CLUB. The Elie and Earlsferry Ladies' Golf Club, which has recently been formed, and, by consent of the joint green committee, admitted to the long links, was, on Thursday, July Ist, inaugurated by an open competition, in which members from the Burntisland, Leven, and Lundin Ladies' Clubs took part. Ten couples started in very favourable golfing weather, from the Golf-house end, when, after making the round of eighteen holes*, they again assembled, tea being kindly provided by Miss Orr Paterson........[At] the close of the proceedings, Mr. Bethune of Blebo, a veteran golfer, who has seen more of the game than most men, in a few well-chosen remarks, congratulated the club upon the auspicious beginning which had been made, referred appreciatively to the immense improvement in ladies' Golf in Scotland, ...and, in conclusion, wished the Elie and Earlsferry Ladies' Golf Club all success in what Mr. Arthur Balfour calls "the most difficult of games." Mr. Bethune's good wishes for the future prosperity of the club have at present every prospect of being fulfilled.

*The winning score for 18 holes was 106.

The only rational explanation we can give for these discrepancies is that there was an Elie Ladies' Golf club and an Elie and Earlsferry Ladies' Golf Club. In 1891 there was this report

> **ELIE AND EARLSFERRY LADIES' GOLF CLUB.**
>
> This club's season was on Friday brought to a close with the most successful meeting of the year. The day was good, and there was a large turn-out of competitors. In the ladies' singles, the Cairnie challenge cup, held by the winner for a year, and the Thomson prize, presented to the lady member of the club making the lowest handicap score, were won by Miss D. Ferguson with the score of 71, less 3=68. For the Taylor prize, presented to the lady member making the lowest scratch score, Miss May Thomson and Miss D. Ferguson tied with a score of 71. In playing off the tie, each returned a score of 35 for the

The report goes on to mention that some gentlemen also took part and the winning score over 18 holes was 62!

In 1897 the club was allowed to play on the "big" course but this was an exception and there was no accommodation in the main club for the ladies. By the turn of the century, notwithstanding the apparent hostility of the GHC there was firmly established on the Recreation Park a 9 hole golf course but no accommodation – the Pavilion was not erected until 1912. However the ingenuity of the fledgling club was exhibited by the building of shelter/shed which ran alongside the wall of Marionville and which they shared with the tennis courts that had recently been built and this was to serve as changing accommodation until 1911.

> **ELIE LADY GOLFERS' NEW CLUBHOUSE**
>
> **INFORMAL OPENING.**
>
> Elie Ladies' Golf Club entered on a new era by the informal opening of their new clubhouse, which is built at the north corner of the golf clubhouse, and communicates with it.
>
> The ladies' clubhouse has a commodious clubroom, cloakrooms, and convenient golf lockers.
>
> The members are grateful to some of the members of the Golf House Club, who subscribed the cost of building their clubhouse, and they themselves met the cost of furniture and furnishings. Already there is a big increase in membership, the roll now standing at 120.

As for acquiring more permanent accommodation after being allowed on one occasion to play on the "big course" that was to come later and the full shenanigans are set out in Drysdale's book on the centenary. A start was made in 1929. But now the Ladies' Golf club have their own very functional and up to date facilities which have been acquired by the simple expedient of persistently adding bits onto the Northside of the GHC clubhouse. The relationship between the Ladies and the GHC have moderated quite substantially over the years and now there is an attempt by the GHC to allow ladies to join the previously all male GHC. The current thinking on diversity being that single sex clubs are anathema to any right thinking people in the 21st Century. It was, naively perhaps, thought that this diversity would have been welcomed by the ladies not least of which it meant that they could play off the first tee before 10 am which the members of the Elie and Earlsferry Ladies club were not permitted to do! Surprisingly (well, perhaps not) very few have taken this opportunity to become lady members of the GHC and indeed attempts to amalgamate the two clubs have been more fiercely resisted by the Ladies' Club than the GHC. Not surprising when the subscription for membership the ladies have to pay is substantially less than that which is paid by a member of GHC. Of course the GHC have to maintain their golf course as well as the clubhouse and the Sports Club whereas the ladies merely make a pro rata contribution to these costs.

Elie and Earlsferry Ladies' Golf Club has been a conspicuous player in the development of golf especially in Scotland. The first Scottish Ladies' Golf Champion in 1903 was a member of the club.

Alexandra (Alexa) Malcolm Glover

1882 - 1933

She was the youngest child of Thomas Craigie Glover an engineer who had made a fortune in India.

It was here in Earlsferry that Alexa Glover became a world class golfer under the tutelage of Andrew Scott (q.v.). She spent countless hours as a young girl playing golf over the Earlsferry tract and latterly the Elie and Earlsferry golf course and the Ladies' course. There is a story that when her father, Craigie Glover, purchased Earlsferry House he had a turret/watchtower added to it from which with an uninterrupted view of the entire golf course he could monitor his beloved daughter's progress. It is said, however, that Alexa was not exactly happy with the scrutiny that this tower provided. If that was the case then his enthusiasm for the talents of his daughter certainly paid off. Alexa Glover was only 19 when she won the first Scottish Ladies Championship. She was a graceful golfer, played in many British events and was a member of that first Scotland international team in 1902. Her golfing progress was well known. But she held a + 4 handicap and the LGU handicap of scratch. She was a teenage prodigy and still only 19 when she won the championship. When the result reach Earlsferry …..intense satisfaction prevailed….. the bell of the town hall was rung and flags were hoisted and later Mr Glover entertained a large company in Earlsferry town hall.

In 1903 there was the first "closed" Scottish Women's Golf Championship which was held at St. Andrews. It was "closed" in that only Scottish golfers could take part. Alexa won the championship at the final hole. This is part of the report of the occasion.

THE CHAMPION Miss Glover, has twice appeared in the Open Ladies' Championship—She also secured a gold medal in a competition held at Cannes. Last year at Gullane she took a conspicuous part in some matches played there, practically carrying everything before her. ....Whenever the result reached Earlsferry, Miss Glover's present residence, intense satisfaction prevailed. The bell of the Town Hall was rung, and flags were hoisted. Miss Glover has for some time past drawn a good crowd to follow her play. The local professionals found themselves unable often to allow her half a stroke a hole. Her round for the links there is 84, and the ladies' golf course (nine holes), 30. Mr A. H. Scott, the golf club professional, initiated her into the game and her success reflects credit on his tuition. Her father, Mr T. C. Glover, has lent considerable aid financially and by personal exertions to have both courses at Elie brought to a perfect state, besides being the means of encouraging professional matches, and that makes the success of Miss Glover all the more popular.

No handicap was enough to deter her exploits.

> Elie Ladies' Links.—The usual Saturday afternoon mixed foursome competition was favoured with a glorious day. Fifteen couples competed. The match caused some excitement by Miss Alexa Glover playing with one hand, having not quite recovered from her cycle accident, and with her partner were only defeated in the final.

By all reports she was a young lady of immense character, hardly ever apparently without a cigarette in her mouth, and occasionally fell foul of the law.

FIFE LADY MOTORIST FINED Miss Alexandra Malcolm Glover, sometime residing at Earlsferry House Elie .. was charged at Cupar Sheriff Court this afternoon of having on Friday 6th October driven dangerously within the High Street and St Andrews Road ..Anstruther at an excessive speed in a manner that was dangerous to James Lawrie builder, William Drysdale police constable and Alexander McHardy police sergeant, and other lieges who were then on the road causing the motor car to swerve from side to side on the roadway, and driving it round a corner at the junction of St Andrews Road and High Street without slackening speed. Police constable Drysdale, Anstruther, deponed that Miss Glover on the day in question was driving her car through the burgh at a speed of between ten and eleven miles per hour; Sergeant McHardy, Mr. Lawrie and himself had difficulty in getting out of the way*. The corner on which she swung round was a very dangerous one, from the Shore Road to the Clydesdale Bank there were five turns. ....James Lawrie a builder in Anstruther in answer to the fiscal said the car was going fast enough for the place it was in – he did not think it was being driven in a manner which was likely to be a danger to the lieges. Sgt McHardy said that his opinion was that Miss Glover had lost control of the car. Lawrie shouted as she passed him that it was something terrible. The Sheriff – he seems to have got over it - his alarm.   Fiscal – he has cooled down but at the time he was very much struck. Sgt McHardy – Yes he was. Proceeding, McHardy said that Miss Glover had so often come through Anstruther and driven her car in such a reckless manner that the people came out of their houses to watch her as she passed. The sheriff found the charge established and fined Miss Glover the sum of £3. He said he could never sanction motor cars going through town and particularly at dangerous corners at so dangerous a speed as 10 miles per hour**.

*I am pleased to say that in my experience the training of police officers is now such as to enable them to get out of the way of motor cars except if there is a possibility of the speed limit being exceeded. However I wonder where these three people were standing.

**One wonders whether this is an expression from the bench that his lordship would have later preferred not to have expounded.

She was a prominent member of Elie and Earlsferry Ladies' Golf club and was responsible for pioneering that club onto the Ladies' Golfing stage to be followed by Madge Maitland and Helen Holm among others.

(For fuller details see Elie and Earlsferry Ladies' Golf club 1884-2022 by Agnes Lind)

Alexa never married but died in 1933. It was a surprise to discover that her death was reported widely in England. No less than seven local English newspapers - after a cursory search - carried a report of her death, such was her popularity.

Chapter 13
Royalty

There were a number of factors which gave rise to the importance of Earlsferry and Elie in the development of the game over the years. The arrival of the Railway line was obviously one of the most important but also the connection with the villages to Royalty increased the profile of the golf course and the Golf House club in particular. The Golf House club would have mounted a major coup had it managed to attract Royalty to its membership. It order to be designated as a "Royal" club it was necessary for a member of the male royalty to become an honorary or actual member. It would therefore have been able to call itself "Royal Elie and Earlsferry". That accolade for such a fledgling club would have been colossal for the future of golf in the East Neuk and Elie and Earlsferry especially. It may have been, therefore, that the first Royal connection, with Prince Leopold one of Queen Victoria's children, had an ulterior motive.

In 1877 a mere two years since the incorporation of the club, it became known that Prince Leopold the youngest son of Queen Victoria was due to visit St Andrews to play in the autumn meeting. He was an enthusiastic golfer and had been Captain of the R and A the preceding year so his attachment to golf was well known. He was a chronic haemophiliac and golf had been recommended by his physicians as the sport least likely to cause injury. All reports suggested he was quite a good golfer. After his game on the Old Course he was expected to visit Balcarres the seat of the Earls of Lindsay. This was was an opportunity not to be missed.

Sir Coutts Lindsay a member of GHC extended an invitation to the Prince to visit the Club. The East Fife Mail reported the events thus:

At the request of Sir Coutts Lindsay, the Elie Golf House Club placed their Golf House at the disposal of the Prince, who was expected to visit the Links on Saturday, but in the morning Mr Ketchen, the secretary, received a note intimating that as His Royal Highness felt slightly fatigued by his journey of the previous day he would not avail himself of the privilege so kindly offered. The inhabitants of Elie and Earlsferry nevertheless did not give up all hope of receiving a visit from the Prince, and there was a very creditable display of flags and bunting--this being the first time the towns were decorated for Royalty since 1822, when George IV sailed up the Firth to Edinburgh. Their labours did not go unrewarded, for it transpired that arrangements had been made for a visit of the Prince to the links to the eastward of Elie. About half past one o'clock the party, which included all the guests of Sir Coutts, Lindsay, left in half-a-dozen open carriages, ... The cortege proceeded ....round by Kilconquhar Mains and Kilconquhar, entering Elie about two o'clock by Park Place.

The prestige that the GHC could have gained had the Prince visited was only slightly dented by the fact that he was a bit tired and did not manage to make it – despite this setback he did visit the villages and spent some time in and around Ruby Bay and the Ladies' Tower. However for a golf club only two years in existence it certainly was a feather in its cap over other such golf clubs. The publicity achieved as a result of the "offer" did not go amiss but the accolade of having invited royalty obviously marked the GHC with the correct pedigree. There is a sneaking suspicion that had he accepted and been able to visit the club an invitation would have been extended to him to become a member.

It was Andrew Scott who managed to secure as much Royal Patronage as Elie and Earlsferry could expect. In 1902 the then Prince of Wales (later George V) changed the Royal warrant holder of golf club maker from Forgan in St. Andrews to Scott of Earlsferry. This connection apart from being very good for Scott's business also put Elie and Earlsferry on the map. It is for certain that the Golf House club may have missed a trick here. Had Andrew Scott been appointed professional to Elie Golf House club we hazard a calculated guess that the Royal connection could have been cemented. However at that time (the GHC was a young club) there was still a resistance to acknowledging the existence of golfers to whom golf was a paid profession. Scott was granted a Royal Warrant to make golf clubs for the then Prince of Wales and he continued the accolade when the Prince ascended the throne as George V. It is likely that the Prince of Wales might have seen some of Scott's clubs at an exhibition in St. Andrews.

However, it was probably the visits of another of Queen Victoria's offspring which put golf and the course firmly on the map. The Duchess of Connaught was the wife of Queen Victoria's third son and her visits to Elie along with her daughter Princess Patricia over the next five or so years firmly put the golf course on the social map. It was hardly surprising that immediate honorary membership was accorded to them. The Marine Hotel thereafter in its publicity referred to the Hotel as "patronised by Royalty" as did Mr. Outhwaite's motor car business in Cupar! It was reported thus:

ROYAL VISITORS TO ELIE. *For some weeks back rumours have been going about Elie and district that a number of Royal visitors were coming to Elie. A fortnight ago, the rumour was to the effect that the children of the Prince and Princess of Wales were to come, but this was denied, and it became known for a certainty by the end of last week that apartments had been taken in the Marine Hotel for H.R.H. the Duchess of Connaught, and her youngest daughter, Princess Patricia of Connaught. Keen interest was everywhere excited over the welcome news, and on Monday forenoon, when the Royal visitors were timed to arrive at Elie station with the train leaving Edinburgh at 8.50, a considerable number of people congregated in and around the station. The Duchess led Princess, with Miss Polly, Captain Graham, and the Hon. Myles Ponsonby, as attendants, and their servants, travelled in a special saloon placed at their disposal by the Railway Company, and reached Elie shortly before eleven o'clock. The saloon was detached from the rest of the train, and brought to the south*

platform. On alighting, the Duchess was immediately recognised, and was heartily cheered, and repeatedly bowed her acknowledgments. The cheering was renewed on H.R.H. stepping into the carriage in waiting. In driving between the station and the hotel, the reception was equally hearty, and the Duchess looked much pleased at the cordiality of her welcome. Accompanying the gentlemen attendants was Mr Marwick, Edinburgh, the secretary of the Hotel Company. From the flagstaff on the Toll Green, the Royal Standard was floating in the breeze, while the burgh flag of Earlsferry was also hung out at the Townhouse of the Royal Burgh. At the Hotel and Golf Clubhouse flags were also displayed. After a short rest, the Duchess and Princess went for a motor drive in the early afternoon, the motor car being lent by Lord Balcarrell, M.P. The drive was to the east as far as Anstruther, and back. At five o'clock the Royal party had their first round of golf on the Elie Links. The wishes of the Duchess to have a quiet game without any followers was generally respected, for on their arrival at the first teeing ground very few people assembled to see the start. Mr A. H. Scott, Earlsferry, one of the local professionals, had previously been engaged to go round with the party, while Mr James Keddie acted as caddie, assisted by two St Monans boys. The Duchess was partnered by Mr Scott, and Miss Pelly by Mr Ponsonby, while the Princess had a single game with Captain Graham, D. Patterson acting as their caddie. A game of 10 holes was played, and except at the third hole, there was nothing like a crowd. The foursome resulted in a win for the Duchess by two up and one to play. In the forenoon, a special meeting of the Golf House Club was held, and on the motion of Captain Outhwaite, the Duchess and Princess were unanimously elected honorary members during their stay in Elie. The weather during the whole of Monday was delightful, and the Royal visitors could not have seen Elie and district under better weather conditions than that which prevailed. The Duchess of Connaught and Princess Patricia had two rounds of golf at Elie on Tuesday. In the forenoon the Duchess, partnering A. H. Scott, played a full round against the Hon. Myles Ponsonby and Captain Graham, the Duchess and partner winning by two holes. Princess Patricia played a round with Miss Polly. During the afternoon the party spent part of the *time on the beach. They had also a visit from the Countess of Crawford. Later the party had another round of the links, the Duchess partnering Mr Scott and Captain Graham Miss Pelly. The Duchess and partner won by three and two. Princess Patricia played a round with the Hon. Myles Ponsonby. The Duchess of Connaught and Princess Patricia were again favoured with fine weather, and played two rounds on the Elie links on Wednesday. In the morning the wind was somewhat gusty, but this did not seem to interfere with Her Royal Highness's game, which was very steady, especially on the putting greens. Partnering A. H. Scott, Her Royal Highness defeated Princess Patricia who was partnered by Captain Graham, the bye being halved. In the afternoon Her Royal Highness played a single game with Miss Pelly, while Princess Patricia, partnering A. H. Scott, took part in a foursome against the Hon. Myles Ponsonby and Captain Graham. Her Royal Highness has expressed her appreciation of the excellent condition of the Earlsferry Links. September 1906.*

For the next few years a similar excursion was enjoyed but the extent of the publicity was much reduced.

She presented a cup to the GHC and the "Duchess of Connaught Cup" is still eagerly competed for by the current membership.

Chapter 14
James Braid

It is only right that James Braid (Jamie) should be given a section all to himself. Although he was not the first Open golf champion to hail from Earlsferry - Jack Simpson predated him - he was without doubt the greatest export and during his reign he was the icon of the game along with Vardon, and Taylor. This was especially at a time when the growth of the game both in this country and abroad resulted in universal approbation.

1870 -1950

Harry Vardon, the record holding six-time winner of the Open, with five-time winner James Braid.

Much has been written of his exploits elsewhere. Bernard Darwin wrote an excellent biography of Jamie and to that source readers should go for fuller information. This entry will be restricted to his activities in and around Elie and Earlsferry.

He was born in Liberty Place according to the birth certificate. It has always been assumed that Liberty Place was in Liberty the small settlement just to the east of Earlsferry which became conjoined with Williamsburgh and Elie in the 1860s. However looking at the census of 1871 the cottages at Grange Farm are described as being in "Liberty Place". Thus whilst Jamie may have been born officially in Liberty Place it seems highly likely that this was at his parents'/grandparents' home at the cottage for the ploughman of Grangehill farm. They eventually moved into Linmara in Earlsferry High Street prior to 1891. Jamie is shown in that census as being a joiner and living in that house. His father by that time was a forester rather than a ploughman.

During his childhood and adolescence like so many of the youngsters of Earlsferry he honed his golfing skills on the golfing tract at Earlsferry and became a proficient and productive member of Earlsferry Thistle Golf club. He did not however take an apprenticeship with any of the golf club makers in Earlsferry at that time so to some extent he was unusual in that he did not consider that golf club making and golf itself was likely to be his future career. Initially he worked as a joiner in St. Andrews then moved to Edinburgh. It is suggested that his parents neither of whom had much inclination for the game counselled against him becoming an apprentice to Forrester. The Earlsferry Thistle Golf club website contains much of this local information.

His victories in the Open Golf Championship 1901, 1905, 1906, 1908 and 1910 are well documented elsewhere. It is his personal life that interests us more.

He spent time as a schoolboy caddying and his first annual caddy competition was at the age of 8, he won the junior class by a margin of 20 strokes. Jimmy Anderson in his career a three times Open Champion took notice of Braid from the age of nine. Anderson was competing in a professional versus amateurs match at Elie and when the match was over Anderson asked Jamie to play a few shots and then told him to play as much golf as he possibly could and practise hard and one day he would be an Open Championship (prophetic words!). He was a scratch player at the age of 16. He won quite a number of medals whilst playing in Earlsferry Thistle. At that time the Simpson brothers and Douglas Rolland (q.v.) were in their ascension and no doubt he honed his competitive skills playing against them. However he did not become a golfer on a full time basis having qualified as the joiner. He initially worked in St. Andrews and often had to travel to jobs around the country. He found that the travelling to and from St Andrews was interfering with his golf so he eventually took a job in Edinburgh which gave him the chance to play more golf in the Edinburgh courses. In particular he was a member of the Edinburgh Thistle Golf Club which played on the Braid Hills golf course and which Jamie exploited to his best of his ability. The well known story tells that he met C. Ralph Smith (q.v.) with whom he had grown up in Earlsferry in Princes St in Edinburgh one day and Smith convinced him to give up his day job in Edinburgh and join him making golf clubs in the Army and Navy stores in London. It is highly probable that he was nervous in relation to this change of career because although he was a strong golfer the actual construction of golf clubs was not one in which he had much experience. However he persisted and for two years he learned how to make golf clubs. In the meantime he had sort of turned professional. He first Professional Golf engagement was at Limpsfield Chart where Dougie Roland (q.v.) was the resident pro. Thereafter having won his Open championships he spent the next five to six years going round various golf courses especially in the South of England proclaiming and demonstrating the appeal of golf. He was good box office and often played before many spectators. There was, at that stage, a fairly close knit community of professional golfers quite a number of whom had originally lived in Earlsferry and with whom he had played on the Earlsferry tract as a youngster. Once he had won his Open Golf championships he was extremely generous in appearing at the various golf courses that his colleagues from Earlsferry had joined. This was a particular time when there was a strong growth of golf courses. Many of his Earlsferry contemporaries had joined fledging clubs and laid out perhaps nine sometimes eighteen holes in a piece of ground and Jamie would be more than happy to attend this course and take part in its inauguration. He went on to design and supervise many golf courses in their construction and layout. He rarely visited his home patch in Fife – he did not enjoy travelling. In 1926 he did visit Elie Golf course. His mother had not been well – she died in October 1925 – and we suspect that it was his mother's death that prompted his visit.

> GOLF COURSE.—Mr James Braid on Thursday visited his native town Elie, and, in company with the captain of the Golf House Club, Lieut.-Col. P. G. Anstruther, of Cairnie, members of the Green Committee, and Mr Prescott, representative from Thistle Club, went over Elie and Earlsferry Golf Course in the forenoon with a view to making certain minor alterations on the course. Mr Braid advised that additional bunkers be made, and recommended that there should be about two bunkers for every green, so making it better sport for the many golfers who frequent the course.

November 1926

His time up north was not wasted, however, since he visited at least another 6 courses including Brechin and Carnoustie with a view to making design improvements. He was much in demand.

He went to Romford as professional, green keeper, designer and jack of all trades before finishing up in Walton Heath in Surrey where he remained for the rest of his life.

On the personal side he married Minnie Alice Wright at Upminster 1st November 1898. They had two children James Jnr who was born in 1899 and Harry Muirfield born in 1901. Although there are no prizes for reckoning the source of his middle name. It commemorates his first Open win.

His younger son Harry had a distinguished career ending up as Chairman of Johnnie Walker Whisky company for which he received an OBE in 1967. He was captain of Walton Heath 1953 - 1955 after his father's death. He inherited his father's prowess on the golf course and won the Elie Links Championship in 1952 as well as being a member of the Golf House club. His father would no doubt have been proud of his achievement and it must have been an emotional time for Harry in 1952 to visit his father's old stamping ground and win the Championship.

Jamie will never be forgotten in Elie – there is a memorial to him on the wall of Earlsferry Town Hall and his residence in Linmara is celebrated with a plaque.

JAMES BRAID READS NOTICE OF HIS DEATH.

DECIDES TO POSTPONE HIS FUNERAL.

This morning it was reported in several papers that James Braid, the well-known professional golfer, had been killed in attempting to board a train in motion at Waterloo Station, London.

This is a mistake. The victim of the accident was another man of the same name. Braid had the mixed pleasure of reading his obituary notices this morning, and discovering what the world thinks of him. They were all favourable, for the golfer is a man of engaging qualities, a giant with a big heart.

After reflecting on his unusual experience, Braid remarked that he would "try to postpone his funeral," and went out to Walton Heath for a game of golf. During the round he pinched himself several times to make quite sure that he was still alive.

No doubt there was some quiet merriment at this error in 1916.

One final aspect of the great man himself is tangential. His mother died in 1925 reputedly the oldest inhabitant of Earlsferry. In the newspapers of the time her life was celebrated by some reminiscences of times in Earlsferry in 19th Century which is a rich resource of the life during these times.

Chapter 15
Miscellanea

There are many events, occurrences and anecdotes associated with golf in Earlsferry and Elie. In this section we mention some things we have come across in our research.

Old Tom Morris

One of the legacies of Andrew Scott (q.v.) was his cuttings book which is currently on loan to the GHC. This is collection of newspaper reports and photographs of many of the well known golfers of the era whom Andrew Scott came across in his long career. On the last page of the book the above photograph appears with the caption in what looks like Scott's handwriting "the last round of golf played by Tom Morris." It is clearly taken at Elie, probably on the last green with Earlsferry being just discernible in the back ground but his playing partner is of itself a historic gem.

James Ludovic Duff was one of the members of the family of Duffs of Hatton in Aberdeenshire who built Earlsneuk, Earlsferry in the late 19th Century. Jimmy Duff as he was known was born in 1889 and became Secretary of the GHC. This photograph however is probably taken in 1899 or later because Old Tom Morris visited Elie in 1899 to advise in relation to some of the layout and he died in 1908. Ludovic Duff looks a little older than 10 in this photograph so we suggest it may have been later than his visit in 1899. Old Tom Morris took more than a passing interest in the goings on in Elie and Earlsferry. He was present on at least one other occasion when the GHC held their annual golf meeting in August in each year. On one occasion he donated a set of golf clubs as a prize for one of the competitions.

Over the years the club has been privileged to have quite a few Scottish international golfers in their membership including A.M.M. Bucher who had the honour of representing the British Isles team in a tour of Kenya in 1957.

The annual Links championship since its inception has attracted may good amateur golfers and the Championship continues. James Braid's younger son Harry won it in the 1950s.

There have been quite a few Secretaries of the GHC over the years. Some have stayed in office for a long time others by happenchance very short time. One died in a car crash and one was removed after helping himself to a small sum of money. A club steward was found guilty of embezzlement by filling empty whisky bottles with cold tea and passing them off as stock in hand to the auditor. It is now a full time job being secretary of a golf club and course which is so often visited by those also touring St Andrews and throughout the summer many small buses arrive and parties of Americans are eager to enjoy the delights of a very playable golf course which requires precision rather than brute strength.

This old photograph shows Georgeville, the house and workshop of George Forrester with Golf Tavern next door. The golfers are playing off what would have been the first tee of the old golfing tract. It is dated about 1906.

In 1925 the fiftieth anniversary of the foundation of the GHC a booklet was produced giving the history to date of the club, authored by Mrs J.B.Clarke in 1975 and a more comprehensive book was published under the authorship of Alistair Drysdale a former Captain of the Club.

Sunday Golf

In true presbyterian fashion Sunday golf was anathema to the citizens of Earlsferry. Pleasures were not expected to be enjoyed on the Sabbath day and in any event it was a long walk to Kilconquhar church where the Rev Dr. Ferrie held sway. In 1957 it must have been on the agenda of the GHC because the Parish Church had indicated very clearly their opposition to Sunday golf notwithstanding that the then minister Rev. K. Dow was an ardent competitor on the golf course – at least 6 days a week. The GHC had firmly rejected the proposal. In February

1958 the Recreation Park/Sports club broke from tradition and decided that the ban on Sunday golf, especially during peak periods in the summer season, was not conducive to prudent financial management and declared that Sunday golf, tennis, putting and whatever else anyone wanted to do on the Recreation Park would be permitted. Elie and Earlsferry Town Council were consulted and indicated they had no objection but later clarified that by stating that they did not necessarily approve of it. Very shortly thereafter the Golf House Club changed the policy allowing Sunday golf.

The Daisies

To greenkeepers especially on golf courses the three most pernicious problems apart from golfers failing to replace their divots, are worm casts, blown sand and daisies. The worms are particularly prolific after wet weather and the worm casts in abundance mar the pleasure of putting on smooth surfaces of greens. They are controllable by dressing put on the surface of the putting green. The normal way this is applied is by spreading it and allowing it to permeate the surface of the green. Blown sand is almost impossible to control or predict but for holes near the sea it is a perennial problem. Nothing can be done other than attempted screening. Daisies, however, present a different problem. A proliferation of daisies on the fairways often means that the golfer cannot see his ball and if these daisies spread to the green they do considerable damage. The only effective way to control them is pesticides dispensed by spraying. In 1979 onwards the procedure of the greenkeepers of the GHC was to spray the fairways with a herbicide. Dr. R.W. Todd who lived on Grange Road running along side the 17th fairway noticed that a number of his plants in his garden and especially his tomato plants seemed to have sufered damage with much reduced growth etc. He suspected that this damage co-incided with the spraying of the fairways with this pesticide. In 1982 he especially noticed that the damage seemed to be prevalent not long after the spraying had been done. He initimated a claim to the GHC seeking to prevent the use of this herbicide and also for compensation for damage to his plants, and reduction in the enjoyment of his garden. He claimed £300. Expert reports were obtained by the club and Dr. Todd which tended to suggest that his hypothesis might be accurate although other causes were also mooted. He raised a court action for interdict against the club and for damages. The club decided vigorously to defend the action and eventually it came for a proof at Cupar Sheriff Court. After hearing the evidence the Sheriff (judge) concluded that the damage to Dr. Todd's plants was indeed caused by this daisy herbicide treatment and he granted interdict and damages in the sum of £150. The club settled that amount together with Dr. Todd's legal expenses amounting to over £2000. One supposes that it would have been considerably cheaper for the club simply to pay Dr. Todd the £300 he sought.

The Hill at the First

Elie's golf course's international claim to fame must be the submarine periscope in the starter's accommodation at the first tee. The first tee shot is blind requiring to clear a hill about 80 yards from the teeing ground. This hill completely obscures the sight of the fairway. Accordingly, to avoid mishaps some way had to be found to enable the starter to be satisfied that the previous match was well clear before acknowledging that the following match could tee off. One method originally adopted was to post a "forecaddie" on the brow of the hill with a system of flags to indicate whether it was safe to play. Ingenious committee members decided to position a mirror on the roof of the clubhouse from which from a point just outside the starter's hut it was possible to see if the course was clear. The starter had to emerge from his comfy though drafty accommodation, consult the mirror and then with the immortal words "Play away please" ringing in the player's ears, the coast was clear. Occasionally the wind would dislodge the mirror but generally it was a very effective if not quirky way of enforcing health and safety on the golf course and of course the starter was reluctant to emerge from his heated hut in inclement weather. In 1968 one member happened to be at an auction of surplus engineering equipment when he spotted for auction the submarine periscope of HMS Excaliber which had recently been decommissioned. With a stroke of genius precognition he made a successful bid and to this day the periscope is comfortably used to advise that the coast is clear. No longer does the starter have to emerge into the inclement weather to consult the mirror. It also enables him to watch the antics of those who have just driven off and out of sight of the clubhouse. One lady was spotted throwing her ball out of the bunker on the right hand side of the fairway whilst her playing partners were distracted.

Etiquette

Stories and reports of the etiquette generally of golfers and more particularly the GHC abound. Shorts required to be of a certain length, long socks were required with shorts, jeans are absolutely a no no, entry to the clubhouse by an incorrect gate would be likely to be greeted at the very least with a frown, despite the clear notice on the gate "Male Members Only", mobile phones going off in the clubhouse smokeroom can attract an immediate fine of a round of drinks, silence was expected on the first tee when players teed off even if at times the wayward first shot scattered the silent spectators standing at almost right angles to the first tee. Holes in one are greeted with the usual festivities and the frequency seem not less or more than other courses – one newspaper report which must be apocryphal suggested that two golfers had halved the seventh hole in one. At least two have gone 2,1 at the tenth and eleventh. Even quite some time ago a newspaper report disparaged:

.... *"James Keddie (q.v.) ought to have his attention called to one circumstance, which, in our judgment, is not only a flagrant breach of etiquette on the part of a professional match player, but a gross want of respect to the members and committee of the club who invited him to play. He lighted and smoked his pipe several times while playing, even disdaining to take the pipe out of his mouth to play his tee shot, and this, too, in a serious match, with a gallery of onlookers. Keddie ought to know that this is not the game."*

However that said it is often a good way of keeping the head still during the shot if one's pipe is firmly clenching in one's teeth. The late Douglas Bader was a fine exponent of such a ruse which combined with his ability to strike his ash from his pipe with a strong metallic "clang" on his metal leg at crucial moments made him a formidable opponent.

"The Huts"

Once the full 18 holes had been created and golf became a frequent exercise there were established against the garden wall of one of the houses in Williamsburgh a series of lean to sheds from which the various golf club makers and professionals had shops to sell their wares. Earlier they operated as ticket dispensers for the Ladies' course, putting green and Tennis Courts. The above photograph shows the sheds in the background beside what is now the car park. The photograph below is a more modern version taken from the top of the hill at the 2nd Green hence its poor quality. James Crowley, George Forrester, James Forrester, Andrew Scott, Jock Ballantine and Tom Reekie all had units there at one time or another. After a time the ability to police those playing on the Ladies' course from 150 yards away resulted in many managing to play golf via the "Aberdeen Gate". One interim solution was a manned wooden box placed at the start of the course where tickets were dispensed and a semblance of order restored. More recently a proper professional's golf shop was built alongside the Pavilion and part of the actual Pavilion. Previously the earlier bowler's locker room had been incorporated into the professional's accommodation whilst the Bowling club acquire their own accommodation nearer the green.

Chapter 16
The Children

One of the more interesting aspects of the history of golf in Elie and Earlsferry has been the involvement of children and introduction of the younger generations to the game and to the competitive aspect thereof. In 1925, Mrs Clarke in her booklet about the first 50 years history of the course refers to the existence of boys and latterly girl's competitions since 1905. There is evidence however that the origins of this competition may be earlier than that. There is a famous photograph dated 1906 showing George Forrester in front of Georgeville accompanied by a lot of youngsters and some not so youngsters. The suggestion is that this photograph, taken by the local photographer J. Gay, was in celebration of a competition for boys and there are some girls in the picture too.

The boys/girls competitions are traditionally held in the first or second week in August and organised not by any of the golf clubs but by an independent organisation which has been going at least since

1921. It was the tradition and indeed the rule that these competitions were for boys and girls specifically on holiday in Elie and Earlsferry – local boys/girls were ineligible – and perhaps this is symptomatic of the then and, somewhat still, division between the locals and the visitors. The competitions are funded by a small entry fee and voluntary contributions from people in the village and the tradition has almost always been that everyone gets a prize – usually a golf ball or more which is then sold back to the parent. There are various categories depending upon the age of the competitors. The under 8s play one hole – the 17th – the rules are enhanced by a get out of a bunker free card (well under penalty of two strokes which often is the better option!). The whole affair over the years has developed a tradition of its own. Mrs Ockleford became associated with the committee in the 1920s and now the whole competition is named "The Ockleford" in her honour. The numbers may be less but the enthusiasm of the players and diligence and persistence of the markers never wanes.

It is significant that the start of the competition for the older boys is always the mound 30 yards in front of the normal 4th tee. One suggests that this harks back to the end of 19th Century when it would have been the first tee of the old golfing tract and the entire tournament for the oldest category of boys takes place on the west side of the Ferry Road. For more on this history of this event see Drysdale's book of 1975. The Sports Club in addition run a competition in the Easter Holidays which is open to all young golfers there being no age categories nor residence restrictions.

Chapter 17
..........and finally

One of the purposes of this work was to highlight the importance of this little place in the history and development of golf and to increase awareness in the local community and of the many visitors, occasional golfers, second home owners and golf club members of its extensive golfing heritage. Had it not been for the "Earlsferry Golfing tract" and the efforts of Earlsferry Town Council and its inhabitants, who so valiantly fought for the right to play golf on this stretch of otherwise infertile land, much of the spreading of the word about the importance of the game between 1880 and 1930 would have been lost. It should be an ambition to honour the many professionals who went to America and elsewhere, and the golf club makers, by the establishment of a Golf Heritage Museum in the village enhanced by a statue of James Braid. Little could they know then how much their pioneering spirit would today be responsible for the popularity of the game. We owe it to them not to forget.

Appendix
List of Golf Clubs associated with Elie/Earlsferry Professionals

A

Albany G.C.	Scotland	George Pearson
Alloa G.C.	Scotland	William Fairful
Ampersand G.C.	USA	J. S. Pearson
Ardeer G.C.	Scotland	William Latto
Argentino G.C.	Argentina	A. Philp
Army G.C.	England	Dougie Rolland
Ascot G.C.	England	W. Thomson
Atherstane G.C.	England	Andrew Bell

B

Banstead Park G.C.	England	Bill Mackie
Barassie G.C.	Scotland	Douglas Given
Barnehurst G.C.	England	Bill Mackie
Bearsden G.C.	Scotland	William Latto
Bellport	USA	Bill Anderson
Bembridge G.C.	England	Archie Simpson
Beverley G.C.	England	Ralph Smith
Bexhill G.C.	England	Dougie Rolland

Bradely Hall G.C.	England	W. Thomson
Brockenhurst G.C.	England	J.S. Pearson
Bromborough G.C.	England	J. Smith
Broomfield Hills G.C.	Mi. USA	W. Graham
		Fred Lamb
Bruntsfield Links G.S.	Scotland	James Sunter
Burlington G.C.	Ont. Canada	Andrew Anderson
Burlington G.C.	Vt. USA	James Crowley Jnr

C

Canoe Brook C.C.	USA	Isaac Mackie
		Ralph Smith
Cape Fear G.C.	N. C. USA	Isaac Mackie
Carnoustie	Scotland	Archie Simpson
Cathcart G.C.	Scotland	R. Elder
Century C.C.	USA	Daniel Mackie
Chesterfield G.C.	England	George Walker
Chevy Chase C.C.	USA	William Webster
Chiswick Park G.C.	Mx. England	George Keddie
Clovernook C.C.	Ohio USA	Archie Simpson
Cowglen	Scotland	James Crowley Jnr
Crieff G.C.	Scotland	William Latto
Cuddington G.C.	England	J Donaldson

D

Deal R. Cinque Ports	England	Andrew Pearson
Denver G.C.	Co. USA	Ralph Smith

Detroit C.C.	USA	Fred Lamb
Dunfermline G.C.	Scotland	William Fairful
Dunwoodie G.C.	USA	William Latto
		Daniel Mackie
		Chris Sunter

E

Edgeworth G.C.	USA	George Keddie
Elie G.H.C.	Scotland	James Sunter
		Tom Reekie
		Andrew Scott
Emporia G.C.	Ky USA	R. Peebles
Epson (RAC)	England	J Donaldson

F

Fairview C.C.	USA	R. Peebles
Falkirk Tryst G.C.	Scotland	William Fairful
Fereneze G.C.	Scotland	James Crowley Jnr
Foresthills CC	N.J. USA	George Pearson
Foxhills CC	S.I. USA	Isaac Mackie
		R. Peebles
Fox Rock G.C.	Ireland	George Elder
Friern Barnet G.C.	England	J Paterson

G

Gravesend G.C.	England	George Walker
Guggenheim G.C.	N.Y. USA	W. Mackie

H

Hastings G.C.	England	James Keddie
		Ralph Smith
Hastings St. Leonards	England	J Paterson
Havana	Cuba	J.S. Pearson
Hawaii	Hawaii USA	James Melville
Highland Park Hotel	Mi. USA	W. Graham
Highland Park Hotel	S. C. USA	Chris Sunter
Homewood C.C.	llinois USA	J.S.Pearson
Hotel Del Monte	Ca. USA	J. Melville

I

Idle Hour C.C.	Ky USA	R. Peebles
Interlaken CC	USA	W. Webster
Irvine Bogside	Scotland	David Given

J

K

Kennet Square G.C.	USA	Harry Anderson
Kelvinside G.C.	Scotland	John Duncan

L

La Grange C.C.	Illinois USA	George Keddie
Lakeshore C.C.	Illinois USA	J.S.Pearson
Lakewood C.C.	N. J. USA	Isaac Mackie
Lanark G.C.	Scotland	James Anderson
Leamington Spa G.C.	England	Andrew Bell
Lee on Solent G.C.	England	George Keddie

Lewistown C.C.	USA	Harry Anderson
Limpsfield Chart G.C.	England	Dougie Rolland
Lynchburgh C.C.	USA	George Pearson

M

Malvern Green	England	Dougie Rolland
Mariemont G.C.	Ohio USA	Archie Simpson
Mcgregor G.C.	Ohio USA	W. Sime
Mexico City G.C.	Mexico	R. Peebles
Millhill/Hendon	England	J Paterson
Miramar G.C.	Argentina	A. Philp
Monterey G.C. Ca.	USA	J Melville
Mortonhall G.C.	Scotland	Alex Simpson

N

Nairn G.C.	Scotland	James Nelson
Netherwood C.C.	N. J. USA	Isaac Mackie
Northampton G.C.	England	David Duncan
		R.Walker
North Middlesex	England	J Paterson

O

Oakwood G.C.	USA	George Pearson
Oakwood Park G.C.	England	J. Smith
Ocala C.C.	Florida USA	George Pearson
		J.S. Pearson
Old Oaks C.C.	USA	Daniel Mackie

P

Peebles G.C.	Scotland	J. Nelson
Philadephia Crick.	Penn. USA	James Crowley Sen.
Poquessie C.C.	USA	Harry Anderson
Port Arthur CC	Canada	W. Thomson
Powelton G.C.	USA	Bill Anderson
		George Keddie
Prestwick G.C.	Scotland	Archie Simpson
Pollock G.C.	Scotland	R. Elder

R

Richmond C.C.	S.I. USA	J.S. Pearson
Rochester G.C.	England	R. Walker
Rochester	Cobham England	George Pearson
Rockaway Hunt G.C.	USA	George Pearson
Roseville G.C.	N. J. USA	Jack Mackie
Royal Aberdeen	Scotland	Archie Simpson
Royal Berkshire	England	W. Thomson
Royal Sydney G.C.	Australia	James Scott
Rye G.C.	England	Dougie Rolland

S

Sacramento G.C.	Ca. USA	J Melville
Shawnee Heights	G.C. USA	R Peebles
Sospel G.C.	France	J. M. Sunter
Southall G.C. (N.Midsx)	England	J.S. Pearson
South Orange C.C.	N. J. USA	R Peebles

Southwood C.C.	Canada	W. Thomson
Stirling G.C.	Scotland	John Duncan
St. Andrews G.C.	Canada	R. Elder
St. Cloud G.C.	Paris France	David Given

T

Tam O'Shanter G.C.	USA	Archie Simpson
Tankerton Whitstable	England	George Keddie
Tooting Bec G.C.	England	Dougie Rolland
Topeka C.C.	USA	R. Peebles
Troon G.C.	Scotland	David Given
Tuckahoe C.C.	USA	R. Peebles
Twyford Abbey G.C.	England	J.S. Pearson

U

Upper Montclair	USA	Andrew Anderson

W

Walton Heath	England	James Braid
		Alex Philp
Wanstead G.C.	England	Andrew Pearson
Warwickshire G.C.	England	Andrew Bell
Wentworth G.C.	Canada	Andrew Anderson
West Middlesex G.C.	England	J.S. Pearson
Whitecraigs G.C.	Scotland	James Crowley Sen
		James Crowley Jnr
Wimbledon Park G.C.	England	W.B. Sime

Winged Foot	USA	Daniel Mackie
		Bill Mackie
Woodbury G.C.	N. J. USA	James Crowley Jnr
Yountakah	USA	J.B. Mackie

Sources and Further Reading

Many of the images of newspapers reports are from British Newspapers on Line from the British Library who granted permission to reproduce them. Excerpts especially from the local newspapers of the time.

History of Elie Golf House Club by Mrs. A.B. Clarke published by J and G Innes St. Andrews 1925

The Golf House Club Elie Alasdair M Drysdale 1975 published privately

Much valuable information was obtained from Ancestry.com and Ancestry.co.uk

Some of the information is available in the archives of Elie History Society www.eliehistory.com

Elie & Earlsferry Ladies Golf Club by Agnes Lind Privately published

Golf websites on the internet especially History of Golf - Wikipedia

Most images are in possession of Elie History Society or are the author's own

INDEX

Anderson, Andrew Mackay, 120-123

Anderson, Harry, 123-124,

Anderson, James, 124-127

Anderson, William, 127-128

Anstruther family 9, 15, 16,

Anstruther Sir John 15

Anstruther Sir Ralph 18, 48, 74

Anstruther Sir Robert, 15, 37, 38

Anstruther T.M. 75, 288,

Babbington, Col., 37, 38

Ballantyne, Jack 128-129, 134, 154

Bell, Andrew 129-130

Brown, William 130-131

Baird, William 9, 39, 40, 46, 50, 66

Braid, James, 43, 61, 62, 78, 97, 111, 118, 131, 133, 143, 147, 151, 155, 156, 157, 163, 164, 172, 183, 188, 189, 190, 192, 194, 212, 213, 214, 219, 230, 231, 233, 240, 241, 242, 243, 247, 258, 262, 263, 265, 266, 269, 274, 275, 306 – 310, 321

Burgh Medal, 37, 38, 57, 128

Coalbaikie 23, 24, 28, 31, 50, 51,52

Connaught Duchess of 93, 233, 288, 303, 305

Crowley James Snr. 62, 112, 115-116, 119, 132, 136, 208, 216

Crowley, John 133-135

Crowley James Jnr. 135-138

Donaldson John, 138-140

Dumbarnie, 15, 16, 18, 35, 38, 56

Duncan David, 140-143

Duncan John 143-145

Earlsferry Abbey Golf Society, 16, 31, 35

Earlsferry and Elie Golf Club, 16, 32, 33, 35-44, 45, 48, 50, 51, 52, 57, 58, 97, 106, 153

Earlsferry Golf Society, 13, 15, 16

Earlsferry Thistle, 42, 49, 53, 56-63, 120, 128, 149, 153, 157, 160, 161, 172, 205, 250, 273, 274, 284, 307, 308

Elder George 146-150

Elder Robert, 145-147

Elie and Earlsferry Ladies 53, 55, 291-294, 298, 299

Elie Ladies Golf Club 291-294

Fairfull William 150-152

Feathery, 11, 13

Forrester, George 32, 33, 36, 41, 43, 45, 48, 61, 62, 63, 92-107, 108, 109, 112, 115, 118, 124, 127, 131, 132, 134, 141, 145, 153, 155, 156, 156, 159, 160, 161, 162, 167, 169, 175, 176, 182, 185, 189, 193, 207, 213, 215, 216, 233, 237, 241, 242, 247, 257, 258, 262, 265, 270, 284, 291, 292, 307, 313, 318, 319

Forrester James 152-156

Georgeville, 35, 43, 45, 63, 97, 106, 313, 319

Given David 156-159

Given Douglas 159-160

Glover Alexa 296-299

Golf House Club, Elie, 32, 40, 41, 42, 43, 44, 45-55, 58, 60, 62, 75, 80, 81, 82, 84, 85, 87, 97, 98, 106, 115, 153, 154, 216, 250, 251, 253, 269, 270, 271, 288, 291, 292, 293, 294, 295, 300, 301, 302, 304, 305, 310, 311, 312, 313, 314, 316

Graham William 160-162

Grange, 11, 13, 20, 22, 25, 26, 27, 28, 29, 31, 32, 33, 34, 35, 41, 45, 54, 56, 83, 84, 212, 307, 314

Hercules Club, 15, 16, 18, 35, 38, 56

Keddie George 162-166

Keddie James 166-168

Ketchen W.R., 38, 39, 45, 46, 54, 58, 65, 68, 70, 71, 74, 84, 85, 86, 301

Lamb Frederick 169-171

Latto William 172-173

Mackie Daniel 174-176

Mackie Isaac 176-180

Mackie Jack 181-182

Mackie William 182-184

Malcolm of Balbedie, 11, 20, 22, 23, 24, 25, 26, 27, 28, 29, 30, 32, 41, 42, 45, 50, 54, 56, 83, 84, 87

Melon Park, 34, 39, 40, 46, 51, 54, 58, 59, 60, 66, 67, 68, 84, 85, 86, 87, 88, 97, 291

Melville James 185-188

Morris Tom, 38, 141, 219, 258, 259, 311, 312

Nelson James 188-192

Outhwaite, 43, 74, 110, 154, 304

Paterson James 192-196

Pearson Andrew 197-199

Pearson George 199-201

Pearson J.S. 201-205

Peebles Robert 207-211

Peebles William 211-212

Philp Alexander 212-214

Plenderleath, Patrick, 15

Professional golfer, 42, 49, 58, 59, 61, 62, 63, 109, 117-287, 308

Recreation Park, 46, 59, 64-82, 120, 216, 289, 290, 292, 293, 294, 295, 314, 320

Reekie John 215-218

Reekie Tom 215-218

Rolland, Andrew 37, 38, 218-220, 221, 223

Rolland Dougie, 38, 49, 61, 97, 111, 117, 163, 164, 219, 220, 221-232, 233, 241, 254, 255, 258, 265, 270, 308

Scott, Andrew, 62, 74, 87, 89, 100, 108-115, 118, 124, 128, 134, 138, 145, 150, 154, 156, 157, 158, 159, 160, 161, 169, 175, 182, 188, 189, 213, 216, 232, 233-237, 273, 277, 280, 284, 286, 287, 296, 297, 302, 304, 305, 311, 318

Scott James 237-239

Sime William 239-245

Simpson family, 43, 111, 173, 248

Simpson Alexander 246

Simpson Archie 246-249

Simpson David 249-252

Simpson Jack 253-257

Simpson Robert 257-262

Smith C Ralph 262-267

Smith James 267-268

Smith Jock 268-270

Sports Club, see Recreation Park

Sunter Andrew 274-276

Sunter Christopher 276-279

Sunter James 271-274

Thomson William 279-282

Walker George 282-284

Walker John 284

Walker Robert 284-286

Webster William 285-287

www.ingramcontent.com/pod-product-compliance
Lightning Source LLC
Chambersburg PA
CBHW041135110526
44590CB00027B/4020